Wissenschaftliche Untersuchungen
zum Neuen Testament · 2. Reihe

Herausgeber / Editor
Jörg Frey (Zürich)

Mitherausgeber/Associate Editors
Markus Bockmuehl (Oxford) · James A. Kelhoffer (Uppsala)
Tobias Nicklas (Regensburg) · Janet Spittler (Charlottesville, VA)
J. Ross Wagner (Durham, NC)

518

D1606601

Dean Furlong

The John also called Mark

Reception and Transformation
in Christian Tradition

Mohr Siebeck

DEAN FURLONG, born 1974; 2009 BA in Classics; 2011 MA in Classical and Near Eastern Studies; 2013 MTS in Biblical Studies; 2015 MA in Teaching with Licensure; 2017 PhD in New Testament Studies; since 2018 Research Fellow, Centre for Contextual Biblical Interpretation.

ISBN 978-3-16-159277-5 / eISBN 978-3-16-159278-2
DOI 10.1628/978-3-16-159278-2

ISSN 0340-9570 / eISSN 2568-7484 (Wissenschaftliche Untersuchungen zum Neuen Testament, 2. Reihe)

The Deutsche Nationalbibliothek lists this publication in the Deutsche Nationalbibliographie; detailed bibliographic data is available on the Internet at *http://dnb.dnb.de*.

The book was printed by Laupp & Göbel in Gomaringen on non-aging paper and bound by Buchbinderei Nädele in Nehren.

Printed in Germany.

Preface

This study will explore the reception in Christian tradition of John/Mark, an important early Christian figure spoken of in the book of Acts and (probably) in the Pauline corpus. In particular, it will examine the portrayals of John/Mark as both a Markan figure (i.e. as a figure identified with Mark the Evangelist) and as a Johannine figure (i.e. as a figure identified with the Beloved Disciple/John the Evangelist).

A shorter version of this study initially formed part of my doctoral dissertation undertaken at the Vrije Universiteit, Amsterdam, under the supervision of Professor Peter-Ben Smit and Professor Aza Goudriaan. [1] While the dissertation focused on the reception of John the Evangelist in early Christian writings, one section considered potential identifications of John with John/Mark. After completing my doctoral work, it became clear to me that the subject matter required a separate treatment focusing on the figure of John/Mark as both a Markan and Johannine figure rather than simply as a potential Johannine figure. This shift of focus, along with the discovery on my part of other sources, led to the study's considerable expansion. The main disadvantage, however, of separating this study from its original context is that the reader has not been familiarised with the arguments for the distinction of John the Evangelist and John the Apostle in early Christian sources which were discussed at length in the first section of the dissertation. Nevertheless, since this view has been widely disseminated, [2] and since a revised version of my own work on the subject is available, [3] this need not be detrimental to the present study.

My own study of this question commenced in the winter of 2004/2005, with the reading of R. Alan Culpepper's *John, the Son of Zebedee: The Life of a Legend*, which discusses the reception of John the son of Zebedee in Christian tradition. In one section of the work, the author discusses scholarly proposals

---

[1] Dean Furlong, "John the Evangelist: Revision and Reinterpretation in Early Christian Sources," (Ph.D. dissertation, Vrije Universiteit Amsterdam, 2017).

[2] E.g. Jean Colson, *L'énigme du disciple que Jésus aimait* (ThH 10; Paris: Beauchesne, 1969); Martin Hengel, *The Johannine Question*, trans. John Bowden (London: SCM Press, 1989); Richard Bauckham, *Jesus and the Eyewitnesses: The Gospels as Eyewitness Testimony* (2nd ed.; Grand Rapids: Eerdmans, 2017).

[3] Dean Furlong, *The Identity of John the Evangelist: Revision and Reinterpretation in Early Christian Sources* (Lanham, Md.: Lexington, 2020).

on the question of the identity of the Beloved Disciple. When I first saw the proposal for John/Mark, I at first turned the page, considering such a suggestion unworthy of serious consideration. I turned back, however, out of curiosity, and after reading the section I had to acknowledge, to my surprise, that the profile of John/Mark did indeed fit remarkably well with that of the Beloved Disciple, and probably more so than that of any other candidate. This started me on a scholarly journey on the question, which I was able to further explore for my undergraduate Honour's thesis at the University of Colorado (2009), under the supervision of Dr Andrew Cain. It was during this time that I came across two short articles by J. Edgar Bruns, who brought to the attention of scholarship potential evidence suggesting that John/Mark had at times been identified with John the Evangelist within Christian tradition.

Further research on this question was suspended for a few years while I was studying at the University of Minnesota, where I discovered an interest in the Qumran community and writings. Indeed, I had planned to pursue this latter line of research for doctoral work, but I eventually decided for various reasons to return to the Johannine Question, and particularly to the question of the early Christian reception of John the Evangelist (the question of the identity of the Beloved Disciple will perhaps provide the subject matter of a future work), which resulted in my dissertation at the Vrije Universiteit, Amsterdam and, in turn, to the present study.

I would like to thank Professor Tobias Nicklas (Universität Regensburg) who read over the initial manuscript of this work and provided invaluable advice on improving it, and who recommended it for publication in the WUNT II series. I would also like to thank Dr Adel Sidarus (University of Évora, Portugal, emeritus), who made me aware of sources and in one case offered me his own private French translation of an Arabic work unavailable in English. I am also grateful to Dr Mark House of the Reformed Theological Seminary, who is engaged in translating the *Acts, Miracles, and Passion of Mark* into English and who graciously shared his work with me, which I was able to consult when working on my own translations. Gratitude is also due to Don Meredith, Bob Turner, and the rest of the staff at the Harding School of Theology Library in Memphis, TN, for all their help over the years.

Collierville, TN, October 2019   Dean Furlong

Table of Contents

Abbreviations XV

Introduction 1

Part 1

John/Mark as a Markan Figure

Chapter 1: Mark in Early Christian Writings 7

1.1. John/Mark

    1.1.1. John/Mark in the New Testament 8

    1.1.2. John/Mark in Other Early Christian Writings 12

1.2. Mark the Evangelist 13

    1.2.1. Mark in Papias of Hierapolis 14

    1.2.2. Mark in Irenaeus 15

    1.2.3. Mark in Tertullian 17

    1.2.4. Mark in Clement of Alexandria 17

    1.2.5. Mark in Origen 18

    1.2.6. Mark the "Stump-Fingered" in the Refutation of All Heresies 18

    1.2.7. Mark in Eusebius of Caesarea 18

1.3. Mark of Alexandria 19

1.4. Conclusion 21

Chapter 2: The Conflation of Mark the Evangelist 23

2.1. Syrian Traditions 23

    2.1.1. The Dialogue of Adamantius 23
    2.1.2. Ephrem the Syrian 26
    2.1.3. The Apostolic Constitutions...................................27
    2.1.4. Victor of Antioch...27
    2.1.5. Severus of Antioch 28
    2.1.6. Isho'dad of Merv..28
    2.1.7. Michael of Antioch...29
    2.1.8. Dionysius bar Salibi...29
    2.1.9. Bar Hebraeus..30
    2.1.10. The Book of the Bee 30

2.2. Greek Sources 31

    2.2.1. Clement of Alexandria's Letter to Theodore 31
    2.2.2. Eusebius of Caesarea...31
    2.2.3. Chrysostom..32
    2.2.4 Epiphanius of Salamis..32
    2.2.5. Sophronius of Jerusalem 33
    2.2.6. Procopius the Deacon 33
    2.2.7. Ps.-Dorotheus 33
    2.2.8. Theophylact 34
    2.2.9. Euthymius 34
    2.2.10. Colophons to the Gospels in Medieval Copies 35

2.3. Western Sources 36

    2.3.1. Jerome 36
    2.3.2. The Monarchian Prologue to Mark............................36
    2.3.3. An Early Commentary on Mark 37
    2.3.4. Bede..37
    2.3.5. Two Hiberno-Latin Manuscripts 37
    2.3.6. Jacobus de Voragine 38
    2.3.7. The Passion of Mark 39

2.4. Conclusion...39

Chapter 3: The Conflation of Mark in Coptic Tradition............41

3.1. The *Encomium on Mark the Evangelist* 41

3.2. The *Encomium of SS. Peter and Paul* 43

3.3. Severus' *Homily on St Mark* 44
    3.3.1. Severus' Defence 47
    3.3.2. The Alexandrian Tradition 48
    3.3.3. Conflation in Severus' Narrative 49

3.4. The *History of the Patriarchs of Alexandria* 50

3.5. Ibn Kabar 53

3.6. *Synaxarion for Baramouda* 54

3.7. Conclusion 54

Chapter 4: John/Mark in Cypriot Sources 55

4.1. The *Acts of Barnabas* 55
    4.1.1. The Division of Paul and Barnabas 56
    4.1.2. The Ministry in Cyprus 57

4.2. The *Encomium of Barnabas* 59

4.3. The *Life of Auxibius* 62

4.4. The Dating of the Cypriot Texts 63

4.5. Conclusion 67

Chapter 5: John/Mark in the *Acts of Mark* 69

5.1. Mark's Background and Conversion 69

5.2. Mark's Travels 71
    5.2.1. Correlating Marks' Travels with the Chronology of Acts 72
    5.2.2. Conflation with the Papian Tradition of Mark 73
    5.2.3. Conflation with the Alexandrian Mark 74

5.3. Shared Material in Greek and Coptic Sources 75

5.3.1. The Acts of Mark *and the* Acts of Barnabas..................................75
5.3.2. The Acts of Mark *and the* Encomium of Barnabas......................78
5.3.3. Comparing Greek and Cypriot Sources..................................80

5.4. Conclusion..84

Part 2

John Who Was Also Called Mark

Chapter 6: The "Johannine" Mark..87

6.1. The Baptist's Disciples (John 1)..87

6.2. The Wedding at Cana (John 2) 88

6.3. The Healing at the Pool of Bethesda (John 5) 89

6.5. Mark at Bethany (cf. John 11) 89

6.6. The Passover (cf. John 13) 90

6.7. The Disciple at the Cross (John 19) 90

6.8. Thomas' Doubting (John 20) 91

6.9. The Gospel of the Divine Logos (cf. John 1; 21) 92

6.9.1. The Acts of Peter *by Peter, Bishop of Alexandria* 92
6.9.2. Ambrose of Milan 92
6.9.3. The Monarchian Prologue to Mark..94
6.9.4. Procopius the Deacon..96
6.9.5. An Epigram on Mark's Gospel..97
6.9.6. The Acts of Mark 98

6.10. Refuting Errors Concerning Christ's Divinity....................98

6.10.1. Chromatius 99
6.10.2. Thomas Aquinas..99
6.10.3. The Refutation of All Heresies..100
6.10.4. Conflation with the Acts of Peter 102

6.11. Conclusion...102

Chapter 7: Reduplicated Traditions...105

7.1. A Levitical Jerusalemite 106

7.2. Of Noble Birth...107

7.3. Mark and John as the One Carrying the Jar of Water............................109

7.4. The Young Man Who Fled Naked 109

7.5. The Virgin 112

7.6. The Theologian and Beholder of God..113

7.7. The Zion Church 114

7.8. Conclusion...121

Chapter 8: The Priest Wearing the Sacerdotal Plate 123

8.1. Mark as a Priest Wearing the Sacerdotal Plate 124

8.2. James as a Priest Wearing the Sacerdotal Plate.......................................125

8.3. Conclusion...132

Chapter 9: The Origins of the Πέταλον Motif...............................133

9.1. Polycrates and the Πέταλον: Proposed Solutions 133

9.2. The Johannine Odist 137

9.3. Epiphanius' Construction of James as Literal High Priest....................142

9.4. Hymns to the Divine Christ 143

9.5. Conclusion...145

Chapter 10: John's Life and Travels 147

10.1. Early Johannine Traditions 147

10.2. Later Sources of Johannine Traditions 153
10.2.1. *The* Suffering of John *and the* Virtues of John 153
10.2.2. *The* History of John..154
10.2.3. *The* Acts of John by Prochorus..................................156
10.2.4. *The* Acts of John in Rome.......................................157

10.3. The Dormition Tradition..158

10.4. The Dormition and the Allotment Tradition...........................161
10.4.1. *The Book of John Concerning the Falling Asleep of Mary* 161
10.4.2. *Ps.-Melito's* Departure of Mary 162

10.5. The Syriac Narrative of John in Ephesus 163
10.5.1. *Moses Bar Kepha*..164
10.5.2. *Mingana 540*..164
10.5.3. *Codex 825*..166
10.5.4. *Syriac Manuscript 16401* 166
10.5.5. *Dionysius bar Salibi*..167

10.6. John's Preaching in Antioch 168
10.6.1. *The Geez Commentary* 168
10.6.2. *The Apocalypse* Andǝmta......................................170
10.6.3. *The Original Context of the Shipwreck Narrative* 171

10.7. Ephesus and Beyond..173

10.8. Conclusion...173

Chapter 11: The Parallel Lives of John and Mark 175

11.1. The Preaching in Antioch 175

11.2. John/Mark's Return to Antioch from Pamphylia....................176

11.3. Publication in Syria 177

11.3.1. The Peshitta 177
11.3.2. The Writing of the Gospel in Antioch 178
11.3.3. The Hebrew Gospel of Matthew 180
11.3.4. A Common Source of the Traditions 180

11.4. The Dormition Traditions 180

11.5. The Desertion 181

11.6. The Further Travels of Mark..182

11.7. Conclusion...185

Chapter 12: The Origins of the Shared Traditions.......................187

12.1 The Source of the Johannine Reduplicated Traditions 187

12.2. The Source of Non-Western Markan Traditions.................191

12.2.1. Hegesippus and the Reduplicated Markan Traditions 191
12.2.2. Proposed Source: Africanus.....................................194

12.3. The Cypriot Mission of Mark and Barnabas 195

12.4. The Source of the Syrian Narrative and Barnabas..............196

12.5. Conclusion...196

Conclusion to the Study 197

Appendix: The *Acts of Mark* Chapter 1–10................................199

Bibliography..205
Index of Sources..221
Index of Modern Authors 232
Index of Subjects...233

Abbreviations

AB	Anchor Bible
ABD	*Anchor Bible Dictionary*, ed. David Noel Freedman (6 vols.; New York: Doubleday, 1992)
ACCSNT	Ancient Christian Commentary on Scripture: New Testament
ACW	Ancient Christian Writers
AJA	*American Journal of Archaeology*
AJT	*American Journal of Theology*
AnBoll	*Analecta Bollandiana*
ANF	*The Ante-Nicene Fathers: Translations of the Writings of the Fathers Down to A.D. 325*, ed. Alexander Roberts and James Donaldson (Buffalo: Christian Literature Publishing Company, 1885–1897; Grand Rapids: Eerdmans, 1951–1956), 10 vols.
ANRW	*Aufstieg und Niedergang der Römischen Welt*
BIS	Biblical Interpretation Series
BSAC	*Bulletin de la Société d'archéologie copte*
BTNT	Biblical Theology of the New Testament
CALP	The Comprehensive Aramaic Lexicon Project
CBP	*Cahiers de Biblia Patristica*
EphMariol	*Ephemerides Mariologicae*
GRBS	*Greek, Roman, and Byzantine Studies*
Hist. Einzel.	Historia Einzelschriften
IEJ	*Israel Exploration Journal*
MJS	Münsteraner judaistische Studien
Mon	*The Monist*
Mus	*Le Muséon*
NAKG	*Nederlands archief voor kerkgeschiedenis*
NPNF	*A Select Library of Nicene and Post-Nicene Fathers of the Christian Church*, ed. Philip Schaff (New York: Christian Literature Company, 1887–1900; Grand Rapids: Eerdmans, 1952–1955), 28 vols. in 2 series
NTOA	Novum Testamentum et Orbis Antiquus
OCA	Orientalia Christiana Analecta
OTP	James H. Charlesworth (ed.), *The Old Testament Pseudepigrapha*
OTRM	Oxford Theology and Religion Monographs
PSBFMi	Publications of the Studium Biblicum Franciscanum. Collectio minor
RE	Paulys Realencyclopädie der classischen Altertumswissenschaft
Scr	*Scripture*
SVTP	Studia in Veteris Testamenti pseudepigraphica
TDSA	Testi e documenti per lo studio dell' antichità
ThH	Théologie historique

Trad	*Traditio*
UCOP	University of Cambridge Oriental Publications
VL	*Vetus Latina: die Reste der altlateinischen Bibel*
WGRW	Writings from the Greco-Roman World

Introduction

While it is often thought that early Christian tradition identified John/Mark, the assistant of Paul and Barnabas spoken of in Acts, with Mark the Evangelist, the putative author of the Gospel of Mark, this study will argue that these figures were originally differentiated; furthermore, it will examine evidence that John/Mark was sometimes identified instead with John the Evangelist. In so doing, it builds primarily upon the work of J. Edgar Bruns, who drew the attention of scholarship to the apparent "confusion" between John and Mark in some Christian sources. [1]

The first part of this study will examine the various conflations of John/Mark with other Markan figures. Chapter 1 will begin with a survey of the three earliest, and apparently unconflated, depictions of a figure named Mark in early sources: that of John/Mark, Mark the Evangelist and the Mark who was associated with the founding of the churches of Egypt.

Chapter 2 will examine the reception of Mark the Evangelist in sources of Syrian, Greek and western provenance, with attention given to the apparent conflation of this figure with John/Mark.

Chapter 3 will discuss the traditions of Mark of Alexandria found in Coptic sources, as well as the various permutations of Coptic narratives which arose from the conflation of this figure with Mark the Evangelist and/or John/Mark.

Chapter 4 will examine a number of Cypriot sources which depict John/Mark's later ministry in Cyprus with Barnabas, culminating in the latter's martyrdom. The variations found in these narratives will be explained as differing attempts at conflating the Cypriot traditions with the narratives associated with Mark the Evangelist and the Alexandrian Mark.

Lastly, chapter 5 will discuss the *Acts of Mark*, a Greek work of unknown date and provenance which preserves a lengthy account of the Judean John/Mark and which shares a number of features in common with the Coptic and Cypriot Markan narratives.

The second part of this study will turn its attention to the lesser-known depictions of John/Mark as a Johannine figure. Chapter 6 will discuss sources which place John/Mark in narratives drawn exclusively from the Fourth Gospel, sometimes in roles associated with the "disciple whom Jesus loved" of the

---

[1] J. Edgar Bruns, "John Mark: A Riddle within the Johannine Enigma," *Scr* 15 (1963): 91; idem, "The Confusion between John and John Mark in Antiquity," *Scr* 17 (1965).

Fourth Gospel (hereafter referred to as "the Beloved Disciple"), including the attribution to Mark's gospel of either a doctrine of Christ's divinity or of a Logos theology.

Chapter 7 will examine traditions that are attributed both to John/Mark and to John, which will be referred to as "reduplicated traditions." These include the description of both as Levitical, aristocratic Jerusalemites, each of whom are said to have had a father named Aristobulus, and the identifications of both as the young man who fled naked and as the one carrying the jar of water to the house in which the Last Supper was eaten. This chapter will also discuss the Church of Holy Mount Zion in Jerusalem, which was said to have been the location of the house of both Mark and John.

There will be a discussion in Chapter 8 of the separate portrayals of both John and Mark as priestly figures who are said to have worn the high-priestly or sacerdotal plate (πέταλον or *petalum*). This chapter will also examine a third figure, James the Just, who is described similarly. A case will be made for considering the possibility that a single source, to be identified as Hegesippus' *Memoirs*, lies behind all three depictions.

Chapter 9 will evaluate the theory of Harris and Mingana that Polycrates' portrayal of John as a priest wearing the sacerdotal plate derived from the *Odes of Solomon*. Attention will also be given to the potential of this theory for elucidating the conclusions of the previous chapter.

Chapter 10 will survey the life and movements of John the Evangelist, as provided by early and medieval Johannine sources. This will lay the groundwork for Chapter 11, in which these traditions will be correlated with the John/Mark narrative. It will be concluded in Chapter 11 that the correlations between these figures are unlikely to have resulted from chance configuration, suggesting that both arose from a single, common narrative.

In the final chapter, an attempt will be made at accounting for the evidence by positing that in the earliest strata of the traditions, John/Mark was identified and not merely confused with the Beloved Disciple and/or John the Evangelist. This identification, it will further be posited, was eventually displaced by a later identification of John/Mark with Mark the Evangelist. A possible theory of transmission will then be laid out to explain how the traditions came to be related under both the name of Mark and of John.

It should be noted that other scholars have argued based upon the internal evidence of the Fourth Gospel for the identification of John/Mark with the Beloved Disciple. [2] This study, however, does not seek to address the historicity

---

[2] E.g. Daniel Völter, *Mater Dolorosa und der Lieblingsjünger des Johannesevangeliums* (Strasburg: Heitz, 1907), 16; idem, *Die Offenbarung Johannis* (2nd ed.; Strasburg: Heitz, 1911), 56; Julius Wellhausen, *Das Evangelium Johannis* (Berlin: Reimer, 1908), 87–88; Carl Erbes "Der Apostel Johannes und der Jünger, welcher an der Brust des Herrn lag," *ZKG* 33 (1912): 159–239; Johannes Weiss, *Earliest Christianity: A History of the Period A.D. 30–*

of the tradition or to examine the profile of the Beloved Disciple for clues as to his identity, though I do hope to write such a study someday.

A Note on Terminology

When discussing the John who was also named Mark, the form "John/Mark" will be employed rather than the ubiquitous "John Mark" as better representing his Hebrew-Latin double name found in Acts (12:12). The form "John Mark" might wrongly suggest to a reader that the name of Mark was analogous to a modern surname,[3] which is not the case. He was not known as "John Mark": rather, Mark was an alternative name that he used in addition to John: he was called John (יוֹחָנָן [Yoḥanan], his Hebrew name), but he was also named Mark (*Marcus*, his Latin name). Thus, in Acts he is variously "John" (13:5, 13), or "Mark" (15:39), or "John, who was also called Mark" (12:12, 25; 15:37).

150, trans. Frederick Grant, vol. 2 (New York: Harper, 1959), 788; Pierson Parker, "John and John Mark," *JBL* 79 (1960): 97–110; idem, "John the Son of Zebedee and the Fourth Gospel," *JBL* 81 (1962): 35–43; John Marsh, *The Gospel of St. John* (Philadelphia: Westminster, 1978), 24–25; Wolfgang Eckle, *Den der Herr liebhatte: Rätsel um den Evangelisten Johannes. Zum historischen Verständnis seiner autobiographischen Andeutungen* (Hamburg: Kovac, 1991).

Oscar Cullmann, *The Johannine Circle*, trans. John Bowden (London: SCM, 1976), 76–77, views John/Mark as a possible identification; Stephen Smalley, *John, Evangelist and Interpreter* (2nd ed.; London: Paternoster, 1997), 85, concedes that the view "is not as wild a suggestion as may at first appear"; while R. Alan Culpepper, *John, the Son of Zebedee: The Life of a Legend* (Edinburgh: T. & T. Clark, 2000), 77, notes that the view "has much to commend it".

[3] Cf. Alfred Plummer, *The Gospel according to St Mark* (CGTSC; Cambridge: Cambridge University Press, 1914), ix; Bauckham, *Eyewitnesses*, 69.

Part 1

John/Mark as a Markan Figure

Chapter 1

Mark in Early Christian Writings

Three narratives concerning a figure named Mark are known in early Christian sources. There is the Mark who was also called John, spoken of in the book of Acts and probably in the Pauline corpus, who is said to have lived in Jerusalem and to have travelled with Paul and Barnabas to Cyprus; there is Mark the Evangelist, who is said to have been a follower of Peter and to have written a Gospel at Rome based upon Peter's preaching; lastly, there is the Mark who is held to have founded the churches of Egypt and to have been martyred in Alexandria.

The traditional view [1] holds that early Christian sources identified Mark the Evangelist with John/Mark. [2] Indeed, Guelich, addressing the theory that the two Marks were distinguished, goes so far as to claim: "We really do not have any basis for this distinction in the Church tradition." [3] Some also associate the Evangelist with Alexandria. [4]

---

[1] It should be noted that this identification has never been universally held, even before the advent of critical scholarship; notable traditionalist scholars who have questioned or rejected it include William Cave, *A Complete History of the Lives, Acts, and Martyrdoms of the Holy Apostles*, vol. 1 (Philadelphia: Solomon Wyatt, 1810), 348; Matthew Henry, *An Exposition of the Old and New Testament*, vol. 5 (London: Bagster, 1811), n.p. (introductory comments on Mark's gospel); Antoine Calmet, *Dictionnaire historique, critique, chronologique, géographique et littéral de la Bible*, vol. 2 (2nd ed.; Geneva: Bousquet, 1730), 661; and Alban Butler, *The Lives of the Fathers, Martyrs and Other Principal Saints*, vol. 2, (New York: P. J. Kenedy, 1903), 155.

[2] E.g. Donald A. Carson and Douglas J. Moo, *An Introduction to the New Testament* (2nd ed.; Grand Rapids: Zondervan, 2005), 174; Craig S. Keener, *The IVP Bible Background Commentary: New Testament* (2nd ed.; Downers Grove, Ill.: IVP, 2014), 126; Jongyoon Moon, *Mark as Contributive Amanuensis of 1 Peter?* (Berlin: LIT Verlag, 2009), 36.

[3] Robert A. Guelich, *Mark 1–8:26* (WBC 34A; Dallas: Word, 1998), xxviii.

[4] Joseph B. Lightfoot, *The Acts of the Apostles: A Newly Discovered Commentary*, ed. Ben Witherington III, Todd D. Still and Jeanette M. Hagen (Downers Grove, Ill.: IVP Academic, 2014), 208; Henry Barclay Swete, ed., *The Gospel according to St. Mark: The Greek Text with Introduction, Notes and Indices* (London: Macmillan, 1898), xviii; Thomas C. Oden, *African Memory of Mark: Reassessing Early Church Tradition* (Downers Grove, Ill.: IVP, 2011), 133.

The claim that early Christian sources identified John/Mark with the Evangelist has not, however, gone without challenge, [5] and this chapter will reopen this question by surveying the earliest forms of these three Markan traditions in early Christian writings. It will commence with sources relating to John/Mark, principally drawn from the New Testament; it will then proceed to discuss the figure of Mark the Evangelist in early Christian writings; lastly, the earliest apparently unconflated account of Mark of Alexandria, entitled the *Martyrdom of Mark*, will be summarised and discussed. It will be concluded that all three Markan traditions likely originated quite separately and in connection with distinct figures.

1.1. John/Mark

1.1.1. John/Mark in the New Testament

The New Testament speaks of a figure named Mark four times in Acts (12:12, 25; 15:37; 39), three times in the Pauline corpus (Col 4:10; Phlm 24; 2 Tim. 4:11) and once in 1 Peter 5:13. All have been suggested at one time or another as references to John/Mark, and the evidence for this will be evaluated below.

1.1.1.1. The Acts of the Apostles

In the book of Acts, John/Mark is indirectly introduced midway through the narrative when Peter, newly freed from prison, is said to have made his way to "the house of Mary the mother of John, the one also called (ὁ ἐπικαλούμενος) Mark" (Acts 12:12). Weiss suggests that the addition of ὁ ἐπικαλούμενος to the name of John was employed to distinguish this John from John the son of Zebedee; this qualification shows, he adds, that he would have normally been known to the readers as John rather than Mark. [6]

The Latin *praenomen* Mark (*Marcus*), which is otherwise unattested among Palestinian Jews, [7] may indicate that John/Mark belonged to the wealthy upper echelon of society whose position depended upon Roman power. [8] As Keener

---

[5] E.g. Johannes Weiss, *Das älteste Evangelium: Ein Beitrag zum Verständnis des Markus-Evangeliums und der ältesten evangelischen Überlieferung* (Göttingen: Vandenhoeck & Ruprecht, 1903), 385–86; Francis Pritchett Badham, "The Martyrdom of John the Apostle," *AJT* 8 (1904): 543–44; Dieter Lührmann, *Das Markusevangelium* (HNT 3; Tübingen: J.C.B. Mohr [Paul Siebeck], 1987), 5–6; Culpepper, *John*, 78.

[6] Weiss, *Das älteste Evangelium*, 387.

[7] Margaret H. Williams, "Palestinian Jewish Personal Names in Acts," in *The Book of Acts in its Palestinian Setting*, ed. Richard Bauckham (BAFCS 4; Grand Rapids: Eerdmans, 1995), 105.

[8] Cf. Keener, *New Testament*, 356.

observes, "the use of the name hardly indicates antipathy toward Rome or its interests in Jerusalem".[9]

The house, which is said to belong to John/Mark's mother Mary, was used as a meeting place for the Christians in Jerusalem (Acts 12:13). Nothing else is related concerning this Mary, though the omission of any mention of her husband may indicate that she was a widow.[10] The mention of the outer gate of the house and the servant girl likely connote wealth.[11]

Mark himself is directly introduced a little later in the narrative, accompanying Barnabas and Saul to Antioch (Acts 12:25), where he is again referred to as the "John also called Mark". He then travels with them to Cyprus (Acts 13:1–5), with the narrative referring to him this time simply as "John," and describing him as Barnabas and Paul's assistant (ὑπηρέτης) (Acts 13:5). Possibly this suggests that he was responsible for the catechetical instruction of new converts,[12] though it may only mean that he was responsible for taking care of the more menial responsibilities such as making travel arrangement or baptising new converts.[13]

The Acts narrative goes on to relate that Barnabas and Paul sailed to Pamphylia in Asia Minor from Cyprus, at which point John/Mark, again referred to as "John," abandoned the mission and travelled back to Jerusalem, though a reason for this is not provided (Acts 13:13). Black provides "scraps of circumstantial evidence" that indicate he might have been offended at Paul's preaching of the gospel to Gentiles: John was clearly a Jerusalemite; his departure occurs following the conversion of a Gentile proconsul; and his re-entry into the narrative follows the endorsement of the Gentile mission by the apostles at Jerusalem.[14] To these may be added one more: it is following John's return to Jerusalem that a law-observant party said to be from James visits Antioch, from whence Paul's mission originated (cf. Acts 12:12, 17), which was perhaps prompted by a negative report of Paul's preaching on John/Mark's part.

---

[9] Keener, *New Testament*, 356.

[10] Ben Witherington III, *The Acts of the Apostles: A Socio-Rhetorical Commentary* (Grand Rapids: Eerdmans, 1998), 386; cf. Charles K. Barrett, *A Critical and Exegetical Commentary on the Acts of the Apostles*, vol. 1 (ICC; Edinburgh: T. & T. Clark, 1994), 583.

[11] Parker, "John Mark," 98; C. Clifton Black, *Mark: Images of an Apostolic Interpreter* (Minneapolis: Fortress, 2001), 27; Keener, *New Testament*, 356.

[12] R. O. P. Taylor, "The Ministry of Mark," *ExpT* 54 (1942–43): 136; cf. Rainer Riesner, "Once More: Luke-Acts and the Pastoral Epistles," in *History and Exegesis: New Testament Essays in Honor of Dr. E. Earle Ellis for his 80th Birthday*, ed. Sang-Won (Aaron) Son (London: T. & T. Clark, 2006), 255; Michael J. Kok, "The Gospel on the Margins: The Ideological Function of the Patristic Tradition on the Evangelist Mark" (Ph.D. dissertation, University of Sheffield, 2013), 138–39.

[13] Swete, *St. Mark*, xvi.

[14] Black, *Apostolic Interpreter*, 40–41.

Following the gathering of apostles and elder in Jerusalem, in which the controversy over circumcision and the Gentile mission had been resolved, Paul and Barnabas travelled to Antioch; while there, Paul proposes to Barnabas that they revisit the cities in which they had formerly preached, but they disagree over Barnabas' insistence that they take Mark with them, who is referred to for the third time as the "John also called Mark" (15:37). Barnabas may have assumed that Mark's presence would have been acceptable to Paul since disagreements over Jewish law had now been settled. This was not the case, and Paul and Barnabas go their separate ways, with Paul travelling through Syria and Cilicia with Silas, and Barnabas sailing to Cyprus with "the afore-mentioned Mark" (τὸν Μᾶρκον with an anaphoric article) (15:39), at which point they disappear from the narrative (Acts 15:37–41). Possibly the use of the Roman "Mark" rather than the Jewish "John" which had been employed prior to the council of Jerusalem indicates his acceptance of a role in the Gentile mission.

1.1.1.2. Mark in the Pauline Corpus

A figure named "Mark" is spoken of in Philemon, an undisputed Pauline letter, [15] as one of the co-workers of Paul that were with him at the time of writing (Phlm 24). Mark is again mentioned in Colossians, a disputed Pauline epistle, along with four of the co-workers that are noted as being with Mark in Philemon: Epaphras, Aristarchus, Luke and Demas (Phlm 23–24; Col 4:10–17). This Mark is said to have been a Jew (Col 4:10–11) and the cousin (ἀνεψιός) of Barnabas (Col 4:10); he is widely believed to be the same John/Mark mentioned in Acts. [16] This Mark was apparently active in Asia Minor, for the imprisoned Paul asks those whom he addresses in the Lycus Valley to receive him, should he come to them (Col 4:10), a statement which possibly presupposes the previous break between Paul and John/Mark (cf. Acts 15:37–39), though this is disputed. [17]

Both Philemon (Phlm 24) and Colossians (Col 4:10) refer to Paul's imprisonment at the time of writing. Traditionally, these letters have been held to

---

[15] M. Eugene Boring, *An Introduction to the New Testament: History, Literature, Theology* (Louisville, Ky.: Westminster John Knox, 2012), 230.

[16] Jac J. Müller, *The Epistles of Paul to the Philippians and to Philemon* (NICNT; Grand Rapids: Eerdmans, 1955), 192; Markus Barth and Helmut Blanke, *Colossians: A New Translation with Introduction and Commentary*, trans. Astrid B. Beck (AB 34B; New York: Doubleday, 1994), 479; James D. G. Dunn, *The Epistles to the Colossians and to Philemon: A Commentary on the Greek Text* (NICNT; Grand Rapids: Eerdmans, 1996), 276; Margaret Y. MacDonald, *Colossians and Ephesians* (SP 17; Collegeville, Minn.: The Liturgical Press, 2000), 180; Joseph A. Fitzmyer, *The Letter to Philemon: A New Translation with Introduction and Commentary* (AB 34C; New Haven, Conn.: Yale University Press, 2008), 124.

[17] Barth and Blanke, *Colossians*, 480.

have been sent from Rome, c. 62, during Paul's final Roman imprisonment, [18] but many now argue that Paul's prison letters were written from Ephesus, c. 54, during Paul's three-year ministry in the city. [19] There is also a minor third position that Paul wrote from Caesarea during his imprisonment there (Acts 24:31–35). [20] The Ephesian hypothesis is not new and is attested in the possibly second-century Marcionite prologue to Colossians, which relates that Paul, "already bound, therefore writes to them from Ephesus" (*ergo apostolus iam ligatus scribit eis ab Epheso*). [21] The prologues to the Philippians and Ephesians, which exhibit the traditional Roman imprisonment view, may be later in date and secondary in importance. [22]

A figure named "Mark" is also spoken of in 2 Tim 4:11 as a co-worker of Paul who was in relatively close proximity to Timothy, somewhere in Asia Minor (cf. 2 Tim 1:15–16; 4:13), during Paul's final Roman imprisonment. While this letter is generally (though not universally) considered not to have been written by Paul, it would still nevertheless reflect early Christian Markan tradition. [23] It depicts Paul as instructing Timothy to bring Mark with him (4:9, 11), presumably to Rome, [24] showing that Mark was held to have arrived in Rome, from Asia Minor, during the reign of Nero, probably in the early to mid-

---

[18] A useful discussion supportive of this view is found in Barth and Blanke, *Colossians*, 126–33. For discussion and bibliography, see Werner Georg Kümmel, *Introduction to the New Testament*, rev. ed., trans. Howard Clark Lee (Nashville: Abingdon Press, 1973), 324–32; Paul Trebilco, *The Early Christians in Ephesus from Paul to Ignatius* (Grand Rapids: Eerdmans, 2007), 83–87.

[19] For a useful summary of the evidence in favour of the view that both Philemon and Philippians (which are generally regarded as having been written around the same time) were written from Ephesus, see Boring, *An Introduction*, 220–23; 232.

[20] Cf. John A. T. Robinson, *Redating the New Testament* (London: SCM, 1976), 65–67. E. Earle Ellis holds that Ephesians-Colossians-Philemon were written at Caesarea and Philippians at Rome; see *The Making of the New Testament Documents* (Leiden: Brill, 2002), 271–72.

[21] The Latin text is taken from Alexander Souter, *The Text and Canon of the New Testament* (New York: Scribner, 1913), 205–6.

[22] For the prologue to Philippians, see John Knox, *Marcion and the New Testament: An Essay in the Early History of the Canon* (Chicago: University of Chicago Press, 1942), 43–44; Boring, *An Introduction*, 221; for Ephesians, see Judith M. Lieu, *Marcion and the Making of a Heretic: God and Scripture in the Second Century* (Cambridge: Cambridge University Press, 2015), 239; for Philemon, see John J. Clabeaux, "Marcionite Prologues to Paul," in ABD 4:520.

[23] Percy Harrison included this verse as one of his proposed genuine fragments of Paul; see *The Problem of the Pastoral Epistles* (London: Oxford University Press, 1921), 115–35.

[24] George W. Knight, *The Pastoral Epistles: A Commentary on the Greek Text* (NIGTC; Grand Rapids: Eerdmans, 1992), 6; William D. Mounce, *Pastoral Epistles* (WBC 46; Dallas: Word, 2000), 590; Luke Timothy Johnson, *The First and Second Letters to Timothy: A New Translation with Introduction and Commentary* (AB 35A; New Haven, Conn.: Yale University Press, 2008), 65.

60s. The description of Mark as "useful for the purpose of ministry" (εὔχρηστος εἰς διακονίαν) (2 Tim. 4:11) may be related to the reference in Acts to Mark as a ὑπηρέτης. [25]

1.1.1.3. Mark in 1 Peter

The final mention of a Mark in the New Testament occurs in 1 Pet 5:13, in which the author, self-identified as Peter, sends greetings from Mark, whom he describes as "my son". This Mark is sometimes identified with John/Mark, [26] though others consider this doubtful. [27] The reference to this Mark as Peter's son may denote that he was Peter's convert, [28] which would be unlikely for John/Mark, the cousin of Barnabas. Some, however, perhaps on account of this unlikelihood, have suggested that the description may only stress the bond that united them in their work. [29]

1.1.2. John/Mark in Other Early Christian Writings

Most of the early sources which speak of a finger named Mark do so when discussing the Evangelist. Two sources, however, Dionysius of Alexandria and Chrysostom, specifically speak of the John/Mark of Acts.

1.1.2.1. Dionysius of Alexandria

Dionysius, who was bishop of Alexandria from 248 to 264 (*Hist. eccl.* 7.25.7), wrote a work entitled *On the Promises* in which he discusses the book of Revelation, the canonicity of which he evidently doubted on account of its millennialism. His work is no longer extant, but the early fourth-century church historian Eusebius discusses Dionysius' views and quotes his work in his *Ecclesiastical History*. In these extracts, Dionysius suggests that another John had written Revelation; but while he discusses John/Mark as a potential author, he questions this on the basis that the book of Acts records this Mark travelling back to Jerusalem rather than accompanying Paul into Asia (Acts 13:13) (*apud* Eusebius, *Hist. eccl.* 7.25.14). His knowledge of this Mark appears to be reliant solely upon Acts and provides no hints that he identified this Mark with either the Evangelist or with the founder of the Egyptian churches.

---

[25] Cf. Riesner, "Once More," 255.

[26] J. Ramsey Michaels, *1 Peter* (WBC 49; Dallas: Word, 1998), 311–12.

[27] Lightfoot, *Acts*, 208; Weiss, *Das älteste Evangelium*, 387; Paul J. Achtemeier, *1 Peter: A Commentary on First Peter* (Hermeneia; Minneapolis: Fortress, 1996), 355.

[28] Cf. Achtemeier, *1 Peter*, 355 (with reservations); Michaels, *1 Peter*, 312.

[29] John H. Elliott, *1 Peter: A New Translation with Introduction and Commentary* (AB 37B; New York: Doubleday, 2000), considers either meaning possible.

1.1.2.2. John Chrysostom

John Chrysostom (344/54–407), the renowned preacher who served as patriarch of Constantinople from 397 until 403 and who straddled the Greek and Syrian worlds, speaks of John/Mark in a series of sermons on the book of Acts (composed c. 400). After citing Acts 12:12, he goes on to discuss how Peter came to the house of Mary, the mother of John/Mark; he then pauses to raise the question of which John this John/Mark was, answering, "perhaps the one who was always with them" (ἴσως ἐκεῖνος ὁ ἀεὶ αὐτοῖς συνὼν [30]) (*Hom. Act.* 26).

Bruns takes this as an evident reference to John the Evangelist, noting in support that two later authors, Oecumenius (tenth century) and the learned Theophylact of Ochrid (d. c. 1107), seem to have understood him this way as well, [31] since they both correct the text. The former writes, "he speaks that he might show that it is not the mother of the John who was always with them" (ἵνα δείξῃ ὅτι οὐ τοῦ ἀεὶ συνόντος αὐτοῖς Ἰωάννου τὴν μητέρα φησὶ, καὶ τὸ παράσημον αὐτοῦ τέθηκε). [32] The latter, paraphrasing Chrysostom, writes: "not that [John] who was perhaps always with them" (Ἰωάννης δὲ οὐκ ἐκεῖνος ἦν ἴσως, ὁ ἀεὶ αὐτοῖς συνῶν), [33] retaining, as Bruns observes, a now redundant "perhaps", [34] before going on to suggest he was "possibly (τάχα)" Mark. While Chrysostom may have suspected John/Mark as being John the Evangelist, it is perhaps informative that he does not suggest that he was Mark the Evangelist.

1.2. Mark the Evangelist

References to Mark the Evangelist in early sources are provided in the context of the authorship of the second Gospel, as would be expected. In none of these is the Evangelist either explicitly identified with John/Mark or distinguished from him, though indications are sometimes given that may suggest that they were differentiated.

---

[30] *PG* 60:201.

[31] Bruns, "Riddle," 91. Raymond E. Brown, *The Gospel According to John (I–XII): Introduction, Translation, and Notes* (AB 29A; New Haven, Conn.: Yale University Press, 2008), xc, and Culpepper, *John*, 87 n. 34, likewise suppose that the reference in Chrysostom is to John/Mark.

[32] Bruns, "Riddle," 91, citing *PG* 118:197–98.

[33] Bruns, "Riddle," 91, citing *PG* 125:683–84.

[34] Bruns, "Riddle," 91.

1.2.1. Mark in Papias of Hierapolis

In the early second century, Papias, bishop of Hierapolis, mentions Mark the Evangelist in his work entitled the *Explanation* (or *Account*) *of the Dominical Logia*. This work, comprised of five volumes, seems to have collected together traditions handed down as from the apostles by a second generation of Christian leaders in Asia named "the elders" (*apud* Eusebius, *Hist. eccl.* 3.39.4). While the work is no longer extant, the church historian Eusebius, who published his *Ecclesiastical History* around the year 324, preserves a fragment in which Papias (quoting a figure named "the Elder" [35]) relates a tradition concerning how Mark the Evangelist wrote his Gospel:

Mark, having become the interpreter of Peter, accurately wrote the things either spoken or done by the Lord, whatever things he remembered, though not with arrangement. For he neither heard the Lord nor followed him, but later (he followed) Peter, as I was saying, who was rendering the teachings according to the needs, but not, as it were, making a complete arrangement of the sayings pertaining to the Lord, so that Mark in no way erred, thus writing singular points as he called them to mind (*apud* Eusebius, *Hist. eccl.* 3.39.15). [36]

Some hold that Papias was likely here referring to John/Mark. [37] Indeed, it is sometimes argued that only John/Mark would have been spoken of as just "Mark" without any further qualification, as he is in this passage. [38] This claim is problematic, however, for Papias in the context is speaking of the Mark associated with the authorship of the second Gospel, which does qualify his use. In any case, since only fragments of Papias' work are extant, it cannot be determined whether Papias provided any further qualification when introducing this Mark.

Furthermore, there are difficulties associating with any identification of this Mark with John/Mark. According to Papias (or rather, "the Elder"), Mark the Evangelist had neither heard nor followed Jesus but had been a follower of Peter and had written down what he had heard about Jesus' life from Peter's preaching (presumably in Rome; *apud* Eusebius, *Hist. eccl.* 2.14.5–2.15.2).

---

[35] Probably Papias' "John the Elder"; see Black, *Apostolic Interpreter*, 202; Elliott, *1 Peter*, 144; Martin Hengel, *Saint Peter: The Underestimated Apostle*, trans. Thomas H. Trapp (Grand Rapids: Eerdmans, 2010), 46.

[36] Translated by the author from the Greek text in Kirsopp Lake, ed. and trans., *Eusebius: The Ecclesiastical History*, 2 vols. (LCL; London: Heinemann; 1926), and so hereafter.

[37] E.g. Carson and Moo, *Introduction*, 174; John Painter, *Mark's Gospel: Worlds in Conflict* (London: Routledge, 1997), 4; Joel Marcus, *Mark 1–8: A New Translation with Introduction and Commentary* (AB 27; New Haven, Conn: Yale University Press, 2008), 22; Michael Bird, "Mark: Interpreter of Peter and Disciple of Paul," in *Paul and the Gospels: Christologies, Conflicts and Convergences*, ed. Michael F. Bird, Joel Willitts (London: T. & T. Clark, 2011), 30.

[38] Richard T. France, *The Gospel of Mark: A Commentary on the Greek Text* (NIGTC; Grand Rapids: Eerdmans, 2002), 37; Carson and Moo, *Introduction*, 174.

John/Mark on the other hand was held to have lived in Jerusalem, rendering it unlikely that he had never heard Jesus himself.

Moreover, John/Mark is said to have been closely acquainted with Barnabas (Acts 13:1–5; Col 4:10), one of the foremost eyewitnesses among the early Christians. This renders it unlikely that Papias would have excused this Mark's lack of "arrangement" in his Gospel on the basis that he was solely reliant upon Peter's preaching for his information, for clearly he would have had access to other potential sources of information. If Papias knew of the John/Mark of the New Testament, he likely did not identify him with Mark the Evangelist.

1.2.2. Mark in Irenaeus

Irenaeus, who was bishop of Lyon in Gaul in the latter part of the second century, seems to echo the Papian tradition concerning the Gospels in his work *Against Heresies*, published c. 185, in which he sought to explain and refute the beliefs of various gnostic groups he considered sub-orthodox. Arguing for the apostolic origin of the faith he defended, he appeals to the role of apostles in producing the four Gospels. Concerning those of Matthew and Mark, he writes:

Indeed, Matthew published a writing of the Gospel also among the Hebrews, in their own dialect, while Peter and Paul were preaching in Rome and establishing the church. After their departure (ἔξοδος), Mark, the disciple and interpreter of Peter, also himself has handed down (παραδέδωκεν) in writing the things preached by Peter (apud Eusebius, *Hist. eccl.* 5.8.2 = Irenaeus, *Haer.* 3.1.1).

Irenaeus, who was familiar with Papias' now lost work (*Haer.* 5.33.4), speaks, like Papias, of Mark the Evangelist as the follower of Peter who wrote down the things preached by Peter. And like Papias, Irenaeus lacks any specific identification of this Mark with John/Mark. However, while Papias is said by Eusebius to have related that Mark wrote while Peter was still alive (cf. the discussion of Clement below), Irenaeus appears to place Mark's writing after the deaths of Peter and Paul, which are usually dated in the 60s. [39] Winn resolves this by positing that Irenaeus was reliant upon a non-Papian source for the tradition of Mark writing after the apostles' deaths; [40] others attempt to reconcile the accounts by noting that the word ἔξοδος can be used of physical departure

---

[39] Thomas W. Manson, *Studies in the Gospels and Epistles* (Philadelphia; Westminster, 1962), 38; France, *Gospel of Mark*, 37; James G. Crossley, *The Date of Mark's Gospel: Insight from the Law in Earliest Christianity* (London: T. & T. Clark, 2004), 6; cf. Eusebius, *Hist. eccl.* 2.22.2; 3.1.2.

[40] Adam Winn, *The Purpose of Mark's Gospel: An Early Christian Response to Roman Imperial Propaganda* (WUNT 2.245; Tübingen: Mohr Siebeck, 2008), 49.

as well as of death, and therefore need not imply that Peter had died.[41] In support of the latter, it has also been observed that Irenaeus uses the present participle κηρυσσόμενος, implying that Peter was still alive at the time "the things being preached by Peter" were written down by Mark.[42]

In addition, a Syriac version of the tradition, related by Ephrem, does speak of Peter's physical departure:

Matthew wrote it [his Gospel] in Hebrew, and it was then translated into Greek. Mark, however, was following Simon Peter. When he had departed to Rome (*cum abiisset Romam*), they [the faithful] persuaded him [i.e. Mark], that they might recall the tradition, and lest it might fall into oblivion after a long duration of time, and he wrote that which he had comprehended (*Comm. in Diatess. Tatiani*).[43]

Thus, this account, which reads similarly to Irenaeus', does not speak of death at all. Furthermore, there is no mention of Paul, a feature which is also absent in the version of the tradition known to the Anti-Marcionite Prologue (second century or later[44]), which relates: "He [Mark] was Peter's interpreter. After the death/departure (*post excessionem*) of Peter he wrote down (*descripsit*) this same Gospel in the regions of Italy",[45] where the Latin *excessio*, like the Greek ἔξοδος, may refer to death or physical departure.

Irenaeus, Ephrem and the Anti-Marcionite Prologue all seem to be independently interacting with the same tradition, presumably derived from Papias, which spoke of Peter's physical departure. The reading in Irenaeus, μετὰ δὲ τὴν τούτων ἔξοδον, may have arisen as a result of a scribe understanding "departure" in the sense of death and then inserting the mention of Paul, since Peter and Paul were held to have died in the same city at about the same time. Possibly this was facilitated by a misreading of τούτου as τούτων (these two words were often confused by copyists[46]), as this would have naturally prompted the insertion of the mention of Paul into the account.

---

[41] Manson, *Studies*, 37–40; Robinson, *Redating*, 111; Ellis, *New Testament Documents*, 362 n. 28; France, *Gospel of Mark*, 37; Crossley, *The Date of Mark's Gospel*, 6–9.

[42] See Ilaria Ramelli, "John the Evangelist's Work: An Overlooked Redaktionsgeschichtliche Theory from the Patristic Age," in *The Origins of John's Gospel*, ed. by Stanley E. Porter and Hughson T. Ong (Leiden: Brill, 2016), 33.

[43] Translated from the Latin text in Kurt Aland, ed., *Synopsis Quattuor Evangeliorum: Locis parallelis evangeliorum apocryphorum et patrum adhibitis edidit* (15th ed.; Stuttgart: Deutsche Bibelgesellschaft, 2001), 560.

[44] Ellis, *New Testament Documents*, 359.

[45] Translation in Crossley, *The Date of Mark's Gospel*, 8.

[46] E.g. Acts 25:20 where the Majority Text is divided, or Mark 10:10 where Aleph reads τούτων against the τούτου of Codices Vaticanus, Alexandrinus, and Ephraemi; cf. LXX Exod 30:23; Num 35:5; Deut 21:6; Ezra 5:17; Neh 5:16; Dan 11:4, 12:8; 2 Macc 10:3; 3 Macc 4:19; Tob 8:6; Josephus, *Ant.* 4.206, 229, 293; 5.318; 8.17; 9.266; 10.255; 11.99; 12.388; idem, *Wars* 1.141; *Mart. Pol.* 23:3.

Nevertheless, those supportive of the traditional identification of Mark the Evangelist with John/Mark often cite this passage as evidence that early Christian sources placed the writing of Mark's Gospel in the late 60s, following the martyrdom of the two apostles, presumably because it is otherwise not easy to integrate all three narratives into a coherent storyline. Thus, while the book of Acts places John/Mark's journeys with Barnabas and Paul in the decade of the 40s, early Christian sources placed Mark the Evangelist in Rome at the time; Mark of Alexandria on the other hand was said to have been active in Egypt from the 40s until the eighth year of Nero (c. 62), a date associated with Mark's death. Furthermore, the Pauline corpus places Mark (presumably John/Mark) in Asia Minor in the early 60s death (for discussion of these points, see below and Chapter 2).

1.2.3. Mark in Tertullian

Tertullian, a native of Carthage in north Africa, wrote a polemical treatise against the Marcionites around the year 208 in which he argues for the apostolic origin of the four Gospels against Marcion's claim to have the original Gospel in a mutilated version of Luke's. In defending their apostolic origin, Tertullian seems to exhibit some familiarity with the Papian tradition of Mark as the one who wrote an account of Peter's preaching:

The same authority of the apostolic churches will defend the other Gospels also, which we accordingly have through them and following them; I speak of John and Matthew – and Mark published a Gospel which may be affirmed as Peter's, whose interpreter Mark was (*Adv. Marc.* 4.5). [47]

The passage is brief, but as with Papias and Irenaeus, Tertullian speaks of Mark only in connection with his writing of the second Gospel, and he provides no indications that he identified this figure with John/Mark.

1.2.4. Mark in Clement of Alexandria

The learned Clement of Alexandria (c. 150–c. 215) is said by Eusebius to have related in his work the *Hypotyposes* (now lost) the story of how Mark was urged to write a Gospel as a written memorial of Peter's preaching, and how Peter later learned of it and sanctioned its public use in the churches; Eusebius adds that this account was also confirmed by Papias (*Hist. eccl.* 2.15.1–2):

Such a light of piety shone in the thoughts of Peter's hearers that they were not content with one hearing or with the unwritten instruction in the divine preaching, but entreated Mark, whose Gospel is extant, being a follower of Peter, with all kinds of exhortations that he might also leave for them in writing a record of the teaching delivered to them by word; nor did they give up until they prevailed upon the man, and in this way they became the cause of the

---

[47] Translated by the author from the Latin text in Ernest Evans, ed. and trans., *Tertullian: Adversus Marcionem*, vol. 1 (Oxford: The Clarendon Press, 1972), 270.

writing called the Gospel according to Mark. They say that the apostle, knowing the deed, it being revealed to him by the Spirit, was pleased with the zeal of the men and confirmed the writing for study in the churches. Clement provides this story in the sixth book of his *Hypotyposes*. The bishop of Hierapolis, Papias by name, also attests the same as him. He (Clement) also says that Peter makes mention of Mark in his first letter, which, it is said, was composed in Rome itself, which he (Peter) himself indicates, speaking figuratively of the city in these words: she who is in Babylon, chosen with you, greets you, and so does Mark my son [1 Peter 5:13] (*apud* Eusebius, *Hist. eccl.* 2.15.1–2).

Clement (and likely Papias) does identify the Evangelist with the Mark whom Peter refers to as "my son" in 1 Pet 5:13; but although he speaks of Mark's association with Peter, he does not mention any association of this Mark with Paul or Barnabas, suggesting that he did not identify him with John/Mark. [48]

Eusebius placed the narrative in the reign of Claudius (41–54) (*Hist. eccl.* 2.14.6) which is inconsistent with John/Mark, who is presented in Acts as having been active in Jerusalem, Antioch and Cyprus during much of this period, rather than in Rome. It is unclear, however, whether Eusebius was following the chronology of Clement and Papias.

1.2.5. Mark in Origen

The Alexandrian scholar Origen (c. 185–c. 254), in a lost work on Matthew's Gospel, relates that Mark wrote his Gospel "as Peter instructed him", before noting, like Clement, that this Mark was the one Peter called his son in 1 Pet 5:13 (*apud* Eusebius, *Hist. eccl.* 6.25.4). Again, he provides no indication that he understood this figure to be John/Mark.

1.2.6. Mark the *"Stump-Fingered"* in the Refutation of All Heresies

The *Refutation of All Heresies*, written in Rome in the early third century (c. 225) and often (perhaps wrongly) attributed to Hippolytus of Rome, [49] briefly mentions a figure named Mark the "stump-fingered" (ὁ κολοβοδάκτυλος) and his Gospel when addressing the teachings of the Marcionites (*Refut.* 7.30.1). [50] Further discussion of this passage will, however, be postponed until Chapter 5.

1.2.7. Mark in Eusebius of Caesarea

Eusebius, bishop of Caesarea (d. c. 339), places the Papian account of Mark writing his Gospel at Rome during the reign of Claudius (41–54) (*Hist. eccl.* 2.14.6–15.2). Whether this was part of the Papian narrative or not is unclear.

---

[48] Cf. Weiss, *Das älteste Evangelium*, 389; Black, *Apostolic Interpreter*, 93.

[49] See the discussion of the issue of authorship in M. David Litwa, *Refutation of All Heresies: Text, Translation, and Notes* (WGRW 40; Atlanta: SBL, 2015), xxxii–xlii.

[50] Greek text in Litwa, *Refutation of All Heresies*, 556.

His account of Peter's encounter with Simon Magus, which immediately precedes the account of how Mark came to write his Gospel, seems to be summarised from second- or third-century *Acts of Peter*, and he may be following its placement of that narrative at that time (*Act. Petr.* 5).

Eusebius also claimed that Mark journeyed to Alexandria after writing his Gospel (*Hist. eccl.* 2.16.1) (cf. Chapter 2), adding that he was succeeded as bishop in the eighth year of Nero (c. 62) (*Hist. eccl.* 2.24.1). This chronology excludes the possibility that Eusebius identified this Mark with John/Mark, since he repeats the discussion of Dionysius in which the Alexandrian bishop speaks of John/Mark's travels in Jerusalem, Syria and Cyprus, during the time in which Eusebius places the Evangelist's activities in Rome and Alexandria.

1.3. Mark of Alexandria

1.3.1. *The* Martyrdom of Mark

The earliest work which purports to give an overview of the life of the Alexandrian Mark is the *Martyrdom of Mark*, likely written in Egypt sometime between the second and fourth century. [51] The story it tells is set in the regions of Libya and Egypt, and much of the narrative is taken up with an account of Mark's martyrdom.

It begins by relating how, at the time when the apostles were dispersed, the lot fell to Mark to preach in Egypt:

> At that time when the apostles were being dispersed throughout the inhabited world, it was the lot of the most holy Mark to go into the environs of Egypt by the will of God, where also the blessed canons of the holy and apostolic Church decreed that he be the first evangelist in the entire region of Egypt, Libya and Marmarice, Ammaniace and Pentapolis to preach the gospel of the visitation of our Lord and Savior Jesus Christ (*Mart. Marc.* 1). [52]

Mark's mission commences with his landing in Cyrene and Pentapolis (3), possibly from Jerusalem, where the tradition of the apostles being allotted their territories is usually located. [53] After preaching the word and performing miracles, Mark, at the direction of the Holy Spirit, sails to Alexandria (4) and disembarks at a place named Mendon. But as he enters the gate of the city, his sandal breaks (5). He brings his sandal to a cobbler, who injures his hand while

---

[51] See the thorough discussion in Allen D. Callahan, "The Acts of Saint Mark: And Introduction and Commentary," (Ph.D. dissertation, Harvard University, 1992), 19–27.

[52] Translation is from Callahan, "Acts of Saint Mark," Appendix 1, from a Greek manuscript (881) held in Paris.

[53] Cf. Dennis R. MacDonald, "Legends of the Apostles," in *Eusebius, Christianity, and Judaism*, ed. Harold Attridge and Gohei Hata (Detroit: Wayne State University Press, 1992), 176–78.

repairing it; Mark spits on the ground and forms clay, with which he anoints the hand, healing it (6). The cobbler then invites Mark to lodge at his house (7). Mark then is said to have instructed the cobbler (whose name is given as Ananias) and to have "enlightened" (i.e. baptised) him along with his household and "a great multitude in that place" (9).

Moved by threats to his life, Mark flees to Pentapolis after choosing Ananias as a bishop (10), but he returns to Alexandria two years later (11), where he finds that the Christians had built a church at a place by the shore called Boukalou. [54] The pagans, hearing of his return, seize him at the church during the Easter service, which takes place at a time corresponding to the festival of Serapis, and they tie a rope around his neck, dragging him along the ground until his body is bloodied. He is thrown into prison for the night where he receives divine visitations (11–15), and the next day he is again dragged around by a rope until he dies from his wounds, after which his persecutors burn his remains (18–19). The account continues by relating that a great storm arose which prevented the fire from consuming the body, and that the Greeks, afraid, returned Mark's corpse to the Christians, who deposited his remains in a place hewn out of rock (19–20). Possibly this is a conflation of an earlier tradition of Mark's body being consumed in a fire [55] and a later claim that his mummified corpse was preserved at the tomb of St Mark in Alexandria (with the relics now in Venice and Alexandria). [56]

While the work relates Mark's commission, ministry and martyrdom, it omits any narrative of his composing a Gospel at Rome, which seems to exclude the possibility that the author associated the Alexandrian Mark with the Mark of the Papian tradition. While it does not explicitly identify its Mark with the John/Mark of Acts either, [57] the inclusion of the allotment tradition, which is usually located in Jerusalem, may presuppose such an identification of the Alexandrian Mark with the Jerusalem-based John/Mark.

---

[54] Birger A. Pearson, "Earliest Christianity in Egypt: Some Observations," in *The Roots of Egyptian Christianity*, ed. Birger A. Pearson and James A. Goehring (Philadelphia: Fortress, 1986), 153, notes that Boukalou had been the Jewish quarter of Alexandria during the first century but would have been destroyed during the unrest in Trajan's reign (115–117) and would have been well outside of the city by the fourth century.

[55] Eutychius (896–940), bishop of Alexandria, recorded simply "his body was burned to ashes" (*corpus eius igne est crematum*); see PG 111:983.

[56] This argues against attempts at dating the *Martyrdom of Mark* on the presumption that the text must have been written after the time from which Mark's tomb was exhibited, as Pearson suggests ("Earliest Christianity in Egypt," 142–43).

For the intriguing theory that the corpse of Alexander the Great, which disappears from the historical record after the fourth century, might have been identified as St Mark's in order to protect it from destruction by anti-pagan Christian zealots at the end of the fourth century; see Andrew Michael Chugg, *The Quest for the Tomb of Alexander the Great* (2007), esp. 200–201.

[57] Cf. Callahan, "Acts of Saint Mark," 4.

1.3.1.1. The Date of Mark's Death

There is confusion in the literary sources of the *Martyrdom of Mark* as to the time of Mark's death. The Greek text places it in the reign of "Gaius Tiberius Caesar," but there was no such emperor, though perhaps Tiberius Claudius Caesar (41–54), as given in the Latin translation of Hieronymus Surianus, was intended. [58] One recension of the Latin places it in the reign of Gaius and one "in the fourteenth year of Nero" (67/68) (*anno Neronis imperii quarto decimo*). [59] The latter date might represent at attempt at bringing the Alexandrian tradition into conformity with that of Mark the Evangelist since, as discussed above, Irenaeus can be understood as placing the writing of Mark's Gospel after the deaths of Peter and Paul, which Eusebius' *Chronicle* places in the thirteenth (Armenian) or fourteenth (Latin) year of Nero, the latter of which is followed by Jerome (c. 347–420). [60]

An Arabic version places Mark's death in the reign of Aghāyūn Tiberius Caesar, [61] while an Ethiopic version claims it occurred in the reign of the emperor Tiberius (14–37). [62] The version of the *Martyrdom of Mark* in the Roman martyrology places it in the eighth year of Nero, [63] while in the version in Mawhub's *History of the Patriarchs of the Coptic Church of Alexandria* (*Hist. Patr. Eccl. Alex.* 1.1), an eleventh-century work written in Arabic, the date is omitted but Mark's successor Ananias is said to have died after twenty-two years of his episcopacy, in the second year of Domitian (85 CE), thus placing Mark's death in 62/63 CE (*Hist. Patr. Eccl. Alex.* 1.3), which is the date Jerome assigns to Mark's martyrdom (*Vir.* 8).

1.4. Conclusion

There appear to have been three separate and independent Markan traditions in early Christian sources. One pertained to the Judean John/Mark, whose journeys in Syria and Cyprus are recounted in the book of Acts; there was also

---

[58] *PG* 115:169.

[59] See Callahan, "Acts of Saint Mark," 7.

[60] See: Jack Finegan, *The Archeology of the New Testament: The Mediterranean World of the Early Christian Apostles* (Boulder, Colo.: Westview Press, 1981), 35.

[61] See: Agnes Smith Lewis, *The Mythological Acts of the Apostles* (HSem 4; London: Clay, 1904), 151; Aghāyūn may be a corruption of "Gaius"; see Callahan, "Acts of Saint Mark," 108.

[62] Ernest Alfred Wallis Budge, ed. and trans., *The Contendings of the Apostles: Being the Histories and the Lives and Martyrdoms and Deaths of the Twelve Apostles and Evangelists*, vol. 2: *The English Translation* (Oxford: Oxford University Press, 1901), 317.

[63] See: Oden, *African Memory*, 65.

Mark the Evangelist, a follower of Peter who wrote his Gospel in Italy, possibly during the reign of Claudius; lastly, there was Mark the founder of the churches of Egypt who was martyred in Alexandria.

There is no evidence from any of these sources that John/Mark was identified with Mark the Evangelist, though there is a possibility that John/Mark was identified with Mark of Alexandria in the *Martyrdom of Mark*. Indeed, the distinct chronological frameworks pertaining to the Evangelist and John/Mark, and Chrysostom's apparent uncertainty over whether John/Mark was John the Evangelist, suggest that they were often viewed as separate figures.

Chapter 2

The Conflation of Mark the Evangelist

The evidence may suggest that narratives pertaining to Mark the Evangelist came to be reconfigured in various ways as a result of his identification with John/Mark and/or the Alexandrian Mark. The conflation of these traditions begins to appear probably no earlier than the turn of the fourth century, suggesting that the Marks of tradition came to be confused from around that time. The conflation of Mark the Evangelist with John/Mark mostly involves nothing more than the appending of the notices concerning John/Mark found in the New Testament to Papias' narrative framework of Mark as a follower of Peter who wrote in Rome. However, two portrayals of Mark the Evangelist portray him as a Judean figure, and these may represent conflations with traditions of John/Mark drawn independently of the New Testament. The first is the portrayal of Mark as a Judean priest, found in Latin sources, and the second is the claim that the Evangelist was one of the seventy or seventy-two disciples sent out by Jesus (Luke 10:1), which is found in Syriac, Greek and Coptic sources. These sources will be discussed in this chapter, with the exception of Coptic ones, which will be discussed separately in the next chapter.

2.1. Syrian Traditions

Syrian sources tend to conflate the Evangelist either with John/Mark or with the Alexandrian Mark. Notices concerning John/Mark are largely drawn from the book of Acts, though a small number of sources of probable Syrian provenance know in common with some Coptic and Greek sources a tradition of Mark the Evangelist as one of Jesus' seventy or seventy-two disciples (Luke 10:1). This motif may represent a conflation of Mark the Evangelist, who had never followed Jesus according to the Papian tradition, with a Judean disciple of Jesus, and possibly with John/Mark.

2.1.1. *The* Dialogue of Adamantius

The *Dialogue of Adamantius* purports to be a record of a debate between an "orthodox" writer, named Adamantius, and a number of "heretical" antagonists, among whom was a Marcionite named Megethius. It is usually thought to have been written in Greek, [1] either in southern Asia Minor or Syria, [2] probably sometime in the period 280–313. [3]

While this work does not specifically identify the Evangelist and John/Mark, it does conflate the Evangelist, the follower of Peter, with the Mark mentioned in Col 4:10, the cousin of Barnabas, who is often identified with John/Mark (cf. Chapter 1). This occurs within the context of a dispute concerning the four Gospels, which the Marcionites rejected, possessing instead their own single Gospel, called the *Gospel of the Lord*, which is believed to have been based upon the Gospel of Luke. In defending this Marcionite Gospel, Megethius claims: "I will show from the Gospels themselves that they are spurious". [4] He proceeds to challenge Adamantius to find a mention of Mark and Luke in these writings, and he concludes from the non-mention of their names that "Christ did not have Mark and Luke as disciples, so you and your party are convicted of producing spurious writings… Let the Gospel be read, and you will find that their names are not recorded."

Adamantius in reply reminds his interlocutor that Jesus had seventy-two disciples who were not named (cf. Luke 10:1), a passage which was presumably also found in the Marcionite Gospel, and he goes on to claim that Mark and Luke were among that number. He adds that Mark and Luke preached with Paul; Megethius replies, "it is impossible that these men ever saw Paul", but Adamantius offers to show Megethius how these two are mentioned in Paul's letters: "I will show that the Apostle himself bears witness to Mark and Luke"; he adds, "I will prove that Mark and Luke worked with Paul." Adamantius then proceeds to quote Col 4:10, 11, 14, which mentions both Mark and Luke among Paul's co-workers (*Adam.* 5). Presumably the Marcionites' own edited version of Paul's letters, which they called the Apostolicon, contained this passage also. The *Dialogue of Adamantius* thus contains the earliest form of the tradition of Mark as one of the seventy-two disciples.

2.1.1.1. Evidence of Conflation?

Adamantius claims that Mark and Luke were disciples of Jesus, but according to Papias, Mark was a follower of Peter who had neither heard nor followed Jesus (*apud* Eusebius, *Hist. eccl.* 3.39.15). Mark the Evangelist thus could not have been one of the seventy-two disciples of Jesus, at least according to the Papian tradition. Luke's Gospel (1:2) seems to exclude the possibility that Luke

---

[1] Robert A. Pretty, trans., *Adamantius: Dialogue on the True Faith in God* (Leuven: Peeters, 1997), 14 n. 38.

[2] Pretty, *Adamantius*, 17–18.

[3] Pretty, *Adamantius*, 16–17.

[4] Translations are from Pretty, *Adamantius*, 41–43. The Greek text is in *PG* 11:1,713–884.

had been an eyewitness disciple also, and Irenaeus speaks of him only as "the disciple and follower of the apostles" (*Haer.* 1.23.1, cf. 3.10.1).

Perhaps, however, John/Mark and Lucius of Cyrene were at one time associated with the seventy(-two) disciples, so that it was the identification of these with Mark and Luke gave rise to Adamantius' claim. John/Mark was a Jerusalemite who was associated with prominent early Christian leaders in the Jerusalem church (Acts 12:12–16; 25), and Lucius seems to have been a Judean disciple too, for he is first mentioned in Acts 13:1 as being in Antioch with those who had been dispersed from Jerusalem on account of the persecution which followed upon Stephen's death (Acts 8:1). He is also said to have been from Cyrene, and he may have been identified as one of those Hellenistic evangelists from Cyrene and Cyprus (cf. Acts 11:20) who brought the gospel to Antioch.

The identification of Lucius with Luke is likely presupposed already in the earlier so-called Western Text of Acts which is probably to be dated to the mid-second century. [5] In Acts 11:28 in this text, the first-person plural pronoun "we", denoting the introduction of the purported author, Luke, into the narrative, is introduced far earlier than in other texts:

Now in these days there came down prophets from Jerusalem to Antioch. And there was much rejoicing; and when we were gathered together one of them named Agabus stood up and spoke, signifying by the Spirit that there should be a great famine over all the world; which came to pass in the days of Claudius. [6]

The context for the placement of the pronoun is a visit of prophets to Antioch from Jerusalem. Since Lucius is later said to have been at Antioch (Acts 13:1), there is a good probability that the pronoun was added to this account due to the identification of Lucius with Luke. [7] Jerome evidently knew this reading as he speaks of Luke as a physician of Antioch, claiming that his writings indicate this (*Vir.* 7; cf. Eusebius' claim that Luke was "of Antiochan stock", *Hist. eccl.* 3.4.6).

While Lucius appears to have been Jewish, the natural inference from Colossians is that the author considered Luke to be a Gentile, since he is mentioned only after Paul's co-workers who were "of the circumcision" are named

---

[5] Bruce Metzger and Bart Ehrman, *The Text of the New Testament: Its Transmission, Corruption, and Restoration* (4th edition; Oxford: Oxford University Press, 2005), 308.

[6] Translation taken, with minor changes, from James M. Wilson, *The Western Text of the Acts of the Apostles, translated from Codex Bezae* (London: SPCK, 1923), 65; cf. Claus-Jürgen Thornton, *Der Zeuge des Zeugen: Lukas als Historiker der Paulusreisen* (WUNT 56; Tübingen: J.C.B. Mohr [Paul Siebeck], 1991), 271.

[7] Hans Conzelmann, *Die Apostelgeschichte* (HNT 7; Tübingen: J.C.B. Mohr [Paul Siebeck], 1963), 68; Thornton, *Der Zeuge des Zeugen*, 271; Markus Öhler, *Barnabas* (WUNT 156; Tübingen: Mohr Siebeck, 2003), 230. Barrett (*Acts of the Apostles*, 564), however, is not convinced.

(Col 4:10–14). [8] Perhaps the idea that Luke had been a proselyte to Judaism before his conversion, which Jerome states was held by some (*Qu. hebr. Gen.* Gen 46:27), represents an attempt at harmonizing the identification of the Gentile Luke with the Jewish Lucius. The same intention is probably also responsible for the view of Jacob of Edessa (c. 640–708), as recorded by bar Salibi, that although Luke was Hebrew, he was educated in the learning and language of the Greeks. [9] Confusion of the two may also have given rise to the reading of Acts 13:1 attested in an early fourth-century African work which Bruce refers to as the *Prophecies Collected from All the Books*, which, like the Western text, inserts the pronoun "we" in Acts 11:28, and which also makes the Greek Titus the foster brother of Lucius of Cyrene. [10] This unique reading probably reflects a mistaken belief that Titus was the literal brother of Luke. Origen (*Hom. 1. in Luc*) [11] identified Luke as the brother "whose praise is in the gospel" spoken of by Paul (2 Cor 8:18; 12:18), who is mentioned immediately after Titus in the account, and some have argued that "the brother" here should be rendered "his [i.e. Titus'] brother", reflecting a common usage of the definite article, which would make Luke the literal brother of Titus. [12] Apparently, some ancient writers thought the same and have subsequently attempted to account for how the Jewish Lucius could be the brother of the Greek Titus by recourse to the convenient expedient of adoption.

2.1.2. Ephrem the Syrian

Ephrem the Syrian (306–373) recounts the Papian tradition of Mark the Evangelist in his commentary upon the *Diatessaron*: [13]

Mark followed Simon Peter. When he went to Rome [the faithful] persuaded him [to write] so that they would remember the tradition, lest it be forgotten after a long time. He wrote what he had grasped. [14]

---

[8] See Frederick F. Bruce, *The Epistles to the Colossians, to Philemon, and to the Ephesians* (NICNT; Grand Rapids: Eerdmans, 1984), 181.

[9] Dionysius bar Salibi, *In Apocalypsim, Actus et Epistulas Catholicas*, CCSO 2.101.23. Cf. Felix Haase, ed., *Apostel und Evangelisten in den orientalischen Überlieferungen* (NTA 9; Münster: Aschendorff, 1922), 288.

[10] See: Frederick F. Bruce, *The Book of the Acts* (NICNT; Grand Rapids: Eerdmans, 1988), 244, n.1.

[11] Cf. Thornton, *Der Zeuge des Zeugen*, 271.

[12] Alexander Souter, "A Suggested Relationship between Titus and Luke," *ExpT* 18 (1907): 285; 335–36; William Ramsay, *Luke the Physician* (London: Hodder & Stoughton, 1908), 17–18.

[13] About 80% of Ephrem's commentary is believed to have been recovered, a translation of which is found in Carmel MacCarthy, trans., *Saint Ephrem's Commentary on Tatian's Diatessaron: An English translation of Chester Beatty Syriac MS 709* (Oxford: Oxford University Press, 1993).

[14] Translation in MacCarthy, *Saint Ephrem's Commentary*, 344.

Ephrem may have identified John/Mark with Mark the Evangelist, for in his commentary on Acts, Ephrem does identify John/Mark and Lucius of Cyrene as Gospel writers:

Saul and Barnabas, who carried food for the saints in Jerusalem, returned with John who was called Mark and so did Luke of Cyrene [cf. Acts 11:25–27; 12:25]. But both these are evangelists and wrote before the discipleship of Paul, and therefore he used to repeat everywhere from their Gospel (*Comm. Acts*). [15]

Ephrem clearly identified Lucius of Cyrene with Luke the Evangelist; however, while for a modern reader, the reference to a Gospel written by "John, who was also called Mark" evokes Mark's Gospel, the possibility cannot be ruled out, in light of the potential Johannine identifications of John/Mark in Chrysostom (see Chapter 1) and other sources (discussed later in this study), that Ephrem might have understood this Evangelist as John rather than Mark. Indeed, Ephrem elsewhere claims that John the Evangelist wrote his Gospel in Antioch (see Chapter 10), [16] the city to which Lucius and John/Mark are said to have returned with Paul.

2.1.3. The Apostolic Constitutions

Like the *Dialogue of Adamantius*, the *Apostolic Constitutions*, a work of probably Syrian provenance written in the latter part of the fourth century, identifies the evangelists Mark and Luke as Paul's fellow workers (*Const. Apost.* 2.57), in an evident allusion to Philm 24 (cf. Col 4:10, 11, 14; 2 Tim 4:11). It also identifies the Evangelist as the one who ordained the first bishop of Alexandria (*Const. Apost.* 7.46). Consequently, the *Apostolic Constitutions* is perhaps the earliest extant work to identify John/Mark, Mark the Evangelist and the Alexandrian Mark.

2.1.4. Victor of Antioch

Victor of Antioch (fifth century) in his *Prologue to the Gospel of Mark* identifies Mark the Evangelist with John/Mark, "the son of Mary, who received the apostles in her house in Jerusalem, as is shown in the Acts of the Apostles" (cf. Acts 12:12), and he goes on to quote Paul's reference to Mark in Colossians and 2 Timothy. He continues by citing 1 Peter 5:13 while adding that after

---

[15] Translation in Henry J. Cadbury, "Lucius of Cyrene," in *The Acts of the Apostles*, vol. 5, ed. F. J. Foakes Jackson and Kirsopp Lake (London: MacMillan, 1933), 494. Conybeare's Latin translation of this passage is found in James Hardy Ropes, "The Text of Acts," in *The Acts of the Apostles*, vol. 3, ed. F. J. Foakes Jackson and Kirsopp Lake (London: MacMillan, 1926), 416.

[16] See Fred C. Conybeare, "Ein Zeugnis Ephräms über das Fehlen von c. 1 und 2 im Texte des Lucas," *ZNW* 3 (1902): 193.

these things, Mark was urged to write his Gospel at Rome, which Peter approved of for use in the churches, [17] following the Papian account. Little is known about Victor, though he may have been a presbyter of the church in Antioch. [18] Among his sources were the works of Origen and Theodore of Mopsuestia (whose commentary on Mark is not extant). [19]

2.1.5. Severus of Antioch

Severus, who was (Monophysite) bishop of Antioch from 512–38, briefly relates that Mark was the disciple of Peter and that he taught the whole of Egypt, showing that he identified the Evangelist with the Alexandrian Mark; [20] he gives no indication as to whether he identified this Mark with John/Mark.

2.1.6. Isho'dad of Merv

Isho'dad (c. 850), the Eastern Syrian bishop, in the preface to his commentary on Mark, gives an account of Mark the Evangelist which combines him with John/Mark and the Alexandrian Mark. [21] He also knows and accepts the tradition that Mark and Luke belonged to the Seventy Disciples (*Comm. Marc.* prolog.), [22] and this has apparently led him to interpret 1 Peter 5:13 to mean that Mark was Peter's biological rather than his convert, presumably because the latter would have conflicted with the narrative of Mark as Jesus' disciple. He cites in support Clement's claim that Peter begat children (cf. *Strom.* 3.6) before relating the tradition that Mary, John/Mark's mother, whose house Peter went to after his deliverance from prison (cf. Acts 12:12), was the wife of Simon (i.e. Peter) and that Mark and Rhoda (cf. Acts 12:13) were his children. Quoting 1 Peter 5:13, he says that Babylon refers to Rome and denotes its opulence (*Comm. Marc.* prolog.).

Isho'dad goes on to recount the story, found in the *Acts of Peter* and Eusebius, of how Peter came to Rome and there opposed Simon the Sorcerer during the reign of Claudius (41–54) (*apud* Eusebius, *Hist. eccl.* 2.14–15). According

---

[17] From the Greek text in John Anthony Cramer, ed., *Catenae Graecorum Patrum in Novum Testamentum*, vol. 1 (Oxford, 1844), 263–64. The Greek text is also given by Weiss, *Das älteste Evangelium*, 404–5. This is an excerpt, and I have not been able to ascertain whether the rest of the text is extant, or whether Victor associated this Mark with Alexandria.

[18] Sean P. Kealy, *Mark's Gospel: A History of Its Interpretation* (New York: Paulist, 1982), 92.

[19] Kealy, *Mark's Gospel*, 92.

[20] See E. W. Brooks, ed. and trans., *The Hymns of Severus and others in the Syriac Version of Paul of Edessa as Revised by James of Edessa*, PO 6 (Paris, 1911), 172.

[21] See Margaret Gibson, ed. and trans., *The Commentaries of Isho'dad of Merv: Bishop of Ḥadatha (c. 850 A.D.)* (HSem 5, vol. 1; Cambridge: Cambridge University Press, 1911), xvi–xvii.

[22] For the English translation, see Gibson, *Commentaries of Isho'dad of Merv*, 123–24.

to the *Acts of Peter*, Peter was in Jerusalem twelve years after the ascension, when he was directed to go to Rome and to confront Simon the Sorcerer (*Act. Petr.* 5). Isho'dad, however, inserts an intervening stay for Peter of two years in Antioch:

but Peter, after he had escaped from that prison [cf. Acts 12:4–10], went to Antioch, and in that very year laid the foundations of the church in Antioch, and made there an altar, and commanded that they should worship towards the East; and [told] that on the first day of the week our Lord dwelt in the Virgin, and on it shall be the Resurrection on the last day. And after two years, on hearing what Simon did at Rome, he appointed Evodios [i.e. Evodius] bishop at Antioch instead of him[self], and he ruled for twenty-five years. [23]

The account adds that Peter "pursued and flew to Rome after Simon" before relating a modified version of the story, found in the *Acts of Peter*, of Peter commanding a dog to deliver a message in a man's voice to Simon (*Act. Petr.* 9). It continues: "Then Peter at once founded a church in Rome, and ruled it for twenty-five years." [24]

Isho'dad also modifies the Papian story of how Mark came to write his Gospel: instead of Mark being exhorted to write after Peter's departure, it is Peter, in view of his coming death, who is exhorted by the Christians at Rome to put the teachings of the gospel in a book. Peter directed Mark to write it, and Mark spoke of Jesus' humanity in order to counteract the teachings of Simon the Sorcerer. [25] Lastly, Isho'dad reports that Mark afterwards "went first to Egypt and preached there, and founded the church at Alexandria." [26]

2.1.7. Michael of Antioch

The Jacobite bishop Michael of Antioch (twelfth century) in a brief comment in his *Chronicle* alludes only to the Papian and Alexandrian traditions: "Mark, the disciple of Peter and his son, was sent to Mizraim [Egypt], and he evangelised the whole of Egypt. He was bishop there for 22 years." [27]

2.1.8. Dionysius bar Salibi

Dionysius bar Salibi (d. 1171), the Jacobite bishop of Amid, relates in his commentary on the Gospels that two apostles and two evangelists wrote, adding that Mark was the disciple of Peter and Luke of Paul (*Comm. in Evang.* 34). He states that Mark wrote his Gospel in Rome, though he notes that according

---

[23] Translation in Gibson, *Commentaries of Isho'dad of Merv*, 124.

[24] Translation in Gibson, *Commentaries of Isho'dad of Merv*, 124–25.

[25] Gibson, *Commentaries of Isho'dad of Merv*, 124–25.

[26] Translation in Gibson, *Commentaries of Isho'dad of Merv*, 125.

[27] Translated by the author from the French translation of Jean-Baptiste Chabot, *Chronique de Michel le Syrien, Patriarche Jacobite d'Antioch (1166–1199)*, vol. 1 (Paris, Leroux, 1899), 156.

to Chrysostom (here called Mar John), Mark wrote in Egypt (*Comm. in Evang.* 37). He adds that Peter directed Mark to write against the teachings of "Simon" (i.e. Simon the Sorcerer), who held that the incarnation of the Lord was not real (*Comm. in Evang.* 40). [28]

2.1.9. Bar Hebraeus

The Jacobite bishop Bar Hebraeus (thirteenth century) seems to follow the account of Isho'dad (c. 850), summarised above, though he confuses Rhoda with Rome, claiming that Rhoda was called Babylon on account of her opulence (*Comm. Marc.* prolog.). [29]

2.1.10. The Book of the Bee

The *Book of the Bee*, written by Solomon, the East Syrian (Nestorian) bishop of Basra in Mesopotamia from about 1222, [30] relates that Mark and Luke were the disciples of Peter and Paul respectively, and that after the martyrdom of the apostles near Rome, they gathered their bodies and brought them back inside the city (*Lib. Apis* 48). [31] It also claims that Mark himself was martyred in Rome and buried there. This narrative contrasts with the more dominant view that Mark was martyred in Alexandria; possibly it reflects a pre-conflated tradition of the Papian Mark dying in Rome.

  The *Book of the Bee* knows the identification of the Evangelist with John/Mark, for it states that some held that Mark was the son of Simon's wife, while others claimed that he was the son of Simon and that Rhoda was his sister (48; cf. 50). However, a little later it distinguishes "Lucius the Cyrenian" and "John called Mark" from the Evangelists Luke and Mark (*Liber Apis* 49). [32] It also places Lucius and John/Mark among the seventy disciples (*Liber Apis* 49), which is consistent with the view posited above that the tradition originally

---

[28] Summarised from the Latin text in I. Sedlácek, ed. *Dionysius bar Salibi: Commentarii in Evangelia* (CSCO 2/98, Scriptores Syri; Rome: de Luigi, 1906) and so hereafter.

[29] Eardley W. Carr, ed. and trans., *Gregory Abu'l Faraj Commonly Called Bar-Hebraeus: Commentary on the Gospels from the Horreum Mysteriorum* (London: SPCK, 1925), 75.

[30] Earnest A. Budge, ed. and trans., *The Book of the Bee* (Oxford: Clarendon Press, 1886), iii.

[31] Another version of the account, found in a Syriac manuscript dated to 874, speaks only of "the Christians" instead of Mark and Luke. See Michel van Esbroeck, "Deux listes d'apôtres conservées en syriaque," in René Lavenant, ed., Third Symposium Syriacum 1980 (OCA 221; Rome: Pont. Institutum Studiorum Orientalium, 1983), 19. It should not be assumed that this version is earlier, however; the reference to Mark and Luke may have been removed in favour of other narratives.

[32] An English translation can be found in Budge, *Book of the Bee.*

pertained to these two figures and was transferred to Luke and Mark by conflation. But this work also seems to have attempted to harmonise this version with the claim that the Evangelists were members of the seventy, for it asserts that "Mark the Evangelist" and "Luke the physician" were later honorary members (along with figures such as Apollos), who replaced original members that had been disqualified on account of heresy (*Liber Apis* 49). In this way, it was able to place Luke and Mark among the seventy without making them disciples of Jesus.

2.2. Greek Sources

Greek works tend to emphasise Papias' narrative of Mark as the disciple and interpreter of Peter. Some, like Eusebius, are silent concerning any identification of this figure with John/Mark, while others combine the New Testament notices of John/Mark with the Papian narrative. Exceptions include a small number of Cypriot works and the *Acts of Mark*, which will be discussed in chapters 4 and 5 respectively.

2.2.1. Clement of Alexandria's Letter to Theodore, *aka "Secret Mark"*

The potentially earliest identification of Mark the Evangelist with the Alexandrian Mark is found in Clement's *Letter to Theodore*, purportedly discovered by Morton Smith in 1958 at the monastery of Mar Saba in Israel. The suspicion of forgery, however, has long hovered over this work, and the reference to Mark the Evangelist as being in Alexandria may be an anachronism which further supports this suspicion, for Eusebius is otherwise the earliest writer to combine the narratives of the two Marks (see below), and it seems to have been unknown to the *Martyrdom of Mark*, which was written sometime between the second and fourth century.

Furthermore, the *Letter to Theodore*'s reference to Mark's journeying to Alexandria "after the death of Peter" seems to have been influenced by Irenaeus' statement that Mark wrote after the death of Peter and Paul. But this might not have been the original reading (see Chapter 1), and no other ancient writer places Mark's stay in Alexandria this late. Indeed, Eusebius places it in Claudius' reign (cf. Chapter 1) and claims, on the basis of an ancient tradition, that Mark's successor was ordained in the ninth year of Nero (c. 62) (*Hist. eccl.* 2.24.1; see below).

2.2.2. Eusebius of Caesarea

After relating the story of how Mark came to write his Gospel (*Hist. eccl.* 2.14.6–15.2), Eusebius goes on to record how "they say" (φασίν) that Mark the Evangelist was the first to establish churches in Alexandria (*Hist. eccl.* 2.16.1).

The relationship between the narratives is unclear. Eusebius may still be relating the accounts of Clement and Papias, so that it is they who made Mark the Evangelist to have travelled to Egypt, [33] but it has also been suggested that Eusebius was combining two separate traditions of both a Mark in Rome (from Clement-Papias) and a Mark in Alexandria (from local Alexandrian oral tradition). [34] Eusebius had already used the verb φασίν of Clement and Papias (*Hist. eccl.* 2.15.2), suggesting he may have still been following their account.

On the other hand, the two accounts do seem to have been variously conflated in later documents (as shall be discussed throughout the course of this study), which may be suggestive of their separate origins.

A Claudian context for the tradition of Mark the Evangelist might partially explain why Eusebius mistakenly conflated Mark's early converts with the sect of the Therapeutae in Egypt, which, he notes, was described by Philo (*Hist. Eccl.* 2.16.2), and which thus would have been in existence prior to Philo's death in c. 50 CE [35] Eusebius apparently assumed that because Philo had taken notice of them during the same general period as Mark the Evangelist's activities, that they must have sprang into existence as a result of his preaching in Egypt. Eusebius adds that Mark's successor in the city was ordained in the eighth year of Nero (c. 62) (*Hist. eccl.* 2.24.1), a date which Jerome understands as that of Mark's death (*Vir.* 8).

2.2.3. Chrysostom

Chrysostom also seems to have identified Mark the Evangelist and the Alexandrian Mark, for he relates that Mark wrote his Gospel in Egypt at the urging of the disciples (*Hom. 1.7 in Matt.*), which probably represents confusion of the Papian and Alexandrian traditions.

2.2.4 Epiphanius of Salamis

Epiphanius (c. 325–403), bishop of Salamis in Cyprus, wrote his *Panarion* or *Medicine Chest* at the end of the fourth century, in which he lists Mark and Luke among the seventy-two disciples (*Pan.* 20.4.4). Later in the work, Epiphanius attempts to resolve the problem of how Mark the Evangelist could have been both Peter's convert (perhaps based on 1 Peter 5:13 and/or Papias) and a personal disciple of Jesus, which he does by having Mark fall away from his discipleship before being later restored by Peter.

---

[33] Ramelli, "John the Evangelist's Work, 31–32.

[34] Stephen J. Davis, *The Early Coptic Papacy*, vol.1 (Cairo: The American University in Cairo Press, 2005), 6–7.

[35] According to the Latin version of Eusebius' *Chronicle*, Peter arrived in the imperial city in the second year of Claudius (42). See Crossley, *The Date of Mark's Gospel*, 11.

And immediately following after Matthew, Mark is instructed by the holy Peter in Rome to set forth the Gospel, and having written it, he is sent by the holy Peter into the region of the Egyptians. But this one was one of the seventy-two, who were scattered at the saying which Jesus spoken: "Unless one eats my flesh and drinks my blood, he is not worthy of me" (cf. John 6:53), as is clear to those reading the Gospels. Nevertheless, having been brought back by Peter, he was made worthy to proclaim the gospel, being filled with the Holy Spirit (*Pan.* 51.6.10–11). [36]

This exegetical manoeuvre similarly enabled him to claim that Luke was likewise one of those who fell away and that he was restored to repentance by Paul (*Pan.* 51.11.6). In this way, he preserved some semblance of the Papian tradition of Mark as Peter's follower and of Luke as Paul's, while maintaining the view that both had been Judean disciples of Jesus.

2.2.5. Sophronius of Jerusalem

Sophronius of Jerusalem (c. 560–638) in his preface to the Gospel [37] reproduces the account found in Jerome's *Lives of Illustrious Men* (8), which related only the Papian and Alexandrian traditions, drawn from Eusebius (*Eccl. hist.* 2.15).

2.2.6. Procopius the Deacon

Procopius the Deacon of Constantinople (d. 815) composed an *Encomium of St. Mark* in which he described Mark as the son of Peter and the "light of the whole of Egypt". [38] While he speaks of him as Peter's son, he also claims that he "was called by the divine voice" and "was numbered with the apostolic assembly of the seventy" (*Encom. in Marc.*). [39] He thus seems to have combined elements of all three Markan traditions into a single figure.

2.2.7. Ps.-Dorotheus

The work *On the Seventy Disciples* (possibly ninth century), found in the *Synopsis* wrongly attributed to Dorotheus of Tyre (d. c. 361), purports to list the names of the seventy disciples sent out by Jesus. In this list, three Marks are distinguished: the bishops of Alexandria, Byblos (in Phoenicia) and Apollonia (it is unknown which city of this name was intended) respectively; confusingly, it refers to the bishop of Byblos as John/Mark and the bishop of Apollonia as

---

[36] Translated by the author from the Greek text in Karl Holl, ed., *Epiphanius* (*Ancoratus und Panarion*), vol. 2, *Panarion haer. 34–64* (GCS 31; Leipzig: Hinrichs, 1922).

[37] The Greek text can be found in Hermann Freiherr von Soden, *Die Schriften des Neuen Testaments in ihrer ältesten erreichbaren Textgestalt*, vol. 1 (Berlin: Duncker, 1902), 308–9.

[38] Literally "fleeting dream," with "dream" used to denote something that is ephemeral, not, as in English, something hoped for or aspired to.

[39] Translated from the Greek text in *PG* 100:1189.

the cousin of Barnabas, though both are distinguished from the bishop of Alexandria, who is referred to as the Evangelist. [40]

2.2.8. Theophylact

The learned scholar Theophylact, of the then Bulgarian city of Ochrid (d. c. 1107), in his *Exposition of Acts*, states, citing Acts 12:12, that John/Mark was "perhaps Mark the Evangelist, through whom they say that Peter preached, for the Gospel of Mark is said to be Peter's" (*Exp. in Acta*). [41]

Elsewhere he combines all three portrayals of Mark, though his account exhibits no independent knowledge of John/Mark outside of the New Testament:

Mark's Gospel was written at Rome ten years after the ascension of Christ. For this Mark was the disciple of Peter, whom Peter also always calls his spiritual son. He is also called John; the cousin of Barnabas and the fellow traveller with Paul. He indeed associated during that time with Peter the most, and in Rome; therefore, the faithful in Rome asked him not only to preach without writing, but also set forth in writing for them the way of life (πολιτεία) according to Christ. He wrote, having been persuaded with difficulty; and it was revealed to Peter from God that Mark had written a Gospel. Therefore, having seen it and having confirmed that it was true, he then sent him out as a bishop to Egypt (*Enarrat. in Evan. Marci* prolog.). [42]

Theophylact only weakly attempts to reconcile John/Mark as Paul's fellow-traveller with Mark as the follower and interpreter of Peter, claiming that Mark had "mostly" associated with Peter. His framework nevertheless leaves no space for the travels of John/Mark with Paul and Barnabas related in the book of Acts.

2.2.9. Euthymius

The twelfth-century Byzantine monk Euthymius Zigabenus may have been dependent upon Victor of Antioch (discussed above), for like him, he identifies Mark the Evangelist with "Mark the son of Mary, who received the apostles into her own house". He adds, citing Acts, that he was also called John and that he accompanied Barnabas, his cousin, and Paul, and that Paul mentions him in his letter to Colossians and Timothy. He continues by alleging that he was then with Peter in Rome, as "the first letter of Peter shows". He notes that according

---

[40] Ps.-Dorotheus, *On the Seventy Disciples*, in Schermann, *Vitae Fabulosae*, 136 (Mark the Evangelist who was made bishop of Alexandria by Peter), 141 (Mark the cousin of Barnabas who was bishop of Apollonia), 142 (Mark who was also called John/Mark, bishop of Byblos).

[41] *PG* 125:684; cf. Weiss, *Das älteste Evangelium*, 405.

[42] Translated by the author from the Greek text in *PG* 123:492.

to Clement in the *Stromata*, Mark wrote in Rome, while according to Chrysostom, he wrote in Egypt. He also claims that Mark wrote his Gospel ten years after the ascension (*Comm. Marc* prolog.). [43]

2.2.10. Colophons to the Gospels in Medieval Copies

The descriptions of Mark the Evangelist in the colophons found in medieval manuscripts of the Gospel of Mark emphasise, as would be expected in this context, the Papian tradition of Mark as the disciple of Peter who wrote his Gospel at Rome. One form, which von Soden refers to as the briefest version, identifies the Evangelist with the Alexandrian Mark:

Mark the Evangelist preached the Gospel to the Alexandrians and to their whole surrounding region, as far as Pentapolis, but it was dictated to him by Peter at Rome and expounded to him. [44]

A longer form is also extant, in which the Evangelist is also identified with John/Mark:

This one was also called John, being the son of Mary who received the apostles in Jerusalem, in her own home; and Peter, having ordained him bishop, sent him from Rome into Egypt. [45]

The reference to Mary receiving the apostles in her house is also found in Victor of Antioch (discussed above).

Another account refers to the Evangelist as "the disciple of Peter and the travelling companion of Paul" [46] in an evident allusion to both the Papian tradition of Mark as the follower of Peter and to the John/Mark of Acts who travelled with Paul during his first missionary journey. The same allusion is found elsewhere in a longer version, in which this Mark is specifically identified as John/Mark:

The Gospel according to Mark was written ten years after the ascension of Christ in Rome. For this Mark was the disciple of Peter, whom Peter names as his son, no doubt a spiritual one, and he was also called John, the cousin of Barnabas, but also Paul's travelling companion. Indeed, he was with Peter the most, and in Rome. The faithful in Rome asked that he not only proclaim verbally [ἀγράφως], but that he put the way of life [πολιτεία] of Christ in written form. [47]

As in Theophylact, this version claims that Mark was with Peter the most and was with him in Rome.

---

[43] From the Greek text in *PG* 129:768–69.

[44] Translated by the author from the Greek text von Soden, *Die Schriften*, 305.

[45] Translated by the author from the Greek text in von Soden, *Die Schriften*, 305.

[46] Translated by the author from the Greek text in von Soden, *Die Schriften*, 314.

[47] Translated by the author from the Greek text in von Soden, *Die Schriften*, 323.

2.3. Western Sources

Western, Latin sources, like Greek ones, tend to combine the narratives of John/Mark, the Papian Mark at Rome and the Alexandrian Mark into a single figure. But unique to the western sources is the claim, evidently drawn from Judean John/Mark traditions, that Mark was an Israelite of the tribe of Levi who had served as a priest in Israel.

2.3.1. Jerome

Perhaps the first explicit identification of John/Mark with Mark the Evangelist (if Ephrem is not included) was made by Jerome in his commentary on Philemon, written sometime in the period 386–388. But Jerome offers it only as his opinion, speaking of Mark, "whom I consider (*puto*) to be the author of the Gospel" (*Comm. Phlm.* 24). [48]

Jerome's account of Mark in his *Lives of Illustrious Men*, written a few years later, in around 393, only summarises Eusebius, depicting Mark as the disciple and interpreter of Peter who wrote his Gospel at Rome and who later went to Egypt, with the exception that Jerome states that Mark died in the eighth year of Nero, whereas Eusebius only states that he was succeeded in his office of bishop in that year (*Vir.* 8). Jerome's account of Mark consequently makes no allusion to the John/Mark of the New Testament and seems to leave no room chronologically for the activities of John/Mark in Asia Minor at the time of Paul's second imprisonment (2 Tim 4:11).

2.3.2. The Monarchian Prologue to Mark

The Monarchian prologues are generally thought to have been composed in Spain, possibly within Priscillianist circles sometime in the late-fourth century. [49] They were later taken up for use as prologues in the Vulgate, and they were consequently influential on later writers. The Monarchian Prologue to Mark speaks of Mark the Evangelist as the disciple of Peter who wrote his Gospel in Rome, but it combines this with a depiction of Mark as a priest in Israel:

Mark, the evangelist of God and the son of the blessed Peter by baptism and the divine word, performing the priesthood in Israel, a Levite according to the flesh, wrote his Gospel in Italy, having been converted to faith in Christ, showing in it what he was owing to his race and what to Christ. [50]

---

[48] Translated by the author from *PL* 26:618.

[49] Bernard Orchard and Harold Riley, *The Order of the Synoptics: Why Three Synoptic Gospels?* (Macon, Ga.: Mercer University Press, 1987), 208.

[50] Translated by the author from the Latin text in Aland, *Synopsis*, 555, and so hereafter.

After providing a description of his Gospel, which will be discussed in Chapter 5, it tells the story of how Mark cut off his thumb in order to disqualify himself from priestly service. It also relates that Mark served as bishop of Alexandria, thus combining its narrative with the Alexandrian tradition:

> Finally, he is said to have cut off his thumb, after coming to faith, in order to be held as rejected from the priesthood (cf. Lev 21:18; 2 Kgs 4:12). But such was the predetermined choice, which was in agreement with faith, that he was not losing in this way what he had formally merited in the work of the word by ancestry, for he was the bishop of Alexandria, of which it was especially his work to know and to administer in himself the things spoken in the Gospel and not to be ignorant of the discipline of the law in himself and to understand the divine nature of the Lord in the flesh.

This work thus combines Mark as the son (convert?) of Peter and bishop of Alexandria with a depiction of a Judean Mark which may reflect a tradition of the John/Mark, who was a Jerusalemite of Levitical heritage.

2.3.3. An Early Commentary on Mark

The earliest extant commentary on Mark, written perhaps in the early seventh century, describes Mark in a similar fashion to the Monarchian Prologue: "Mark, the Evangelist of God, the disciple of Peter, a Levite by birth and a priest, wrote this Gospel in Italy." [51] It adds that he was "the first bishop of Alexandria." [52]

2.3.4. Bede

A little later, Bede (672–735) follows Jerome's account (derived from Eusebius) and makes Mark the interpreter of Peter who wrote his Gospel in Rome before being sent to Alexandria (*In Marci Evang. Exp.* Epist. ad Accam). [53] But he also notes, possibly from the Markan prologue, that Mark "was drawn from the Israelite nation and the priestly lineage", adding that he was one of those of whom it was written, "for great crowds of priests were obeying the faith" (cf. Acts 6:7). [54]

2.3.5. Two Hiberno-Latin Manuscripts

Mark is also depicted as a priest in two Hiberno-Latin manuscripts of the mid-ninth century, with a text possibly to be dated to around 750, containing biblical

---

[51] See, Michael Cahill, trans., *The First Commentary on Mark: An Annotated Translation* (Oxford: Oxford University Press, 1998), 21.

[52] See, Cahill, *First Commentary on Mark*, 22.

[53] *PL* 92:131–33.

[54] *PL* 92:133.

commentary. [55] The first one contains a short notice about Mark: "Mark, of the tribe of Levi, was a priest in Jerusalem. Mark means exalted one (*Marcus interpretatur excelsus*), [56] he who first proclaimed the gospel of Christ in Alexandria." [57] The second text, like the Monarchian prologue, relates the Papian story of Mark writing his Gospel at Rome:

> Peter preached in Rome to the faithful ones of the Romans. They asked Mark to write for them the preaching of Peter. He wrote under their care until it had been finished and showed it to Peter. And Peter approved it for a perpetual Gospel for the churches. This is a laudable theft. [58]

It then tells the story of the amputation:

> He was of Jewish descent, a Levite. And he had cut off the thumb of his right hand in order not to undertake his office (*principatum*). Nevertheless, he would not consent to that selection, but he had consented to the end and to death. Then he was ordained a bishop in the city of Alexandria. Mark is called "exalted with respect to the commandment", who, after he founded the church in Alexandria and disseminated the gospel through Egypt and joined his family to Christ, and triumphed over the riches of the world, died in the fourteenth year of Nero and was buried with honour in Alexandria. [59]

The claim that the name Mark means "exalted one", found in these texts, may have been derived from Jerome. [60]

2.3.6. Jacobus de Voragine

Jacobus de Voragine (c. 1230–1298) also claims that Mark's name means "exalted with respect to the commandment" (*Leg. aur.*); and he likewise relates that Mark cut off his thumb so that he would not have to serve as a priest, adding that he was a Levite and a priest. He goes on to claim that Mark was the spiritual son of Peter because he had been baptised by him, and that he therefore accompanied him to Rome, where Mark was asked to put Peter's preaching into writing. Mark is said to have shown his Gospel to Peter, who approved it and commanded it to be read at Rome. Peter then sent Mark to preach in

---

[55] Robert E. McNally, "Two Hiberno-Latin Texts on the Gospels," *Trad* 15 (1959): 387–401; cf. J. L. North, "*ΜΑΡΚΟΣ Ο ΚΟΛΟΒΟΔΑΚΤΥΛΟΣ*: Hippolytus, *Elenchus*, VII. 30," *JTS* 28 (1977): 388.

[56] The name of Mark was often held to have been derived from a Hebrew word. See Tjitze Baarda, "The Etymology of the Name of the Evangelist Mark in the *Legenda Aurea* of Jacobus a Voragine," *NAKG* 72 (1992): 1–12.

[57] Translated from the Latin text in McNally, "Two Hiberno-Latin Texts," 391.

[58] Translated from the Latin text in McNally, "Two Hiberno-Latin Texts," 396.

[59] Translated from the Latin text in McNally, "Two Hiberno-Latin Texts," 396–97; North, "*ΜΑΡΚΟΣ Ο ΚΟΛΟΒΟΔΑΚΤΥΛΟΣ*," 500.

[60] Jerome interprets the name as *excelsus mandato* ("exalted by the commandment") (*Nom. hebr.* 1.1, cited by Baarda, "Etymology," 3). Likewise, Greek onomastica interpreted his name as ὑψηλὸς ἐντολῇ (cited by Baarda, "Etymology," 3).

Aquilegia, and later to Alexandria. Jacobus goes on to summarise the account found in the *Martyrdom of Mark*, beginning with the story of Mark's sandal strap breaking and concluding with his martyrdom. [61]

2.3.7. *The* Passion of Mark

A fragment from the otherwise lost work of unknown date and provenance entitled the *Passion of Mark*, which was quoted by Henri de Valois (1603–1676) in a marginal note to his edition of Eusebius' *History* (5.24), [62] likewise speaks of Mark as a priest:

> The histories (*syngraphae*) of famous men have declared blessed Mark, according to the rite of the carnal sacrifice, to have borne the sacerdotal plate of the high-priestly crown (*pontificalis apicis petalum*) among the Jewish people: from which it is manifestly given to understand that he was of Levitical descent, indeed that he had Aaron for the origin of his sacred priestly succession. [63]

The text of the *Passion of Mark* cites its sources as the "histories of famous men"; although these cannot be identified, the presence of two Greek loanwords, *petalum* (πέταλον) and *syngraphae* (συγγραφαί), suggests a Greek derivation. The reference to the sacerdotal plate, which seems to relate to the crown worn by the high priest on the Day of Atonement (cf. Exod 28:36, LXX), will be discussed later in the study.

2.4. Conclusion

The identification of John/Mark with Mark the Evangelist appears to have been made by the turn of the fourth century. In Syrian, Greek and Latin sources, the Papian tradition of Mark the Evangelist is dominant, and even where this figure is identified with John/Mark, the latter's journeys in Judea, Syria and Cyprus are often neglected or displaced altogether in favour of the Evangelist's Claudian residence in Rome and later ministry in Egypt.

A number of primarily Syrian sources exhibit evident conflation of Mark the Evangelist with a Judean disciple of Christ by making the Evangelist one of the seventy(-two) disciples of Jesus, which is inconsistent with the Papian narrative of Mark as a disciple of Peter who had never heard or followed the Lord. The original form of the tradition may have spoken of John/Mark and Lucius

---

[61] Jacobus de Voragine, *The Golden Legend, or, Lives of the Saints*, trans., William Caxton, ed. Frederick S. Ellis, vol. 3 (London: Dent, 1900), 134–37.

[62] See Eusebius, *The History of the Church from our Lord's Incarnation to the Twelfth Year of the Emperour Mauricius Tiberius, or the Year of Christ 594*, ed. Henricus Valesius, trans. anon (Cambridge, 1683), 87.

[63] Translated from the Latin text in Badham, "Martyrdom of John," 544 n.16. Cf. *PG* 5: 1360.

of Cyrene, with the later identification of these figures as Mark and Luke resulting in the latter's inclusion among the seventy(-two). This then resulted in
various attempts at reconciling the tradition of Mark as a disciple of Jesus with
that of Mark as Peter's convert; thus, in Epiphanius, Mark is restored to the
faith through Peter, not converted through him, while in Isho'dad and Bar Hebraeus, Mark was said to have been Peter's literal son rather than a spiritual
one.

Lastly, Latin sources seem to exhibit an apparently separate conflation of
Mark the Evangelist by portraying him as a Levite who had served as a priest
in Israel and who had cut off his thumb in order to be disqualified from office.
This too perhaps reflects tradition which originally pertained to the Judean
John/Mark.

Chapter 3

The Conflation of Mark in Coptic Tradition

While Greek, Latin and Syriac sources tend to employ the Papian template of Mark the Evangelist for their Markan narratives, the emphasis of Coptic sources, understandably, is on the Mark who was associated with the founding of the Egyptian churches. While Greek, Syriac and Latin sources tend to string together the three Markan traditions in a generally consistent pattern, commencing with the John/Mark of Acts before transitioning to the Papian and Egyptian narratives respectively, the Coptic sources are more diverse, and the Papian tradition is variously woven around this narrative, while one source does not interact with it at all. Coptic sources do, however, tend to utilise John/Mark traditions for constructing this Mark's background, though in different ways. While some writers simply summarised New Testament references to Mark, others seem to have been familiar with independent John/Mark traditions, some of which are independently attested in the Cypriot John/Mark traditions and in the *Acts of Mark*, to be discussed in more detail in the following chapters.

3.1. The *Encomium on Mark the Evangelist*

John, of the city of Shmun in Egypt (Arabic: El Ashmunein; near ancient Hermopolis), who was active in the late sixth and early seventh century, wrote a Coptic work entitled the *Encomium on Mark the Evangelist* which is extant only in fragments which Orlandi published with an accompanying Latin translation.[1] While the account is fragmentary, it seems to relate how Mark's mother delivered him to Barnabas for instruction. It then takes up the story

---

[1] Tito Orlandi, ed., *Studi Copti. 1. Un encomio di Marco Evangelista. 2. Le fonti copte della Storia dei Patriarchi di Alessandria. 3. La leggenda di S. Mercurio* (TDSA 22; Milan: Cisalpino, 1968). There is a discussion and partial English translation of the encomium in Mark Sheridan, "The Encomium in Coptic Sermons of the Late Sixth Century" in *Christianity in Egypt: Literary Production and Intellectual Trends. Studies in Honor of Tito Orlandi*, ed. Paola Buzi and Alberto Camplani (Rome: Institutum Patristicum Augustinianum, 2011), 451–53.

from Acts concerning how Barnabas and Paul took Mark with them from Jerusalem to Antioch (cf. Acts 12:25). [2]

Another fragment goes on to describe John/Mark's repentance, presumably for abandoning the mission (cf. Acts 13:13). It continues by recounting Paul and Barnabas' subsequent split over Barnabas' insistence that they take John/Mark with them (cf. Acts 15:36–41), only in this account, which is simply an interpretative expansion of the Acts story, the apostles argue over whether Mark's repentance should be accepted as a valid reason for allowing him to accompany them:

> Barnabas said: "Let us take Mark with us." Paul said: We will not take him on account of the former error." Barnabas said: "We will take him, who has demonstrated repentance." Paul, however, was unwilling to take him with them. Barnabas said: "It is not right to shut the door of repentance at the beginning of preaching." Paul said: "It is not good reasoning for the faithful to reinstate the weaker (or "rather cowardly") ones, in order that they labour thus." [3]

Presumably earlier in the narrative the account had attributed cowardice as the motive of John/Mark's departure.

After relating the separation of Paul and Barnabas, the account adds that Mark went to Peter: "For Peter received him joyfully, and made him his disciple, indeed, he became his genuine son." It thus omits Mark's later accompaniment of Barnabas to Cyprus (Acts 15:39) in favour of the Papian narrative, though it later weaves the John/Mark narrative back into the account:

> Paul observed and heard these things. He rejoiced on account of him, he softened his spirit towards him, although he had been separated from him in a dispute. He received him warmly, even though he had been an adversary in his heart; he wrote to the churches that they receive him, even though he had reproached him before by the providence of God.

The account goes on to quote Paul's words to the Colossian church that they were to receive him, should he come (cf. Col 4:10).

A later fragment depicts Mark taking the gospel to Alexandria, thus drawing together into one narrative the three Markan traditions. Unlike Greek, Latin and Syriac sources, John of Shmun's *Encomium* has made a conscious effort to weave the Pauline depictions of John/Mark into its narrative, though in order to do so it omitted Mark's second journey to Cyprus with Barnabas, inserting instead the narrative of Mark's following of Peter.

---

[2] Summarized from the Latin text in Orlandi, "Un encomio," and so hereafter.

[3] Translated by the author from the Latin text in Orlandi, "Un encomio," and so hereafter.

3.2. The *Encomium of SS. Peter and Paul*

The *Encomium of SS. Peter and Paul* is a Coptic work which claims to be a translation of a Greek encomium of bishop Severian of Gabala in Syria (late fourth and early fifth century). This claim, however, is considered "highly suspect", and it is thought that it was probably written in Coptic in the sixth or seventh century. [4]

This work attempts to weave the three Markan narratives into a coherent storyline built around the notices of John/Mark given in the New Testament. It begins by claiming that after Paul was abandoned by Demas, Hermogenes, Phygelus and Alexander (cf. 2 Tim 1:15; 4:10, 14), he took Mark with him, before going on to relate a version of the story of Mark's desertion:

When he realised their betrayal, he cast them out and abandoned them. He took Mark the young lion cub, who was strong in the faith and who was the nephew of Barnabas. When he took him out the first time, Mark saw the hardship and became afraid. He turned back and went to his mother Mary, with whom Peter the great apostle would often stay, and he (Peter) spoke with the faithful inside his house and he (Mark) paid attention to the words that Peter was saying. He repented until (his) death (*Enc. Petri et Pauli* 102). [5]

Here (unlike in the New Testament) the reason for Mark's abandonment of the mission is given as fear, which echoes the claim of John of Shmun that Mark departed on account of cowardice. The mention of Mark listening attentively to Peter's words seems to be an allusion to the Papian tradition.

It is then related that Barnabas and Paul separated, as Barnabas was wishing to bring John/Mark along with them on their journeys, while Paul refused. As a result, Barnabas is said to have taken Mark with him to preach (*Enc. Petri et Pauli* 103). When Paul later learned that Mark was "teaching uprightly and preaching the gospel that Peter proclaimed", he wrote to Timothy, saying "Take Mark and bring him with you when you come to me, for he is useful to me for service. For he was worthless to me at that time, but now he is useful to me in the Lord", in a reinterpretation of 2 Tim 4:11 (*Enc. Petri et Pauli* 104). Mark does come to Paul, and Paul rejoices greatly and brings him to Jerusalem, where the apostles and priests ordain him "a great bishop". They then cast lots for him, and it falls to him to go to Alexandria (*Enc. Petri et Pauli* 105; cf. the account of this in the *Martyrdom of Mark* discussed in Chapter 1).

The text then recounts the story from the *Martyrdom of Mark* of how Mark's shoe broke as he entered the city and how he healed the hand of the cobbler,

---

[4] *Encomiastica from the Pierpont Morgan Library: Five Coptic Homilies Attributed to Anastasius of Euchaita, Epiphanius of Salamis, Isaac of Antinoe Severian of Gabala, and Theopempus of Antioch*, trans. Paul Chapman, Leo Depuydt, Michael E. Foat, Alan B. Scott and Stephen E. Thompson (CSCO 545; Leuven: Peeters 1993), x.

[5] English translation from Michael E. Foat, trans. "Encomium on SS. Peter and Paul Attributed to Severian of Gabala," in *Encomiastica*, 89–92; 98–101.

Anianus, with clay made from spittle (*Enc. Petri et Pauli* 107–8). As in that work, Mark is told to leave Alexandria, but instead of travelling west, he returns to the apostles and priests in Jerusalem to report to them all the wonders that God had done through him in the city (*Enc. Petri et Pauli* 117). Later, Mark returns to Alexandria, and the text recounts the story of Mark's martyrdom, relating how he was seized in the house of Anianus (rather than in the church as in the *Martyrdom of Mark*) and dragged through the streets of the city (*Enc. Petri et Pauli* 142–43). After being placed in a prison that night, he was dragged up by his feet the following day and then let loose, so that he landed on his head, which shattered his skull and killed him (*Enc. Petri et Pauli* 146–47). This version does not include the story of the thunderstorm.

This work, like John of Shmun's, seems largely dependent upon the New Testament for its account of John/Mark. It has conflated all three Markan traditions, though it has attempted to form a coherent storyline out of them without much regard for the chronology of the New Testament (thus, Paul's workers in Asia are said to have forsaken him before the split with John/Mark, which occurred far earlier according to the Acts chronology). It has also only weakly followed the Papian narrative by relating that Mark heard Peter's words in the house of Mary and that he later preached the gospel that Peter proclaimed.

3.3. Severus' *Homily on St Mark*

Severus, bishop of the city of Nastrawa in Egypt, delivered a homily on Mark in Coptic during the ninth century [6] which was written down and appointed to be read publicly in the churches twice in the liturgical year. [7] While the original has not survived, an Arabic translation made about 1300 is extant, which was translated into French by Jean Joseph Léandre Bargès in the nineteenth century.

Severus begins his sermon by expressing his desire to "clear up" the matter of Mark's genealogy:

let us try to clear up the genealogy of the great St. Mark, the apostle of the Saviour, the brilliant light that enlightened Egypt and the entire world. It is a somewhat obscure question, because the Scripture, which speaks of St Mark, only makes mention of his mother, saying absolutely nothing about his father. However, whoever begot him was not at all of the Israelite race; only his mother belonged to this nation, as we will have the occasion to establish in the course of this speech. [8]

---

[6] For a discussion of the origin of this homily, see the preface in Jean J. L. Bargès, trans., *Homélie sur St Marc, apôtre et évangéliste par Anba Sévère, évêque de Nestéraweh* (Paris: Leroux, 1877).

[7] On the feast day of St. Mark (25 April) and on the feast of the Manifestation of the Holy Head of Mark in Alexandria (27 October). See: Bargès, *Homélie sur St Marc*, xlvi.

[8] Translated from Bargès, *Homélie sur St Marc*, and so hereafter. Here, p. 10.

Severus' account of Mark's genealogy begins with two "very rich" brothers who lived in Jerusalem, Abraham and Jacob, who are said to have been of the tribe of Levi. On account of a dispute, Jacob is said to have left Jerusalem and to have sailed to the city of Tunis, near Carthage, where he took a wife named Tecla. From there, he set sail again and came to Alexandria. Meanwhile, in the city of Ashmunein (near ancient Hermopolis in Egypt) there was a rich pagan named Agathon. While his parents, who had died when he was a young man, had worshipped a sacred calf, Agathon himself saw the folly of idols and refused to serve them. [9]

Later, Agathon travelled to Alexandria on business, and while there, an angel appeared to Jacob, instructing him to teach Agathon about the God of Israel and to give him his daughter for a wife. [10] Following the marriage, an angel promises Agathon that they would have a son named John, whose son, Agathon's grandson, would be one of the seventy-two disciples of the Son of God at the time of his incarnation. [11] Agathon himself, however, dies before the child is born. [12]

When Agathon's son John was a young man, Jacob, who had since returned to Tunis, decided to visit his brother Abraham in Jerusalem, and he brought John with him. There, he discovered that his brother had a daughter named Hannah, who was then given to John as a wife. [13] John takes his wife Hannah and his grandfather Jacob and returns to Tunis; later, upon Jacob's death, Abraham travels to Tunis to bring John and his wife Hannah back to Jerusalem, and there Mark was born, who was called John by Abraham, in the thirtieth year of Jesus' incarnation. [14] It adds that Abraham's son Levi had settled in Cyprus, where his son Barnabas was born. [15] The account continues:

Now John, otherwise called Mark, was three years old at the time when our Saviour Jesus Christ was crucified, that is to say in the thirty-fourth year of his incarnation. As for Hannah, Mark's mother, she secretly joined herself to the holy women who were witnesses of the crucifixion of the Saviour and who brought perfumes to his tomb. [16]

The claim that Hannah joined the holy women secretly was presumably made to account for the absence of the mention of anyone of this name among those women spoken of as being near the cross in the canonical Gospels. Nevertheless, the claim that Mark's mother was at the crucifixion is potentially significant and will be noted again later.

---

[9] Bargès, *Homélie sur St Marc*, 11.
[10] Bargès, *Homélie sur St Marc*, 13.
[11] Bargès, *Homélie sur St Marc*, 16–17.
[12] Bargès, *Homélie sur St Marc*, 18.
[13] Bargès, *Homélie sur St Marc*, 19–20.
[14] Bargès, *Homélie sur St Marc*, 20.
[15] Bargès, *Homélie sur St Marc*, 21.
[16] Bargès, *Homélie sur St Marc*, 22.

Severus continues by relating how Mary, the mother of Jesus, had been entrusted into the care of John, the Beloved Disciple, who brought her into his house. He adds that Hannah would spend time with Mary, John's mother:

Now, the immaculate mother, the mother of God, after the crucifixion of her beloved son, lived another fifteen years in this earthly world. During this interval, Hannah, the mother of Saint Mark, went every hour of the day to the holy virgin, the mother of God, accompanied with her young son John, who was subsequently called Mark, and after having been blessed by the hand of the mother of God, she used to return to her house with her son. [17]

He goes on to inform his hearers that after the descent of the Spirit on the Day of Pentecost, Hannah and John (whose name is usually given as Mark in the narrative) were baptised by John the Evangelist, and that their names were subsequently changed to Mary and Mark:

Hannah, the mother of Mark, having presented herself with her son John before the very pure virgin, the holy Mary, the mother of God, requested that she confer on her the grace of baptism, to her and to her son John. The virgin Mary, yielding to her desire, commanded Saint John, the Beloved Disciple, the Evangelist, to baptise both of them, John and his mother Hannah, and in the same moment they were baptised in the name of the Father, and of the Son, and of the Holy Spirit.

The name of John was then changed to that of Mark, and Hannah, his mother, received that of Mary.

While the hand of Saint John the Beloved was raised above the head of Saint Mark, to baptise him, our lady, the virgin Mary, caught sight of the hand of the one and only Son, Jesus Christ, lying on the head of Saint Mark, as though to testify that the one who was baptising him was our Saviour Jesus Christ himself. [18]

The account adds that the Holy Spirit visibly descended on Mark's head as a dove and enveloped his entire body. [19]

This narrative departs from the tradition of Mark as the disciple of Christ, which was perhaps associated with John/Mark, though it may have been attempting to partially assimilate this when it relates that following Mark's baptism, Mary saw Jesus' hand on him, as though "the one who baptised him was our Saviour, Jesus Christ himself."

A little later Severus relates how Mary proposed to Barnabas that he take Mark with him wherever he would go. This is followed by the story, found in Acts, of Mark travelling with Barnabas and Paul. In this version, however, Mark sees the persecution and suffering that the apostles undergo and "he felt his chest tightening with pain; he was indignant, as an inconsiderate young man". Seeing how the apostles had no rest and how even the bread they ate was provided by the charity of others, he decided to return "to Jerusalem, to his

---

[17] Bargès, *Homélie sur St Marc*, 23.

[18] Bargès, *Homélie sur St Marc*, 23–24.

[19] Bargès, *Homélie sur St Marc*, 24.

mother", where he would be able to find food without difficulty. When Mary later found out the motives for his return, she was greatly sorrowed in her heart. [20] This echoes the claims of the *Encomium of SS. Peter and Paul* that Mark abandoned the mission when he saw the hardships and was afraid, and that he returned to his mother Mary in Jerusalem.

Paul and Barnabas returned to Jerusalem and spoke of the marvellous things they had witnessed, and when Mark saw the honour in which they were held for the things they had undergone for the salvation of others, he repented and felt great sadness. Barnabas is said to have known about Mark's repentance by divine illumination, and he subsequently attempted to bring Mark with him on his next journey with Paul, but Paul would not allow it. After the resulting controversy between them, Barnabas took Mark to Cyprus while Paul took Silas to visit the churches. [21] Barnabas then remained in the island for five years, until his death, and "his body was buried in a city of Cyprus, where it can still be found in our days". [22]

At this juncture, Severus weaves into his narrative the Papian tradition of Mark as the follower of Peter:

As for the great Saint Mark, he returned to Saint Peter, the chorus-master of the apostles, and he attached himself to him as a disciple for an entire year. It is during this time that Saint Peter composed the Gospel which bears the name of Saint Mark, and which he preached in the great city of Rome and in the country of the Latins. [23]

Severus departs from the Papian tradition by claiming that Peter composed the Gospel which bears Mark's name.

3.3.1. Severus' Defence

It is noteworthy that Severus anticipates opposition to his reconstruction:

Perhaps there will be found among you those who like to contradict, who will say to me, "where have you drawn the knowledge of such a so profound mystery?" Because it is not found in any part of the holy scripture; it was not known by Luke the doctor, who recounts the Acts of the Apostles, nor by the historian Josephus [Hegesippus?], nor by Philo, Jewish writers who have brought to light the deeds of our Saviour; not even by Saint Clement, the disciple of Saint Peter. All of these authors have carefully consulted the writings about our holy fathers the apostles to trace out their lives. They have spoken about the conduct of the mother of Saint Mark, that the disciples were seeking a refuge with her, as she provided for their expenses. But as for the father of the holy Evangelist, they have not said a single word. [24]

---

[20] Bargès, *Homélie sur St Marc*, 26–27.

[21] Bargès, *Homélie sur St Marc*, 27–28.

[22] Bargès, *Homélie sur St Marc*, 29.

[23] Bargès, *Homélie sur St Marc*, 29.

[24] Bargès, *Homélie sur St Marc*, 33.

Severus goes on to relate a dream he had experienced in which Saint Mark himself appeared to him and informed him concerning his parentage, and he seems to expect that by relating this he could dispel all doubts. [25] In this dream, he relates that he enquired of Mark as to why only his mother was mentioned in the scripture. Mark then instructs him about Agathon, John and Hannah, and the other details Severus had just described, which things, Mark directs, are to be written in a book for the edification of all. [26]

3.3.2. The Alexandrian Tradition

Severus resumes the narrative by relating that after the death of Peter, Mark was commissioned by the Lord to go to Alexandria, who informed him that his power would be over "Egypt, Nubia and the Pentapolis, on the province of Africa and the whole western country of this land, as well as on two islands of Cyprus and Crete", [27] with the mention of Cyprus perhaps reflecting knowledge of Mark's Cypriot ministry.

Mark first sails to Jerusalem to receive a blessing from his mother Mary before her death. [28] Later, while searching for a ship, the virgin Mary appears to him and instructs him to go to Egypt [29] (an explanation for which will be offered in Chapter 10). Although Mark seeks a ship that will take him to a city named Ifrikiah (Bargès suggests that Barca in Pentapolis is intended [30]), he boards one going only as far as Alexandria. [31]

The storm carries the ship to Ifrikiah, Mark's originally-intended destination, where Mark performs many healings by making the sign of the cross. [32] After ordaining Alinus, a rich prince whom he had healed of leprosy, as bishop of the city, Mark sails to Alexandria, at which point the story of Mark breaking his sandal upon entering the city is related. [33] As in the *Martyrdom of Mark*, he takes his sandal to a cobbler named Anianus, who injures his hand while trying to fix it, but in this work he makes the sign of the cross before forming clay out of spittle and healing him. [34]

Mark leaves Alexandria when persecution looms, as in the *Martyrdom of Mark*, and he goes to Pentapolis, where he remained for two years. [35] After that

---

[25] Bargès, *Homélie sur St Marc*, 33–36.
[26] Bargès, *Homélie sur St Marc*, 35–36.
[27] Bargès, *Homélie sur St Marc*, 39–41.
[28] Bargès, *Homélie sur St Marc*, 41–42.
[29] Bargès, *Homélie sur St Marc*, 42–43.
[30] Bargès, *Homélie sur St Marc*, 188.
[31] Bargès, *Homélie sur St Marc*, 43–44.
[32] Bargès, *Homélie sur St Marc*, 47–50.
[33] Bargès, *Homélie sur St Marc*, 52–53.
[34] Bargès, *Homélie sur St Marc*, 53–54.
[35] Bargès, *Homélie sur St Marc*, 56.

time, he again departs for Alexandria, in order to appraise the condition of the church there. When he returns, pagans seize him on "the holy day of Sunday," place a rope around his neck and drag him around until night time, when they throw him into a prison. They again dragged him by a rope the next day, and Mark "gave up his soul to the Saviour". [36] As in the *Martyrdom of Mark*, his persecutors attempted to burn the body but were prevented by a storm. [37]

3.3.3. Conflation in Severus' Narrative

Severus' account has attempted to harmonise the three traditions pertaining respectively to John/Mark, the Alexandrian Mark and Mark the Evangelist. His chronological framework for Mark's ministry and journeys is straightforward: he first follows the Acts chronology and the tradition of Mark's Cypriot mission and transitions from this to the Papian narrative of Mark at Rome, before concluding with the Alexandrian narrative.

Severus' Mark is of mixed heritage, having an Egyptian paternal grandfather named Agathon, a Jewish/Egyptian father named John and a Jewish mother of Levitical descent named Hannah. This likely represents a conflation of the Egyptian Mark with the Judean John/Mark, which Severus has woven together into a single story by means of multiple travels between Tunis, Egypt and Jerusalem, in an account that seems reminiscent of the travels of the Hebrew patriarchs.

Severus expected opposition to his own reconstruction. A tradition of a Judean Mark, without any Egyptian heritage, is found in the work of the Coptic historian Mawhub, discussed below, and in some Greek sources (see Chapter 7), which identify Mark's father as a Judean named Aristobulus. Possibly such traditions informed the opposition that Severus anticipated.

Bargès, the editor, who holds (as here) that Mark the Evangelist was conflated with John/Mark, suggests that Hannah was originally the name of the Egyptian Mark's mother. [38] If the name was not simply a literary creation on Severus' part inspired by the story of Samuel (cf. 1 Sam 1), it seems more likely that the name of Hannah was originally associated with John/Mark, as she is said to have been from Jerusalem and to have been born to a Levitical family. [39]

Severus' claim that Mark was only three years old at the time of the crucifixion is discordant with the promise given to Agathon, recorded earlier in the narrative, that his grandson through John would be one of the seventy-two disciples of Christ during the time of his incarnation. Possibly it reflects a tradition

---

[36] Bargès, *Homélie sur St Marc*, 57–60.

[37] Bargès, *Homélie sur St Marc*, 60.

[38] So Bargès, *Homélie sur St. Marc*, 24 n.1.

[39] If John/Mark was identified as the Beloved Disciple, then the name of Mary would have been that of his adoptive mother, the mother of Jesus (cf. John 19:25–27), not that of his birth mother, whose name may well have been Hannah.

originally pertaining to Mark of Alexandria, though this would mean that he would have only been in his 30s when he was martyred around the year 62, though Severus evidently believed this. Possibly Eusebius wrongly dated Mark's ministry in Alexandria to the reign of Claudius on account of his identification of Mark the Evangelist with the Alexandrian Mark and on account of his mistaken correlation of the Therapeutae, described by Philo who died c. 50, with Mark's disciples.

3.4. The *History of the Patriarchs of Alexandria*

Mawhub's *History of the Patriarchs of the Coptic Church of Alexandria* was written in Arabic, though based on older Greek and Coptic sources. [40] It is traditionally ascribed to Sawirus ibn al-Muqaffa, or Severus, bishop of El Ashmunein near ancient Hermopolis in Egypt, who lived at the end of the tenth century, but it is now widely believed to have likely been compiled and translated under the direction of an eleventh-century Alexandrian deacon named Mawhub ibn Mansur ibn Mufarrij. [41]

The work provides a history of Mark and his successors in the episcopal seat of Alexander, and its Mark is, as expected, a conflated figure. According to Mawhub, Mark was raised in Cyrene, a city of Pentapolis in North Africa, where his father Aristobulus and his father's younger brother Barnabas, who were evidently Judeans, had great possessions. They later lost everything to raids from local tribes, and they fled to Judea, where Aristobulus settled with his son John near Jerusalem (*Hist. Patr. Eccl. Alex.* 1.1).

Mawhub's Mark is a disciple both of Peter and of Christ. He thus relates that Peter's wife was the cousin of these two brothers, and that consequently, "the said John whom they had surnamed Mark, used to visit Peter, and learn the Christian doctrines from him out of the holy Scriptures." [42] But he also later claims that Mark was one of the seventy disciples of Christ (*Hist. Patr. Eccl. Alex.* 1.1). This perhaps represents another attempt at reconciling the Papian tradition of Mark as Peter's disciple with that of Mark as a disciple of Christ by having Mark first learn from Peter before becoming a disciple.

---

[40] For an English translation, see Basil Evetts, ed. and trans. *Severus of Al'Ashmunein (Hermopolis), History of the Patriarchs of the Coptic church of Alexandria* (*PO* 1; Paris: Firmin-Didot, 1904).

[41] Cf. Johannes den Heijer, "Réflexions sur la composition de *l'Histoire des Patriarches d'Alexandrie*: les auteurs des sources coptes," in *Coptic Studies, Acts of the Third International Congress of Coptic Studies*, ed. Wlodzimierz Godlewski (Warsaw: PWN-Éditions scientifiques de Pologne, 1990), 107–13; cf. L. I. Conrad, "Ibn Mufarrig." *Encyclopedia of Arabic Literature*, vol.1, ed. Julie Scott Meisami and Paul Starkey (London and New York: Routledge, 1998), 351. But contra Oden, *African Memory*, 69–70.

[42] Evetts, *Severus*, 136.

Mawhub recounts two anecdotes relating to Mark. In the first, he relates an encounter with lions near the Jordan river which precipitated the conversion of Aristobulus and Barnabas:

And when Aristobulus saw them approaching him, and perceived the violence of their rage, he said to his son Mark: "My son, do you see the fury of this lion which is coming to destroy us? Escape now, and save yourself, my son, and leave them to devour me, according to the will of God Almighty." But the disciple of Christ, the holy Mark, answered and said to his father: "Fear not, my father, Christ in whom I believe will deliver us from all danger". And when the lions approached them, Mark, the disciple of the Lord Christ, shouted against them with a loud voice, and said: "The Lord Jesus Christ, son of the Living God, commands that you be rent asunder, and that your kind be cut off from these mountains, and that there be no more offspring to you here for ever". Then the lion and the lioness burst asunder in the midst at that moment, and perished straightway; and their young were destroyed (*Hist. Patr. Eccl. Alex.* 1.1). [43]

Seeing this, the brothers are said to have become disciples of Christ.

The second anecdote relates how Mark miraculously felled an olive tree to which the people of a certain town used to pray:

There was in those regions, in a town called Azotus, a very large olive-tree, the size of which was greatly admired. And the people of that city were worshippers of the moon, and prayed to that olive-tree. So when the holy Mark saw them pray, he said to them: "As for this olive-tree, which you worship as God, after eating its fruit and burning its branches for fuel, what can it do? Behold, by the word of God whom I worship, I will command this tree to fall to the ground, without being touched by any tool" (*Hist. Patr. Eccl. Alex.* 1.1). [44]

Mark then prayed and there was great darkness, and the moon itself is said to have rebuked the townspeople. The olive tree fell, but those who worshipped it grew angry, seized Mark and threw him into prison. During the night, he saw in a dream Christ promising to Peter that he would "bring forth all those that are in prison". When Mark awoke, the prison doors were open and the jailers asleep, so that all the prisoners were able to depart. [45]

At this point, Mawhub notes that Mark was one of Jesus' seventy disciples; he then provides some specific occasions on which Mark was present with Jesus:

And Mark was one of the Seventy Disciples. And he was among the servants who poured out the water which our Lord turned into wine, at the marriage of Cana in Galilee. And it was he who carried the jar of water into the house of Simon the Cyrenian, at the time of the sacramental Supper. And he also it was who entertained the disciples in his house, at the time of the Passion of the Lord Christ, and after his Resurrection from the dead, where he entered to them while the doors were shut (*Hist. Patr. Eccl. Alex.* 1.1). [46]

---

[43] Evetts, *Severus*, 136–37, with minor changes.
[44] Evetts, *Severus*, 137.
[45] Evetts, *Severus*, 138–39.
[46] Evetts, *Severus*, 139–40.

The account contains two allusions to the Johanne narrative, which will be discussed in more detail in Chapter 6: the mention of Mark as being one of the servants at the wedding at Cana (cf. John 2:1–10), and the reference to the disciples being at his house after the resurrection, when "the doors were shut" (cf. John 20:19).

While he claims that Mark entertained the disciples at the time of the crucifixion, he also claims that Mark was the one who carried the jar of water at the time of the Last Supper (Mark 14:13; Luke 22:10). He adds that he brought the jar into the house of Simon the Cyrenian, which conflicts with the earlier claim that the Passover was eaten at Mark's house. He probably knew two rival traditions, one of which made Mark the owner of the house, and one of which made Simon the owner and Mark the servant.

Mawhub goes on to relate a unique tradition of Mark preaching with Peter in Bethany following the ascension:

And after his Ascension into heaven, Mark went with Peter to Jerusalem, and they preached the word of God to the multitudes. And the Holy Spirit appeared to Peter, and commanded him to go to the cities and villages which were in that country. So Peter, and Mark with him, went to the district of Bethany, and preached the word of God; and Peter remained there some days (*Hist. Patr. Eccl. Alex.* 1.1). [47]

The account seems to refer to the Bethany that was near Jerusalem, the home of Lazarus (cf. John 11:1; 18; 12:1), rather than the Bethany across the Jordan (cf. John 1:28; 10:40).

Mawhub's version omits any record of the journeys of John/Mark in Syria and Cyprus recorded in Acts, displacing it in favour of the Papian tradition of Mark in Rome during the reign of Claudius and the Alexandrian tradition which follows it:

And he saw in a dream the angel of God, who said to him: "In two places there is a great dearth". So Peter said to the angel: "Which places do you mean?" He said to him: "The city of Alexandria with the land of Egypt, and the land of Rome. It is not a dearth of bread and water, but a dearth arising from ignorance of the word of God, which you preach". So when Peter awoke from his sleep, he told Mark what he had witnessed in his dream. And after that Peter and Mark went to the region of Rome, and preached there the word of God. And in the fifteenth year after the Ascension of Christ, the holy Peter sent Saint Mark, the father and evangelist, to the city of Alexandria, to announce the good tidings there (*Hist. Patr. Eccl. Alex.* 1.1). [48]

Mawhub goes on to summarise the *Martyrdom of Mark*'s account of Mark's ministry in Egypt and North Africa and martyrdom in Alexandria.

---

[47] Evetts, *Severus*, 140, with minor changes.
[48] Evetts, *Severus*, 140, with minor changes.

3.5. Ibn Kabar

The *Lamp of Darkness* is an Arabic work, written by the Coptic priest Ibn Kabar (thirteenth-century), which summarises the lives of the apostles and the early disciples. [49] Some of the traditions found in Mawhub are also found in this work, though in modified form; thus, after relating that Barnabas and his uncle Mark had preached with Paul, it continues:

His father was from the western Pentapolis, and his name was Aristobulus; the name of his mother was Mary. When he had previously wasted his wealth, having been reduced to poverty, he withdrew far from his land and resided near Jerusalem. His mother was the cousin of the wife of Peter, the chief of the apostles. [50]

In this version, only Aristobulus (and not his brother) was in Pentapolis, and it was Mark's mother Mary, rather than Aristobulus, who was the cousin of Peter's wife. Ibn Kabar adds that Mary taught John three languages: Latin, Hebrew and Greek.

Ibn Kabar also relates the story of the lions near the Jordan, though his version is much simpler: Mark commanded the lions to be split in half, and his father Aristobulus believed as a result (the conversion of Barnabas is not mentioned).

Ibn Kabar goes on to claim that Mark was "one of the disciples who drank from the water made wine at the wedding at Cana", and he also identifies him as the one who carried the jar of water at the time of the Passover meal. He adds: "he went, moreover, into the house of Simon the Cyrenian, where the sacred dinner was prepared." He goes on to claim that Mark preached the gospel in Rome with Peter, writing his Gospel in Latin twelve years after the ascension, and that he afterwards preached in Egypt. As with Mawhub, this account leaves no room for the travels of Mark with Paul and Barnabas, as recorded in Acts.

Mawhub concludes his account by relating the martyrdom of Mark, though his version differs from other accounts in alleging that he was beheaded and then buried, though he notes that others hold that an attempt was made at burning Mark's body.

---

[49] A complete scholarly edition of this work does not exist, but a Latin translation of the section on Mark can be found in Haase, *Apostel und Evangelisten*, 284–85. An English translation was made by William A. Hanna, Ibn Kabar, *The Lamp that Lit the Darkness* (St Louis: 2000), 76–78. Cf. Roelof van den Broek, *Pseudo-Cyril of Jerusalem On the Life and the Passion of Christ: A Coptic Apocryphon* (VCSup 118; Leiden, Brill, 2012), 15 n. 22.

[50] Translated by the author from Graf's edition, and so hereafter.

3.6. *Synaxarion for Baramouda*

The Coptic synaxary (a liturgical account of the life of a saint or martyr) called the *Synaxarion for Baramouda* claims that following the "departure" (i.e. death) of Barnabas, Mark travelled from Cyprus to Africa, where he visited Barca, the five cities, and finally Alexandria. [51] This account omits the Roman narrative entirely, in a conflation of traditions which is similar (accidentally or not) to that found in the Cypriot *Acts of Barnabas* (see Chapter 4).

3.7. Conclusion

As the founder of the Coptic Church, Mark of Alexandria was of central important to Coptic writers. Consequently, the Papian tradition of Mark the Evangelist at Rome is more tangential and is variously woven into the Markan narrative, or in one case is omitted altogether. Also distinctive of the Coptic sources is the emphasis given to the figure of Mark the Judean disciple of Jesus, which no doubt bolstered the standing and independency of the Church in a way that Mark, the disciple and follower of Peter, could not have done.

However, John/Mark traditions often provide only the background for the Alexandrian Mark, with John/Mark's later travels with Paul and Barnabas often omitted. An exception to this is the *Synaxarion for Baramouda*, which affirms John/Mark's later ministry on Cyprus with Barnabas, though at the cost of the Papian narrative, mention of which it has been obliged to entirely pass over.

While the Greek, Latin and Syriac sources could more comfortably navigate the three Markan traditions by placing the Papian narrative at their centre, the Coptic sources struggled to find a cohesive narrative which could affirm the central role of Africa and Egypt in their retellings of the Markan narrative.

---

[51] See Oden, *African Memory*, 60.

Chapter 4

John/Mark in Cypriot Sources

The following two chapters will examine sources which appear to have preserved independent John/Mark traditions and which place John/Mark at the
centre of their narratives. In this chapter, three works of Cypriot origin will be
examined, namely the fifth-century Greek *Acts of Barnabas*, the sixth-century
Encomium of Barnabas and the possibly early seventh-century *Life of Auxibius*,
all of which preserve traditions concerning the mission to Cyprus undertaken
by Barnabas and Mark following the Jerusalem Council, referred to but not
described in the book of Acts (15:39). According to these works, this mission
concluded with Barnabas' martyrdom in Salamis, at which time Mark left the
island (cf. the *Synaxarion for Baramouda*). But these sources variously conflate their accounts with the Papian and Alexandrian narratives in ways which
will may prove informative for reconstructing the earlier, non-conflated versions of the traditions.

4.1. The *Acts of Barnabas*

The Greek *Acts of Barnabas* is believed to have been written in Cyprus during
the late fifth century. [1] It tells its story in the first person, from the perspective
of John/Mark, but the John/Mark of this text is neither an eyewitness disciple
of Jesus nor a follower of Peter, but rather a former servant of Cyrus, a chief-
priest of Zeus, who was converted by Paul, Barnabas and Silas, who baptised
him in Iconium in Anatolia (see the discussion of this in Chapter 5). [2] Thus, he
describes himself as John,

who followed Barnabas and Paul, the holy apostles, being previously a servant of Cyrillus
the high priest of Zeus, but now has received the grace of the holy spirit through Paul and

---

[1] See the discussion of the document in Glenn E. Snyder, "The Acts of Barnabas: A New
Translation and Introduction," in *New Testament Apocrypha: More Noncanonical Scriptures*, vol. 1, ed. Tony Burke and Brent Landau (Grand Rapids: Eerdmans, 2016), 317–26.

[2] An English translation can be found in Snyder, "Acts of Barnabas," 327–36. The references are given according to the section numbers given in Richard. A. Lipsius and Max Bonnet, eds., *Acta Apostolorum Apocrypha*, vol. 2/2, *Acta Philippi et Acta Thomae, accedunt
Acta Barnabae* (Leipzig: 1903).

Barnabas and Silas, who are worthy of the calling and who baptised me in Iconium (*Act. Barn.* 1–2). [3]

After being baptised, the Mark of the narrative relates that he saw in a vision a man clothed in white who informed him that he had been given understanding in order to know the mysteries of God (3).

Following Mark's baptism, he accompanies Paul, Barnabas and Silas to Seleucia, presumably to the city of this name near Antioch, [4] where they board a ship for Cyprus; they journey through the island, with John/Mark ministering to them, and then they sail to Perga in Pamphylia. The apostles depart from Pamphylia but John/Mark remains there for a while, until he later reunites with them in Antioch:

And finally, I remained there [i.e. Pamphylia] about two months, wishing to sail away to the western parts" (τὰ δυτικὰ μέρη [5]); and the Holy Spirit did not permit me. Turning my attention again, I sought the apostles, and having learned that they were in Antioch, I journeyed to them (5).

Upon finding the apostles, he discovers that Paul was very grieved with him because he had delayed in Pamphylia; a little later it is explained that Paul felt this way because while John/Mark was in Pamphylia, he had in his possession the "parchments" (μεμβράναι) (cf. 2 Tim 4:13); Paul is furthermore said to have refused to accept his repentance (6).

4.1.1. The Division of Paul and Barnabas

The *Acts of Barnabas* contains its own reworking of the story of the division that took place between Paul and Barnabas. In the Acts of the Apostles (15:36–41), the division occurs after Paul and Barnabas decide to revisit the cities of their previous ministry, when Barnabas insists that they bring John/Mark with them, which Paul refuses on account of John/Mark's prior desertion of them in Pamphylia (cf. Acts 13:13).

In the version of the division in the *Acts of Barnabas*, however, the division occurs in Antioch over their differing travel plans. They thus

took counsel together to journey to the eastern places, and afterwards to go to Cyprus and to oversee all the churches in which they had spoken the word of God. But Barnabas urges Paul to go first to Cyprus and to oversee his [Barnabas'] own people in his own [Barnabas'] village; and Lucius urges him that he oversee his own town of Corina [Κορίνη]" (5.7).

Paul is directed in a dream to return to Jerusalem; in response, Barnabas urges that they first go to Cyprus and then to Jerusalem, and a great contention

---

[3] Author's translation from the Greek text of Lipsius and Bonnet, *Acta Barnabae*, and so hereafter.

[4] One Greek manuscript and the Latin recension place this in Seleucia on the Calycadnus. See Snyder, "Acts of Barnabas," 328 n. g.

[5] Greek text in Lipsius and Bonnet, *Acta Barnabae*, 293.

(φιλονεικία; not παροξυσμός as in Acts 15:39) arises between them, which is heightened by Barnabas' insistence that they take John/Mark with them, which Paul refuses to do (8). [6] In the end, Paul recounted how the Lord appeared to him in the night, instructing him to allow Barnabas to journey to Cyprus, and they amicably go their separate ways, with Paul travelling to Jerusalem and with Barnabas taking John/Mark with him to Cyprus.

At this point in the narrative, Lucius of Cyrene (cf. Acts 13:1) is abruptly mentioned, and he is said to have hailed from a city named Cyrene, or Κορίνη, in Cyprus. [7] Possibly this was because Lucius was said to have been at Antioch (Acts 13:1). While Lucius plans on journeying to Cyprus with Barnabas, he is not mentioned again in the narrative or depicted as actually accompanying Barnabas and Mark to the island.

4.1.2. The Ministry in Cyprus

Having separated from Paul, Barnabas went down to Laodicea [8] with John/Mark, where they looked for a ship sailing to Cyprus (9–11). They first sail to Corasium (either Corycus or Coracesium, [9] both in Cilicia on the southern coast of modern Turkey) and from there sail to the island of Pityusa, [10] where they remained for three days on account of a storm, lodging at the house of a certain Euphemus (11). They resume sailing and reached the city of Anemurium, where Barnabas baptised two Greeks (12–14). They finally arrived in Cyprus, at a place named Crommyacita, [11] where they found two temple servants, Timon and Ariston, with whom they lodged (14), with the account adding that Barnabas healed Timon of a fever (15). It then notes that Barnabas would heal the sick by placing on them "lessons, a book in God's voice (Hebrew?), a writing of wonders and instructions", which he had received from Matthew.

Barnabas and Mark are said to have arrived at the city of Lapithus, but they were refused entry into the city on account of a pagan feast that was being

---

[6] Snyder's interpretation of this passage differs considerably from that of Matthew Brown Riddle (ΛNF 8:493–96) and my own. Snyder takes πρότερον not to mean that they "first" go to Cyprus, but as an adjective modifying Paul (thus: Paul, the "foremost in Cyprus"); he consequently understands the Paul in question as probably Sergius Paulus ("The Acts of Barnabas, 329 e).

[7] Greek text in Lipsius and Bonnet, *Acta Barnabae*, 294.

[8] No doubt Laodicea (ad mare) in Syria; cf. Acts 13:4–14a (Snyder, "Acts of Barnabas," 330 n. f.)

[9] See: Snyder, "Acts of Barnabas," 330 n. h.)

[10] Probably the same as the island of Pittyusa (Riddle, ANF 8:494), also called Dana (Snyder, "Acts of Barnabas," 331 n. b.), located off the southern coast of Turkey, north of Cyprus.

[11] Probably the "peak of Krommion," a peak near the city of Lapithus on the northern peak of the island (Snyder, "Acts of Barnabas," 332 n. a)

celebrated there; instead, after resting at the gate (16), they resumed their journeys, travelling across the mountains to the city of Lampadistus, where Timon is said to have held property. There they are shown hospitality by Heracleius, who was of the city of Tamasus, and who is said to have been baptised and renamed Heracleides by Paul and Barnabas in Citium. Barnabas and Mark ordained Heracleides as bishop of Cyprus and strengthened the church of Tamasus (17).

From there they travelled to Old Paphos, where they met Rhodon, a temple servant who came to believe and then accompanied the group (18). Later they met a Jew named Bar-Jesus who forbade them from entering Paphos and who continued to resist them on their journeys throughout the island, in a legendary accretion to the tradition which was no doubt inspired by the account of Bar-Jesus' resistance of Paul on the island (cf. Acts 13:6–12) and which is absent from the other accounts of this Cypriot mission found in the *Encomium of Barnabas* and the *Life of Auxibius*, discussed below.

Instead of entering Paphos, the group travelled towards Curium; when arriving near the city, they witnessed a race by the road involving naked runners, in a place where cheating and other wicked acts are also said to have occurred. Barnabas rebuked the place, and the western part collapsed, with many fleeing to the temple of Apollo (19).

After reaching Curium they were again prevented from entering the city, this time by a great number of Jews who had been under the influence of Bar-Jesus (19). After resting under a tree near the city they continued on their journey. The next day they reached a village where a certain leper named Aristoclianus lived, who is said to have been healed at Antioch and to have subsequently been ordained as a bishop by Paul and Barnabas and to have been sent back to his village in Cyprus (20). After staying with him for a day, they resumed their travels and arrived at Amathus, where they found a crowd of Greeks pouring out libations in the temple. Furthermore, Bar-Jesus had anticipated their arrival and had stirred up the Jews so that they could not enter. Instead, they rested for an hour at the house of widow who lived outside of the city (20).

After this, they journeyed through desert places, accompanied by Timon, and they arrived at Citium, where they heard of a great disturbance in the hippodrome. No-one there received them, and so they rested for an hour at the gate, near the aqueduct (21), before sailing away in a ship to Salamis on the other side of the island. After disembarking, they found Heracleides (it is not explained why he is so far from Tamasus), whom they instructed to preach the gospel of God, establish churches and appoint ministers.

After entering the city, Barnabas went into a synagogue, rolled out the scroll of Matthew and began to teach from it (22). After two days, however, Bar-Jesus is said to have arrived and to have stirred up the crowds against Barnabas; they then bound him, intending to hand him over to the governor, but upon learning that a pious Jebusite (possibly a corruption for "Eusebius"), a relative of Nero, had arrived in Cyprus, they instead seized him and dragged him by the neck with a rope to the hippodrome. Having passed through the gate they burned his body, so that his bones became dust. That night they took the ashes and placed them in a cloth with lead, planning to cast the ashes into the sea (23), but Mark, Timon and Rhodon were able to steal the remains away (24).

These three fled to a certain place where Jebusites were said to have formerly dwelt, where they deposited the ashes in a cave, along with the "lessons" (μαθήματα) which Barnabas had received from Matthew (24). Being pursued by the Jews, they fled from there to a village of the Ledrians, and finding another cave nearby, they hid in it for three days (25). From there they journeyed to a village named Limnes (unknown) and they afterwards came to the shore. Finding a ship headed for Egypt, they boarded it, sailing to Alexandria (26). There Mark is said to have remained, teaching and baptising. The account concludes with Mark, still in the first person, relating that he had taught there the things he had heard from the apostles of Christ, who had renamed him Mark in the waters of baptism (10). The Papian narrative is omitted altogether.

4.2. The *Encomium of Barnabas*

The *Encomium of Barnabas* was written by the Cypriot writer Alexander the Monk, probably in the sixth-century.[12] Alexander, whose monastery was at the site of Barnabas' supposed tomb near Salamis in Cyprus, informs his readers that he had reluctantly written out of obedience to a request (6–15; 29–37), and that he had consulted for his work the *Stromata*[13] and other ancient writings (136–39).

He relates that although Barnabas was born in Cyprus, his parents brought him to Jerusalem, where he was trained under Gamaliel. As a young man he joined a priestly course and excelled in virtue and self-control (161, 177–91). It then adds:

And it came to pass at that time that Jesus was in Jerusalem and healed the paralytic in the sheep gate and worked many other signs and wonders in the temple. Having seen these things, the blessed one was amazed, and having immediately gone to him, he fell at his feet

---

[12] Peter van Deun, ed., *Hagiographica Cypria* (CCSG 26; Turnhout and Leuven, 1993), 15–21. An English translation is available in Michael R. Cosby, *Creation of History: The Transformation of Barnabas from Peacemaker to Warrior Saint* (Eugene, Oreg.: Cascade, 2017) Appendix B.

[13] The word means "miscellanies" and is usually given as the title of a work by Clement of Alexandria, but Clement's work does not contain any biographical details concerning Barnabas' life.

and began requesting that he be blessed by him. And the one who enters hearts, Christ, having accepted his faith, received him with good will and gave him a share in his divine intervention (192–200). [14]

At this point in the narrative, mention is made of the house of John/Mark:

Having quickly arrived at the house of Mary the mother of John, the one called Mark, who was said to be his aunt – on which account they called him "John/Mark, the cousin of Barnabas" – he spoke to her: "Come, O lady, behold those things which our fathers have desired to see. For there is a certain prophet from Nazareth of Galilee, Jesus, in the temple, working wonders by divine power, and, as it appears to many, this is the Messiah who is to come" (200–208).

Mary is then said to have gone to the temple, where she found Jesus, whom she entreated to visit her house:

Seeing the Lord and Master of the temple, she fell at his feet, requesting and saying: "Lord, if I have found favour before you, come to the house of your maidservant and bless your household slaves by your visit. And the Lord assented to her request, whom, having come, she joyfully received into her upper chamber. From that day, therefore, whenever the Lord came into Jerusalem, he used to rest there with his disciples ... (209–19).

It adds that Jesus kept the Passover at this house, and it claims that Mark was the disciple who carried the jar of water:

there he kept the Passover with his disciples; there he initiated the disciples through participation in the secret mysteries. For an account has come to us from the elders (γέροντες) that the one carrying the jar of water whom Jesus instructed the disciples to follow was Mark, the son of that blessed Mary. And the Lord said with restraint (οἰκονομικῶς), "to a certain one", as the fathers say, interpreting this place, teaching us through this riddle that to everyone readying himself, the Lord dwells with him. In this upper chamber, therefore, the Lord kept the Passover; in it he appeared to those around Thomas, having been raised from the dead. There the disciples went up after the ascension, coming from the Mount of Olives with the rest of the brothers, of whom the number was about 120, among whom was Barnabas and Mark. There the Holy Spirit descended in tongues of fire upon the disciples on the day of Pentecost. There has now been established the great and most holy Zion, the mother of all the churches (219–37).

The claims that Mark was the one carrying the jar of water and that his house was the site of Pentecost are also found in Coptic sources, as discussed in the previous chapter. The *Encomium* further identifies the house of Mark with the Christian church on Mount Zion, which shall be discussed in Chapter 6.

4.2.1. The Cypriot Mission

After relating some things about Barnabas, the account continues by recounting Mark's journey with Paul and Barnabas through the island of Cyprus and his

---

[14] Translated by the author from the Greek text in Van Deun, *Hagiographica Cypria*, and so hereafter.

abandonment of them in Pamphylia (ll. 398–412), though unlike in Acts, it interprets Mark's departure in terms of cowardice on his part, as in the Coptic *Encomium on Mark the Evangelist* by John of Shmun (cf. the Coptic *Encomium of SS. Peter and Paul* and Severus' homily, which attribute it to fear):

> But after Mark saw the apostles joining battle together against the dangers on account of the good news, and that they, having left where they were going to be honoured, were advancing to the war with unbelievers, he waivered before the dangers, inasmuch as he was a young man (μειράκιον), cowardly and imperfect with respect to the contempt of death, and having left the apostles, he turned back towards Jerusalem, to his own mother (405–12).

Later, Mark, seeing how Paul and Barnabas were honoured in Jerusalem, and recalling how they had remained steadfast through so many dangers, was greatly ashamed and went weeping at the feet of Barnabas, seeking forgiveness (ll. 420–28; cf. Severus' similar version of the story). The account continues by relating the story of Barnabas and Paul's falling out over Barnabas' desire for Mark to accompany them on their journeys; they then went their separate ways, with Barnabas taking Mark with him to Salamis in Crete (ll. 438–65).

As in the *Acts of Barnabas*, the account concludes the Cypriot mission with the story of Barnabas' martyrdom. Thus, while Barnabas and Mark were in Salamis, Jews from Syria are said to have confined Barnabas and to have taken him outside the city at night, where they stoned him to death (there is no mention of Bar-Jesus in this version). Though they attempted to burn his body, the fire did not damage it (ll. 536–44), and Mark, with some other unnamed helpers, took the body and buried it in a cave, about five stadia away from the city (ll. 544–49). At that time a persecution arose against the Christians in Salamis, and Mark, leaving the island, sailed to Ephesus, where he found Paul:

> But Mark, having sailed away from the land of the Cypriots, came to Paul in Ephesus and informed him of Barnabas' perfection (i.e. his martyrdom). Having heard that, he lamented with great weeping over him, but he kept Mark with himself (κατέσχε παρ᾽ ἑαυτῷ) (553–57).

The final words, Paul "kept Mark with himself", may suggest that the source material knew a tradition according to which Mark remained with Paul, as in the *Life of Auxibius*, discussed below, which relates that Mark travelled with Paul to Rome and remained with him until his death. But in this version of the story, which assimilates the Papian tradition of Mark the Evangelist, John/Mark does not remain with Paul but later journeys with Peter to Rome. Thus, it relates:

> After these things, Peter, departing to Rome according to a revelation of God, took Mark with him, in a certain manner giving birth to him. There he composed the evangelical history. When Peter read it and was satisfied, he knew that it was God-breathed. And having laid his hands on Mark, he sent him to Alexandria, Egypt, Libya and Pentapolis, as very sufficient (for the task) (557–64).

The *Encomium of Barnabas* here exhibits yet another attempt at reconciling the tradition of Mark as the son of Peter (probably spiritually, through baptism) and that of Mark the disciple of Jesus, by interpreting Mark's sonship in terms of Peter's choosing of Mark for his Roman mission. The account adds that as a result of Mark's preaching, many believed (ll. 564–67), and it concludes by relating that Mark died in Alexandria after nine years (ll. 567–69).

Thus, the account has conflated all three Markan portrayals into a single narrative. The Acts account is followed until Mark and Barnabas' second journey to Cyprus, at which point the narrative follows the local tradition of their ministry in Cyprus, culminating with Barnabas' martyrdom. The story then transitions to the Papian tradition by having Mark sail to Rome from Ephesus. Lastly, Mark is sent from Rome to Alexandria.

4.3. The *Life of Auxibius*

The *Life of Auxibius*, a Cypriot work which dates perhaps from the early seventh century, [15] tells the story of Auxibius, a young man who arrived in Cyprus after fleeing from his pagan parents in Rome (*vit. Aux.* 1–6). At around the time of his arrival on the island, Barnabas and Mark are beginning their tour of Cyprus, disembarking at Lapithus on the northern shore (cf. the reference to nearby Crommyacita in the *Acts of Barnabas*), with the narrative picking up their story where Acts left off (*vit. Aux.* 7; cf. Acts 15:39).

The account only briefly mentions Barnabas' martyrdom in Salamis, and it relates, as in the *Acts of Barnabas*, how Mark, accompanied by Timon and Rhodon, had to flee the Jews, hiding in a cave in Ledra for three days before crossing the mountains and arriving in Limnetes (*vit. Aux.* 7), where Auxibius, who is not mentioned in the *Acts of Barnabas*, was staying (8). Mark is said to have instructed and baptised Auxibius, and, after bestowing the Holy Spirit on him by the laying on of hands, to have appointed him a bishop before sending him to Soloi (8). Mark himself then departed from the island: "Mark, finding an Egyptian ship boarded it, and after they sailed away, he came to Alexandria; and there he was preaching the gospel and teaching the things concerning the kingdom of God" (8).

The account continues relating the narrative of Auxibius' life, but Mark is reintroduced into the story a little later:

---

[15] Jaques Noret, ed., *Hagiographica Cypria* (CCSG 26; Turnhout: Leuven University Press, 1993), 158. A partial English translation of this work by Hans A. Pohlsander is found in Hans A. Pohlsander, ed., *Sources for the History of Cyprus, 7: Greek Texts of the Fourth to Thirteenth* Centuries (Greece and Cyprus Research Center, 1999), 57–60.

While he [i.e. Auxibius] was staying in that place, Mark came preaching the good news of Christ in Alexandria. After many believed and were baptised, Mark went away to seek the apostle Paul, and when he had found and greeted (or "bowed before"; προσκυνέω) him, Paul welcomed Mark with great joy. And Mark explained to Paul the things concerning Barnabas, and how, having been martyred in Salamis, he finished the good race. That Paul truly received Mark, he himself bears me witness, writing to the Colossians: "Receive Mark, the cousin of Barnabas" (Col 4:10); and to Timothy he says: "Having taken Mark, bring him with yourself, for he is useful to me for the ministry." (2 Tim 4:11). Mark then remained with him until Paul's death (*vit. Aux.* 12).

Unfortunately, the account does not record where Mark found Paul and therefore it cannot be determined whether it was at Ephesus, as in the *Encomium of Barnabas*. Nor does it state where Paul died, though presumably it did not deviate from the established tradition of his martyrdom at Rome late in Nero's reign.

The narrative continues by relating that as a result of hearing of Barnabas' martyrdom in Cyprus, Paul sent his co-workers, Epaphras and Tychicus, to the island to help Heracleides (13). The rest of the narrative continues the account of Auxibius' life, and Mark is not mentioned again.

4.4. The Dating of the Cypriot Texts

The present form of the texts can be dated with relative accuracy, though this would not preclude their use of earlier sources. The *Acts of Barnabas*, which seems to have been composed in Cyprus, [16] refers to the ashes of Barnabas, and this serves as an important indication of the date of the work, since it must have been written prior to the discovery of the alleged tomb containing Barnabas' corpse, [17] for, as Czachesz notes, "it makes no sense writing about the ashes when the whole body is thought to be found". [18] This discovery, as Czachesz observes, is said by three sixth-century sources to have been made during the reign of the emperor Zeno (474–491). [19] The earliest of these sources, Theodorus Lector, died in 527, providing the latest possible date for the origin of this

---

[16] According to István Czachesz, the geographical references found in work are accurate, providing it with "an air of truth"; see István Czachesz, *Commission Narratives: A Comparative Study of the Canonical and Apocryphal Acts* (Leuven: Peeters, 2007), 189.

[17] Czachesz, *Commission Narratives*, 190.

[18] Czachesz, *Commission Narratives*, 190. Snyder counters that "the martyrdom (8:4–6) may have been composed with an alternate description of the gathering and burial of Barnabas" (Snyder, "Acts of Barnabas," 324). However, it is the body of Barnabas, not merely his relics, that plays a prominent role in the debate of the late fifth century and this could hardly have been ignored; nor would there have been any apologetic value for the Cypriot church in modifying the tradition in this way.

[19] Czachesz, *Commission Narratives*, 189.

claim. [20] This "rediscovery" of Barnabas' relics was no doubt apologetically-motivated, coming as it did at a time when Cyprus was seeking to assert its ecclesiastical independency from Antioch, since the possession of the relics of Barnabas would have bolstered Cyprus' claim of independence. [21]

If the notice of the discovery of the corpse in the reign of emperor Zeno is accurate, the *Acts of Barnabas* must have been written prior to its discovery, or before 491. By contrast, the *Encomium of Barnabas* relates that Barnabas' persecutors tried to burn his body and were unsuccessful, which is consistent with a composition of this work in the late fifth century or later, after the "rediscovery" of Barnabas' corpse.

Noret, the editor of the *Life of Auxibius*, thinks that this work was probably written after 600 and certainly before 649. [22] It does not contain any account of Barnabas' relics, instead simply relating that Barnabas was martyred, and while it speaks of Mark fleeing from Salamis and hiding in a cave in Ledra, it does not claim that Mark fled the city with Barnabas' relics or that he buried them in a cave near the city before coming to Ledra. It may therefore reflect an earlier, simpler version of the narrative than that known to the older *Encomium*.

Noret argues that the *Life of Auxibius* was dependent on the *Acts of Barnabas*, since it seems to explicitly cite the *Acts of Barnabas* when it states:

It happened that Barnabas the apostle of Christ came to Cyprus in his second journey, after separating from Paul by face, not in heart. And taking Mark along, they landed at Lapithus. And going around all the island, we came to Salamis – now called Constantia – as Mark says (*vit. Aux.* 7). [23]

The reference to what "Mark says" thus refers, according to Noret, to the *Acts of Barnabas*, which is written as though by Mark (or rather by "John") in the first person.

Noret also argues that the author of the *Life of Auxibius* follows the *Acts of Barnabas* "avec une fidélité totale" in the sections dealing with Barnabas and Mark's Cypriot mission, which concludes with an account of Barnabas' martyrdom (*vit. Aux.* 7–8). Indeed, he provides two examples where the wording is very similar – Barnabas and Mark's charge to Heracleides, shortly before Barnabas' martyrdom, and the account of Mark, Timon and Rhodon fleeing to the city of Limnetes following Barnabas' martyrdom. [24]

However, consideration must be given to the possibility that the *Life of Auxibius* has used an earlier version of the *Acts of Barnabas*, or even that both

[20] Czachesz, *Commission Narratives*, 190.
[21] However, see Czachesz, *Commission Narratives*, 184, 189, 193.
[22] Noret, *Hagiographica*, 158.
[23] Noret, *Hagiographica*, 159.
[24] Noret, *Hagiographica*, 159.

works follow a common written source that claimed to have been written by John/Mark in the first person and which depicted the Cypriot mission. For although the *Acts of Barnabas* is the oldest account of the Cypriot mission, neither the *Encomium of Barnabas* nor the *Life of Auxibius* have included the obvious accretions to the narrative found in that work, such as the inclusion of the Bar-Jesus legend and the retelling of the disagreement between Paul and Barnabas as a disagreement over travel plans.

While Noret points to the similarities in the depictions of Barnabas' martyrdom in the *Acts of Barnabas* and the *Encomium*, it should be noticed that both works seem to have reworked their martyrdom narratives using the account of Mark's martyrdom given in the *Martyrdom of Mark* as a template, whereas this feature is entirely absent from the *Life of Auxibius*. Thus, the *Acts of Barnabas* records that Barnabas died by being dragged with a rope around his neck and it relates that his persecutors burned his body to dust. In the *Martyrdom of Mark*, Mark is similarly dragged by the neck with a rope, and his persecutors attempt to incinerate his body. In the *Encomium*, Barnabas is stoned to death, but his killers are prevented by a storm from burning his body, as Mark's killers are in the *Martyrdom of Mark*.

Also missing from the account in the *Life of Auxibius* is any claim that Mark deposited the relics and/or body of Barnabas in a cave, as found in the *Acts of Barnabas* and the *Encomium of Barnabas* respectively. Instead, the narrative passes directly to the story of Mark fleeing and hiding in a cave for three days (also found in the *Acts of Barnabas*), before escaping to Limnetes. While these features can be explained on the basis that the *Life of Auxibius* only provides a summarised account, it might be significant that the clearly accretionary traditions are absent from its version.

4.4.1. The Conflation of Markan Traditions

Also suggestive that the three texts interact independently with a common Cypriot narrative is the differing attempts exhibited in each at conflating the John/Mark narrative with that of the Alexandrian Mark. Thus, the *Acts of Barnabas* has John/Mark sail to Alexandria from Cyprus following Barnabas' martyrdom, where he remains (*Act. Barn.* 23). It consequently omits both the Pauline tradition of the later activities of John/Mark in Asia Minor and the Papian tradition of Mark as Peter's follower at Rome.

The *Encomium of Barnabas*, however, has Mark instead sail to Ephesus following Barnabas' martyrdom, where he finds Paul, whom he informs of Barnabas' martyrdom (*Encom. Barn.* 550–57). But instead of having Mark later travel with Timothy to Paul in Rome, as in 2 Tim 4:11 and the *Life of Auxibius*, the text transitions to the Papian tradition by relating that Peter received a revelation to sail to Rome, and that he brought Mark with him, thereby "in a certain manner giving birth (τεκνοποιέω) to him" (*Encom. Barn.* 559–60; cf. 1

Peter 5:13), in an apparent attempt at reconciling the narratives of Mark the follower (if not convert) of Peter and Mark the disciple of Jesus. Mark then writes his Gospel in Rome and is later sent to Alexandria, where he teaches the faith of God for nine years until his martyrdom (*Encom. Barn.* 557–69).

The *Life of Auxibius* claims that Mark sailed directly to Alexandria from Cyprus following Barnabas' martyrdom (*vit. Aux.* 8), as in the *Acts of Barnabas*. However, unlike that work, it resumes the John/Mark narrative by having Mark later find Paul, whom he informs concerning the events of Barnabas' martyrdom (*vit. Aux.* 12). Mark's journey to Paul is also found in the *Encomium of Barnabas*, where it occurs immediately after Barnabas' martyrdom, with no intervening journey to Alexandria.

It could be argued that the *Life of Auxibius* has combined the narratives of both the *Acts of Barnabas* and the *Encomium*, though it can be noted that it does not demonstrate any familiarity with the Papian tradition of Mark, found in the *Encomium*, or with the legendary accretions found in the *Acts of Barnabas*. Furthermore, *Auxibius* adds that Mark stayed with Paul until Paul's death, presumably in Rome, which is not found in either of the other accounts.

Possibly the *Life of Auxibius* was modifying the same common source known to the two other texts. The *Life of Auxibius* would have sought to maintain the narrative of John/Mark's accompaniment of Paul until his death while also seeking to include the Alexandrian narrative. To accomplish this, it would have departed from the tradition of Mark's martyrdom in Alexandria so that it could insert the Alexandrian ministry parenthetically into the account and resume the narrative of John/Mark's later accompaniment of Paul. The other two texts, on the other hand, have apparently privileged the Alexandrian martyrdom tradition at the expense of Mark's accompaniment of Paul, though, as noted above, the *Encomium* seems to have left a vestige of this tradition in its claim that Paul kept Mark with himself.

Table 4.4.1: Conflation in the Cypriot Narrative

Order of Events	*Acts of Barnabas*	*Encomium of Barnabas*	*Life of Auxibius*	*Reconstructed Common Source*
1	Cyprus	Cyprus	Cyprus	Cyprus
2	Alexandria	With Paul in Ephesus	Alexandria	With Paul in Ephesus
3		With Peter in Rome	With Paul (in Ephesus?)	With Paul in Rome
4		Alexandria	With Paul (in Rome?)	

4.5. Conclusion

The three Cypriot narratives cluster around the ministry of Barnabas and Mark in Cyprus, and a common underlying narrative linking them all can be discerned, which likely related their travels through the island, Barnabas' martyrdom and John/Mark's journey to Ephesus to find Paul.

Although the Cypriot texts merge their John/Mark with the Alexandrian Mark, they accomplish this in diverse ways. The *Acts of Barnabas* has Mark travel to Alexander from Cyprus following Barnabas' martyrdom, while the *Encomium of Barnabas* has Mark leave Cyprus to find Paul, before transitioning to the Roman and Alexandrian Markan narratives. The *Life of Auxibius* inserts the Alexandrian tradition between Barnabas' martyrdom and his journey to Ephesus to find Paul, and it implies that Mark thereafter went to Rome with Paul, in accordance with 2 Tim 4:13, thus bridging the gap between the Acts narrative and the Pauline corpus and perhaps preserving an account that was, in the other two versions, displaced by the Alexandrian narrative.

All three texts likely preserve differing aspects of a now lost Cypriot tradition, which they have variously conflated with the Papian and Alexandrian narratives. The original narrative likely depicted the travels of Barnabas and Mark through the island, though without the later Bar-Jesus accretion. It went on to relate Barnabas' martyrdom, but it lacked the later story of the attempt at burning the body. Following the martyrdom, John/Mark would have sailed away to Ephesus, where he found Paul and informed him of Barnabas' death. He would then have remained with Paul until his death. The differing attempts at conflating this narrative with the Papian and Alexandrian traditions have obscured, but not entirely erased, the more primitive version of the story.

Chapter 5

John/Mark in the *Acts of Mark*

The work entitled the *Acts, Miracles, and Passion of Mark*, or simply the *Acts of Mark*, [1] provides the fullest purported account of the life and journeys of John/Mark. This little-known work, preserved in a single thirteenth-century codex discovered in the Stavronikitas monastery on Mount Athos, is of unknown date and provenance. [2]

The Mark of this work, which is divided into thirty-five chapters, is a composite figure, and the account weaves together the narratives of John/Mark, Mark the Evangelist and the Alexandrian Mark into a single story. The first eight chapters are primarily concerned with the travels and ministry of the Judean John/Mark, and these will be the focus of the present chapter. The narrative then transitions in chapter nine to the Papian narrative of Mark writing his Gospel at Rome. The rest of the account, from chapter 10 onwards, mostly reworks the narrative of the Alexandrian Mark found in the *Martyrdom of Mark*, though with some significant and informative conflations with independently-attested John/Mark traditions.

5.1. Mark's Background and Conversion

Following a prologue in praise of Mark, the *Acts of Mark* begins by relating some facets of Mark's background and of his upbringing in Jerusalem:

This glorious apostle Mark, the lamp of the never-setting light and the very great (or "greatest") herald of the evangelical teaching concerning the divinity, was descended from pious-minded ancestors who were adorned with worthy practices and were drawn from the Levitical tribe (*Act. Marc.* 2). [3]

---

[1] Not to be confused with the *Martyrdom of Mark*, which is also sometimes referred to as the *Acts of Mark*.

[2] François Halkin, "Actes inédits de saint Marc," *AnBoll* 87 (1969): 343.

[3] Translated by the author from the Greek text in Halkin, "Actes," 343–71, and so hereafter. I also consulted the unpublished partial translation by Dr Mark A. House ("Deeds and Miracles and Testimony of the Holy and All-praiseworthy Apostle and Evangelist Mark").

The narrative goes on to note his privileged status: "Having his home in Jerusalem, he was allotted much wealth from his ancestors", adding: "He distributed this to the needy and poor" (*Act. Marc.* 3). This Mark thus inherited great wealth, but in accordance with his godly character he is said to have remembered the poor.

The text then relates how Mark was called John until his baptism by Peter (cf. 1 Peter 5:13), in an obvious conflation with the Papian tradition:

> And at first this blessed apostle was called John. But when he received the washing of regeneration by the holiest and the all-venerable Peter, the leader of the apostles, he received the name of Mark, and he took the position of his adopted son (*Act. Marc.* 4).

The account adds that Mark's mother Mary was also converted to an honourable and God-pleasing life", and it relates, as in the *Encomium of Barnabas*, how she received Jesus into her house:

> Seeing the crowded multitude following Christ our God, who became man for the salvation of the human race and accomplished very great and incredible wonders, she goes to him with great speed and earnestly intreats and beseeches him to come into her house. The most benevolent Jesus of great mercy, the God-man, hearkened to her, and the Creator of all things came into her house, the one who is present everywhere and fills all things with his divine and all-controlling power (*Act. Marc.* 4).

The account also provides another version of John/Mark's conversion, relating that Mark had at first been a disciple of John the Baptist and that he later came to follow Jesus (here, without Peter's instrumentality):

> Therefore, the glorious apostle Mark first began following the holy and most loud-voiced John, the forerunner; but when the one and only Son of God (or "only begotten"' τοῦ μονογενοῦς υἱοῦ τοῦ Θεοῦ) was going from Jerusalem into Galilee, he followed him (*Act. Marc.* 5).

The allusion in the passage is to the Johannine account in which two disciples of John the Baptist, one of whom is unnamed, begin following Jesus (John 1:35–40), after which Jesus goes into Galilee (John 1:43) where he attended the wedding at Cana in Galilee (John 2:1–2) (cf. the discussion of these passages in Chapter 6).

The narrative then abruptly shifts to relating, from Acts 12:1–12, that Peter, following his imprisonment by Herod and subsequent miraculous release, "having run a straight course, came to the house of the thrice-happy Mark" (*Act. Marc.* 5), in what appears to be another insertion into the narrative resulting from conflation with Papias' Petrine tradition.

The mention of Mark's house segues into a notice of the tradition, also found in Coptic sources and the *Encomium of Barnabas*, that Mark was the one carrying the jar of water and that his house was the place in which the Passover (i.e. the Last Supper) was eaten:

And this has reached to us from tradition and by succession that the one carrying the jar of water and the one having have heard from those who were sent: "Christ, who sent us, will keep the Passover at your place" – for his willing suffering had drawn near – was the divinely-sounding Mark (*Act. Marc.* 6).

While in the Gospels the one carrying the jar of water (Mark 14:13 and Luke 22:10) is distinguished from the master of the house who heard the reported words (cf. Matt 26:18; Luke 22:10–11; Mark 14:14), here they are identified (see below for discussion of this point).

5.2. Mark's Travels

The *Acts of Mark* goes on to provides an account of Mark's ministry following the ascension, relating his journeys to Antioch, Seleucia and Cyprus:

Having received from the apostles in Jerusalem, wise in divine things, the saving teachings that were set forth in writing, the divinely-voiced evangelist Mark arrived in the great Antioch, the most conspicuous of cities, with the most holy and admirable apostle Barnabas. And they began (to preach) the God-given and most saving proclamation, and they were very readily received by the Antiochians. And many who were abandoning the error and wickedness of idols though the teaching of these inspired apostles converted to the Christian way (Χριστιανισμός) and have become sons of light (*Act. Marc.* 6).

Mark later departs from Antioch and arrives at the nearby port city of Seleucia, where too he preaches the word and where he meets opposition from an influential citizen of the city:

Departing from there, the divinely-minded Mark came to Seleucia. Then the one entrusted with the work of the commanding authority of that district, impious and an idol worshipper, happening to meet other citizens, having heard that the divine apostle Mark came to reside there and was freely preaching the word of godliness, was exceedingly troubled and ordered them to restrain him (*Act. Marc.* 6).

After Mark was imprisoned, this man "was then examining with what death he might kill him." Mark, however, is miraculously delivered: "After a few days had passed, an angel of the Lord delivered him from those very grievous chains"; the angel then instructs him to go to the people of Caesarea in Palestine, where he again converts many (*Act. Marc.* 6).

Mark then sailed to Cyprus, where he journeyed around the island, preaching and healing the sick, before sailing to Pamphylia on the southern coast of Asia Minor, where he again is said to have spent some time (7).

From Pamphylia, Mark had hoped to visit "the western lands of the Gauls (Galatians?)" but was prevented, and he travels instead to Antioch:

Then the most holy Mark wished to reach the western lands of the Gauls; this was not carried out, on account of a divine revelation; but having learned that the most holy Paul, the herald of truth, was spending time in great Antioch with the glorious Barnabas, who were openly preaching the divinely-given and saving teachings, he left for them. And having spent time with them there for not a short time and having announced the word of godliness to all, he was filled with gladness and joy, seeing the flock of Christ growing yet more daily (*Act. Marc.* 8).

Mark's travels conclude with his return to Jerusalem:

After these things, leaving them, he came to Jerusalem together with Simeon, called Niger. Coming into the temple, having gathered all the brothers, and having lifted up befitting sup-plication and laudatory hymn singing to the master of all things with them, to Christ the God for sufficient days, he rejoiced, being spiritually overjoyed (*Act. Marc.* 8).

The reference to Mark leading the brothers in praise to the divine Christ in the temple will be discussed in more detail in Chapter 9 of this study.

5.2.1. Correlating Marks' Travels with the Chronology of Acts

Mark's journeys to Antioch, Seleucia, Caesarea and Cyprus may have been understood as occurring within the context of the missions of the Jerusalem Christians who were said to have preached "as far as Phoenicia, Cyprus and Antioch" (Acts 11:19) following the persecution that arose in the wake of Ste-phen's martyrdom (cf. Acts 8:1), which probably took place sometime between 34–37 CE. [4]

Thus, following Mark's departure from Cyprus, he is said to have sailed to Pamphylia before journeying to Paul and Barnabas in Antioch, and the mention of these two apostles as being in Antioch at the time may be connected to the placement of both in the city following the dispersion. According to Acts, when news of those who were spreading the message to Phoenicia, Cyprus and An-tioch reached Jerusalem, they sent Barnabas to Antioch; he then departed to Tarsus in order to bring Paul to the city, where they remained together for one year (cf. Acts 11:22–27; 13:1).

Prominent among those who were scattered were "Cypriot and Cyrenian men" (ἄνδρες Κύπριοι καὶ Κυρηναῖοι) (Acts 11:20); interestingly, perhaps, Cypriot tradition is said to have located the birthplace of both Barnabas and Mark at Salamis on the island [5] (cf. Acts 4:36, which states that Barnabas was from Cyprus).

The Cyrenian men are usually identified with Cyrene (Κυρήνη) in North Africa, perhaps because the καὶ is thought to distinguish two separate groups (i.e. Cypriots and Cyrenians), but there was a city named Kyrenia (modern day

---

[4] Pierson Parker, "The Posteriority of Mark," in *New Synoptic Studies: The Cam-bridge Gospel Conference and Beyond*, ed. William R. Famer (Macon, Ga.: Mercer Univer-sity Press, 1983), 132, without knowledge of the *Acts of Mark*, already made the suggestion that Mark was involved in this missionary work.

[5] John Hackett, *A History of the Orthodox Church of Cyprus* (London: Methuen, 1901), 379.

Girne, but known in modern Greek as Κερύνεια or Κυρήνεια) in Cyprus, and the καὶ may be epexegetical: "Cypriot, that is Cyrenian men"; alternatively, it may be distinguishing Cypriots in general from Kyrenians in particular (cf. Luke 5:17 and 6:17 which refer to both Judea and Jerusalem). [6]

Admittedly, a Flavian inscription attests to the spelling of Keryneia (Κερύνεια) for the Cypriot city, speaking of ὁ Κερυνήτων δῆμος (the district of the Keryneians), [7] but alternative forms like Κυρηνία, Κυρήνεια, Κυρήνη, Κορύνεια and Κορώνεια are attested in the Byzantine era, [8] and Hackett states that the Cypriot city and the North African one were frequently confused by ancient writers. [9] As noted in the previous chapter, Lucius, the travelling companion of Mark and Barnabas, was said to have been a native of Cyrene or Κορίνη in Cyprus by the *Acts of Barnabas* (*Act. Barn.* 7), where the spelling appears to be a variation of Κυρήνη; it is also close in form to Corinaeum, the name given to the city by Pliny in the first century (*Nat. Hist.* 5.130).

5.2.2. Conflation with the Papian Tradition of Mark

The account then shifts to relating the Papian narrative of Mark the Evangelist, with whom it identifies John/Mark. But because the *Acts of Mark* transitions to the Papian narrative at a point in the Acts chronology that precedes its introduction of John/Mark, it never directly relates any of the John/Mark material found in the book of Acts.

The seam by which the John/Mark narrative and the Papian tradition have been joined seems to have been the tradition of Peter receiving a revelation in Jerusalem to sail to Rome in order to confront Simon the Sorcerer, as related in the *Acts of Peter*, an apocryphal work written perhaps as early as the end of the second century (*Act. Petr.* 5). This revelation, according to this work, was given in the twelfth year following the ascension of Christ (c. 41/42) (*Act. Petr.* 5), thus explaining why the *Acts of Mark* has placed Mark's journey to Rome with Peter so early.

The tradition of Peter's vision found in the *Acts of Peter* has, however, been reworked to accommodate the inclusion of Mark, who was not mentioned in that text. Thus, in this version of the story, Peter receives a revelation while in Antioch (the account does not previously record that he was there) and then proceeds to Jerusalem, where Mark is located, and from there he sails to Rome, taking Mark with him:

---

[6] Cf. Eric F. F. Bishop, "Simon and Lucius: Where did they come from? A Plea for Cyprus," *ExpT* 51 (1939–40): 152.

[7] Cited by Terence B. Mitford, "Further Contributions to the Epigraphy of Cyprus," *AJA* 65 (1961): 132.

[8] Eugene Oberhummer, "Keryneia 2," RE 11 (1921): 344–47.

[9] Hackett, *History of the Orthodox Church*, 387.

Peter, the all-reverend and inspired speaker (θεορρήμων) and chorus leader (κορυφαῖος), leaving Antioch on account of a divine revelation (ἐκ θείας ἀποκαλύψεως), came to the glorious Mark. Having spent some time there with him, they both, having departed from Jerusalem, set out for old Rome.

It goes on to provide a slightly modified version of the Papian tradition of Mark writing his Gospel at Rome:

After a short time, the admirable and inspired-speaking (θεορρήμων) Mark began to explain through a prose exposition (λογογραφικῆς ἀποδείξεως), the Spirit-moved and God-breathed oracles of the evangelical teaching concerning the divinity (τῆς εὐαγγελικῆς θεολογίας), with the wonder-worthy and loud-voiced Peter the apostle agreeing and approving him in this, and dictating (or "suggesting": ὑπαγορεύω) to him the greatest and most beautiful and highest sayings (λόγια) filled with truth and divine discourse (*Act. Marc.* 9).

This version of the narrative assigns a greater role to Mark than is traditionally given in the Papian version. It also seems to combine a tradition of Mark writing concerning the divinity with the Papian account of Peter dictating the sayings of Jesus to Mark, for reasons which will be discussed in Chapter 6.

5.2.3. Conflation with the Alexandrian Mark

Lastly, the account transitions to the Alexandrian Markan narrative, depicting Peter as commissioning Mark to preach in Egypt (10). Mark leaves Rome, but the voyage to Alexandria is interrupted by a storm, which Mark is said to have calmed by making the sign of the cross (10); Mark and the crew then made a straight course for the island of Pityusa, where Mark baptises many (11).

The journey is resumed, and Mark arrives in Alexandria, where he preaches the gospel (12). Among other wonders, it relates that Mark found Timon the deacon and healed him of a fever (15). Later he visits a place called Mendesion (16; cf. Mendion in *Mart. Marci* 5) and thereafter he preaches in Cyrene of Pentapolis (19). He is then said to have departed for Libya (21) and to have later preached in a certain Marmarican country (22), evidently the region stretching from the east of Pentapolis to the frontier of Egypt.

Following, with modifications, the story in the *Martyrdom of Mark*, Mark returns to Alexandria, with the narrative taking notice of the church at Boukalou, as in that work (27). Mark is likewise arrested, though in this version it is both the Jews and the Greeks who seize him (28). And as in the *Martyrdom of Mark*, he is dragged with a rope by the neck in Boukalou and dies (33). His persecutors then burn his body but are interrupted by a storm, and the Christians place his body in a carved-out rock (34).

5.3. Shared Material in Greek and Coptic Sources

5.3.1. The Acts of Mark *and the* Acts of Barnabas

Both the *Acts of Mark* and the *Acts of Barnabas* seem to depict the same initial Cypriot mission. Thus, in both accounts, Mark travels to Seleucia, Cyprus and Pamphylia before journeying to Paul and Barnabas in Antioch. Also in both, Mark wishes to travel west from Pamphylia; he desires go to the "western parts" in the *Acts of Barnabas*, while he wishes to preach in "the western lands of the Gauls" in the *Acts of Mark*. In both cases he was forbidden to go west, and in both he is said to have gone to Paul and Barnabas in Antioch instead.

However, unlike the *Acts of Barnabas*, the *Acts of Mark* does not relate the later Cypriot mission of Barnabas and Mark which culminated with Barnabas' martyrdom, since, as noted above, the *Acts of Mark* shifts its narrative from John/Mark to Mark the Evangelist at a point in the story prior to John/Mark's introduction in the book of Acts and therefore prior to the later, post-Acts Cypriot mission which he undertook with Barnabas.

The *Acts of Mark* is, however, aware of traditions relating to the Cypriot mission that are found in the *Acts of Barnabas*, and it has conflated them with its Alexandrian narrative. Thus, the story of the landing at Pityusa (i.e. Dana off the southern coast of Turkey) and the three-day stay on the island on account of a storm, found in the *Acts of Barnabas*, has been transformed into the story of Mark calming a storm on the ship before stopping at the island *en route* from Rome to Alexandria. [10] Likewise, the healing of Timon's fever by Barnabas in Cyprus, also related in the *Acts of Barnabas*, has been transformed into a healing of Timon's fever in Alexandria by Mark.

Furthermore, in the *Acts of Mark*, Mark is martyred by both Jews and pagans, whereas in the *Martyrdom of Mark* only pagans are involved; the account in the *Acts of Mark* may have been remodelled on the story of Mark fleeing from the Jews who caused Barnabas' martyrdom, as related in the *Acts of Barnabas* and the *Encomium of Barnabas*.

Table 5.3.5: Conflation of Cypriot and Alexandrian Narratives in the *Acts of Mark*

	Acts of Barnabas	*Martyrdom of Mark*	*Acts of Mark*
Pityusa	Between Cilicia and Cyprus	X	Between Rome and Alexandria
Healing of Timon	In Cyprus	X	In Alexandria
Persecution of Mark	By Jews	By Greeks	By Jews and Greeks

[10] Cf. Halkin, "Actes," 344.

5.3.1.1. The Conflation of the Acts of Barnabas *and the Book of Acts*

Halkin sees these features as evidence that the *Acts of Mark* was dependent upon the *Acts of Barnabas*,[11] but dependency, or at least sole dependency, would not account for the material found in the *Acts of Mark* which is not shared by the *Acts of Barnabas*. While Halkin attributes this to "l'imagination de l'hagiographe",[12] he does not address why some of this unique material reappears in other sources of John/Mark tradition. Thus, the tradition of Mark as the one carrying the one carrying the jar of water at the time of the Passover, although not found in the *Acts of Barnabas*, shows up in both the *Encomium of Barnabas* and in Coptic sources; the *Acts of Mark* also seems to presuppose knowledge of the Coptic tradition that Mark was at the wedding at Cana by relating that he was one of those who followed Jesus into Galilee after he began following him (*Act. Marc.* 5; John 1:35; 43; 2:1–2). In addition, both the *Acts of Mark* and some western sources attribute a Johannine-type Gospel to Mark, as will be discussed in Chapter 6. The question of the provenance of the traditions known to the *Acts of Mark* is clearly more complex than simple dependence on the *Acts of Barnabas*, supplemented by the imagination.

Furthermore, sometimes the priority of the tradition does appear to be with the *Acts of Barnabas*, at other times the *Acts of Mark* exhibits awareness of traditions that appear to be known to the *Acts of Barnabas* in only a later, conflated form. Thus, the *Acts of Barnabas* has clearly conflated a Markan Cypriot mission with Paul's first missionary journey, in which Paul and Barnabas travel to Syrian Antioch, Seleucia, Cyprus and Pamphylia and Pisidia in southern Asia Minor, before returning to Syrian Antioch (Acts 13:4–14:25).

Thus, while John/Mark travels alone in the *Acts of Mark*, he is in the company of Paul and Barnabas in the *Acts of Barnabas*, reflecting his accompaniment of them during the first missionary journey. In the *Acts of Mark*, Mark is said to have spent some time in Perga in Pamphylia while Paul and Barnabas proceeded to Antioch, where Mark later finds them; the *Acts of Barnabas*, however, has conflated this stay in Perga with Mark's abandonment of Paul and Barnabas at this city during the first missionary journey (Acts 13:13), so that Paul is angry at Mark on account of his delaying at (and not departing from) Perga with certain parchments.

The *Acts of Barnabas* has further conflated the account with that of the separation of Paul and Barnabas in Acts, who part ways in Antioch following the council in Jerusalem (Acts 15:36–41). In the *Acts of Barnabas*, this division occurs after the return of Mark to Antioch following the Cypriot mission, and it is further claimed that Paul and Barnabas separated as Paul wished to travel

---

[11] Halkin, "Actes," 345; cf. Wilhelm Schneemelcher, ed., *New Testament Apocrypha*, vol. 2 (Cambridge: James Clarke, 1992), 465; Czachesz, *Commission Narratives*, 194.

[12] Halkin, "Actes," 345 n. 1.

to Jerusalem and Barnabas to Cyprus. Paul and Barnabas go their separate ways, with Barnabas taking Mark with him to Cyprus, which allows the narrative to incorporate the account of Barnabas' final Cypriot mission at this point in the story. In this version, however, prominence is given to Bar-Jesus, a figure introduced in Acts during Paul's first missionary journey (Acts 13:6–12), in another example of conflation with the first missionary journey.

Table 5.3.6.1: Conflation of Missions in the *Acts of Barnabas*

	Paul's first Missionary Journey in Acts	First Cypriot mission in the *Acts of Mark*	First Cypriot mission in the *Acts of Barnabas*
Agents	Paul, Barnabas, Mark, Bar-Jesus	Mark	Paul, Barnabas, Silas, Mark, Bar-Jesus
Places			Iconium,
	Antioch	Antioch	
	Seleucia	Seleucia, Caesarea	Seleucia
	Cyprus	Cyprus	Cyprus
	Perga	Perga	Perga
	Iconium		Iconium
	Lystra		
	Derbe		
	Antioch	Antioch	
Event	Mark abandons Paul at Perga	Mark stays in Perga	Mark's stay at Perga offends Paul
Event		Mark desires to travel west	Mark desires to travel west
Event		Mark travels to apostles in Antioch	Mark travels to apostles in Antioch
Event	Paul and Barnabas separate in Antioch		Paul and Barnabas separate in Antioch

5.3.1.2. Further Conflation in the Acts of Barnabas

The *Acts of Barnabas* also contains a distinctive portrayal of Mark as a pagan convert who was baptised at Iconium in Asia rather than a Levite and eyewitness disciple of Christ from Jerusalem. Since this Mark was converted by Paul at Iconium, it is probable it is probable that the sources of this narrative originally contextualised it in the time of Paul's visit to the city during his first missionary journey (Acts 14:1–4). The identification of this Mark with John/Mark then likely resulted in the conflation of Paul's first missionary journey with the initial Cypriot ministry of John/Mark found in the *Acts of Mark*.

Neither the conflation of John/Mark with an Iconium Mark nor any subsequent conflation of Mark's initial Cypriot mission and Paul's first missionary journey are present in the *Acts of Mark*, arguing against its direct dependence on the *Acts of Barnabas*. Further evidence for the priority of the version in the *Acts of Mark* will be provided in chapters 10 and 11 of this study, where it will be argued that the same Markan narrative found in the *Acts of Mark* is preserved in Syriac and Ethiopic sources under the name of John.

Possibly this Iconium Mark was the same Mark spoken of in Cypriot oral tradition as the bishop of Apollonia in Asia Minor. Thus, whereas the *Encomium of Barnabas* has Mark travel to Ephesus following Barnabas' martyrdom, Cypriot oral tradition claims that Mark journeyed to Apollonia in Asia upon Barnabas' death, where he became bishop of the city and later underwent martyrdom, which was remembered on 30 October. [13] Possibly this reflects an earlier form of the conflation of the Iconium Mark with John/Mark, which the *Acts of Barnabas* presumably further conflated by substituting the journey to Apollonia in Asia Minor with one to Alexandria.

Supporting evidence for a separate Mark of Apollonia is also provided by Ps.-Hippolytus' list of the seventy disciples, which differentiates Mark the bishop of Apollonia from John/Mark, the bishop of Byblos in Phoenicia (the region in which John/Mark was active, according to the *Acts of Mark*); it also exhibits conflation of the two by referring to the bishop of Apollonia as the cousin of Barnabas (*De LXX Discip.* 56; cf. 14; 65).

5.3.2. *The* Acts of Mark *and the* Encomium of Barnabas

Van Deun thinks that the *Acts of Mark* has recycled the *Encomium of Barnabas* in several places, of which he provides a list, though he adds that it takes over the details "très librement il est vrai". [14] Thus, both works relate that Mary the mother of John/Mark urged Jesus to come into her house, both identify Mark as the one carrying the jar of water and both state that the Passover was held in this house. Furthermore, both record Mark being sent to Alexandria from Rome by Peter, after writing his Gospel, and both provide accounts of Mark's martyrdom in Alexandria that share the detail that he died in the city after preaching there for nine years, which is not found in the *Martyrdom of Mark*.

Nevertheless, these similarities might only represent the shared use of material rather than dependence. One example is particularly informative in this regard. In the *Encomium*, Mark sails from Cyprus to Ephesus to inform Paul of Barnabas' martyrdom; Peter thereafter receives a vision to go to Rome, and he takes Mark with him (557–59). In the *Acts of Mark*, however, Peter, receiving a revelation, leaves Antioch and goes to Mark in Jerusalem, and a little later they sail to Rome, probably sometime in the early 40s (*Act. Marc.* 9; cf. discussion above).

---

[13] Hackett, *History of the Orthodox Church*, 379.
[14] Van Deun, *Hagiographica Cypria*, 76.

As was noted above, the contours of the narrative of Peter receiving a revelation before going to Rome seem to have been drawn from the second- or third-century *Acts of Peter*, which recounts how Peter, who was in Jerusalem at the time, was directed by God in a vision, in the twelfth year after the ascension (c. 41/42), to go to Rome in order to confront Simon Magus (*Act. Petr.* 5). Eusebius alludes to the story in his *Ecclesiastical History* (c. 324), placing it in the reign of Claudius (*Hist. eccl.* 2.14.6). The *Acts of Peter*, however, speaks only of Peter going to Rome, with no mention of Mark.

Because the *Encomium* follows the Acts narrative of John/Mark's travels with Paul and Barnabas and has told the story of Barnabas and Mark's later mission to Cyprus, it has been obliged to place Mark's departure with Peter to Rome, along with the revelation which led Peter to go, after Barnabas' martyrdom, at the cost of the original chronological context of the revelation twelve years after the ascension.

The *Acts of Mark* has maintained both the chronological context and the role of Jerusalem as the place from which Peter departed, but it has modified the story in order to accommodate the inclusion of Mark. Thus, Peter receives a revelation to go to John/Mark in Jerusalem, rather than to go to Rome, as in the *Acts of Peter*. Furthermore, the original early chronological placement of this revelation in the *Acts of Peter* has resulted in the *Acts of Mark*'s omission of the narrative of John/Mark's travels with Barnabas and Paul, related in Acts, as well as of the later Cypriot mission.

It is clear that in both cases independent attempts were made at harmonizing an original John/Mark narrative with the tradition of Peter's journey to Rome drawn directly or indirectly from the *Acts of Peter*. This being so, the *Acts of Mark* could not have been dependent upon the *Encomium of Barnabas*; both were working with common sources for their construction of the John/Mark narrative which they separately conflated with the Petrine narrative.

5.3.2.1. The Rearrangement of Material in the Acts of Mark

The *Encomium of Barnabas* may, however, have preserved the original order of narratives common to both works. The account given in the *Acts of Mark* is disjointed, relating that Mark was baptised by Peter, becoming his son in the faith, that Mary too was converted, and that Mary invited Jesus into her house during his Jerusalem ministry. It then claims that Mark had first been a disciple of John the Baptist before following Jesus into Galilee, which seems to conflict with the earlier claim that Mark was Peter's convert. It then summarises the account in the book of Acts of Peter's visit to the house of Mark following his release from prison. Again, without any clear transition, it goes on to identify Mark as the one carrying the jar of water and as the master of the house at the time of Jesus' final Passover meal.

The version found in the *Encomium of Barnabas* likewise interprets Mark as the one carrying the jar of water and speaks of the house as that of his mother, Mary (221–28), but it does so after relating that Mary invited Jesus into her house at the time of the healing of the paralytic at the sheep gate (192–95; 209–15; cf. John 5:1–8), and that he lodged in the upper part of the house thereafter, whenever he visited Jerusalem (209–19). It adds that Jesus kept the Passover at that house, with his disciples (219–21). [15] Thus, the mention of Jesus coming into Mary's house naturally segues into notices of Jesus' other visits to the house.

This probably represents the original arrangement of the material, into which the author of the *Acts of Mark* has likely attempted to insert the Papian tradition of Mark as Peter's disciple, which in turn has required the reordering of some of the material. Without the interpolated Petrine material, the narrative could be arranged more logically, in way that corresponds to the *Encomium of Barnabas*:

Table 5.3.2.1: Rearrangement of Material in the *Acts of Mark*

Acts of Mark	Minus Petrine Interpolations	*Encomium of Barnabas*	Proposed Original Sequence
Mark baptised by Peter			
Jesus invited into house by Mary	Jesus invited into house		Mark as disciple of the Baptist
Mark as disciple of the Baptist	Mark as disciple of the Baptist		Mark follows Jesus into Galilee
Mark follows Jesus into Galilee	Mark follows Jesus into Galilee	Jesus invited into house by Mary	Jesus invited into house by Mary
Peter visits house of Mark		Jesus lodges at house	Jesus lodges at house
One carrying jar of water at Passover	Mark carries jar of water at Passover	Mark carries jar of water at Passover	Mark carries jar of water at Passover
Master of the house	Master of the house	Master of the house	Master of the house

5.3.3. Comparing Greek and Coptic Sources

Many of the traditions shared by the *Acts of Mark* and Cypriot sources are also found in Coptic sources, perhaps suggesting that they all derive from a common source or sources.

---

[15] Greek text in Van Deun, *Hagiographica* 83–122.

5.3.3.1. Conflation with the Acts of Peter

Like the *Encomium* and the *Acts of Mark*, the Coptic historian Mawhub inter-acts with the narrative known to the *Acts of Peter*; in his version, Peter is in Jerusalem when he receives a dream, as in the *Acts of Peter*. In Mawhub Peter is instructed concerning the needs of both Rome and Egypt, whereas he is only instructed to go to Rome in the *Acts of Peter*.

Furthermore, after Peter and Mark went to Rome, Peter is said by Mawhub to have sent Mark to Egypt, in the fifteenth year after the ascension (c. 44/45), suggesting that this work maintained the original chronological context of the dream found in the *Acts of Peter*, of the twelfth year after the ascension (as in the *Acts of Mark*), rather than the later timeframe presupposed by the *Encomium of Barnabas*. But this early chronology for Mark's journey to Rome has apparently obliged Mawhub, like the *Acts of Mark*, to omit the Acts narrative of John/Mark entirely (*Hist. Patr. Eccl. Alex.* 1.1).

By maintaining Jerusalem as the place in which Peter received the dream and in placing the events in their original chronological context, Mawhub follows the *Acts of Peter* more closely than either the *Acts of Mark* or the *Encomium of Barnabas*.

5.3.3.2. Mark's Abandonment

The narratives of Mark's abandonment of Paul and Barnabas in Cypriot and Coptic sources also share common elements. Thus, in both Severus and the *Encomium of Barnabas*, Mark departs from Paul and Barnabas and returns to Jerusalem after seeing the many dangers that they underwent, "like an inconsiderate young man" in Severus' *Homily* and "being a young man" in the *Encomium*. The Coptic *Encomium of SS. Peter and Paul* similarly states that he abandoned them after seeing the hardships they experienced. Mark is also said to have returned "to Jerusalem, to his mother" in all three sources (though not in the book of Acts).

Again, in both Severus and the *Encomium of Barnabas* Mark's repentance is prompted by the praise heaped upon Paul and Barnabas for hazarding their lives, following their return from their mission. In the *Encomium*, however, Mark goes to Barnabas and weeps at his feet, while in Severus, Barnabas learns of his repentance by divine revelation.

5.3.3.3. The Chronology of the Cypriot Mission

Coptic and Cypriot sources may also reflect very similar chronological constructions of the Cypriot ministry. According to Severus, Barnabas and Mark spent five years preaching in Cyprus, culminating in Barnabas' martyrdom.[16]

---

[16] Bargès, *Homélie sur St Marc*, 29.

The book of Acts relates that Barnabas and Mark departed for Cyprus follow-ing the council of Jerusalem, which is generally dated in modern reconstruc-tions to c. 49/50. [17] If Barnabas was martyred five years later, it would have taken place c. 54/55. The *Acts of Barnabas* places Barnabas' martyrdom at a time when a pious relative of Nero arrived in Cyprus, indicating that the mar-tyrdom was placed in Nero's reign, which began in the year 54. And according to the *Encomium of Barnabas*, Mark sailed to Ephesus following Barnabas' martyrdom and found Paul; the dating of five years would be consistent with this, as Paul's Ephesian ministry was likely conducted in the period 52–55. [18] Severus' chronology thus aligns well with Cypriot sources as well as with mod-ern chronological reconstructions based on the book of Acts.

5.3.3.4. The One Carrying the Jar of Water

Mawhub (*Hist. Patr. Eccl. Alex.* 1.1) and Ibn Kabar among Coptic sources claim that Mark was the one who carried the jar of water into the house in which the sacramental supper was eaten (cf. Mark 14:13; Luke 22:10), a tradi-tion which also appears in the *Encomium of Barnabas* (190–225) and the *Acts of Mark* (6). Mawhub and the Greek texts also claim that Jesus ate the Passover in Mark's house, but he could not have both carried the jar of water, a work reserved for a servant, and have been the host. Indeed, the incongruity of these two claims is particularly illustrated by the *Acts of Mark*, which also identifies the "master of the house" (Matt 26:18) as Mark (6), when the Gospels clearly distinguish the "master of the house" from the one who carried the jar of water (Mark 14:14; cf. Matt 26:18).

Mawhub and Ibn Kabar perhaps attempt to correct this when they claim that the one carrying the water led the disciples into the house of Simon the Cyre-nian, though Mawhub retains the conflicting claim that the disciples were en-tertained in Mark's house at the time of the Passion.

The name of Simon was also associated with the wedding feast at Cana. According to Ibn Kabar, Simon the Canaanite "is from Cana, and he is the bridegroom of the wedding, at which the Lord turned water into wine". [19] There is also a notice found in a Greek work entitled *The Names of the Twelve Apos-*

---

[17] E.g. Ralph P. Martin, *2 Corinthians* (WBC 48; Dallas: Word, 1986), liv (c. 50 CE); Witherington, *Acts of the Apostles*, 82 (49 CE); Joseph A. Fitzmyer, *The Acts of the Apostles: A New Translation with Introduction and Commentary* (AB 31; New Haven, Conn.: Yale University Press, 2008), 502 (49 CE); Keener, *New Testament*, 794 (c. 49 CE).

[18] E.g. Calvin J. Roetzel, *Paul: The Man and the Myth* (Minneapolis: Fortress Press, 1999), 107; Frederick F. Bruce, *Paul: Apostle of the Heart Set Free* (Grand Rapids: Eerd-mans, 2005), 407; Trebilco, *Early Christians*, 53 (52/53–55 CE).

[19] Haase, *Apostel und Evangelisten*, 299–300.

tles and Their Parents, written probably no earlier than the eighth or ninth century, [20] which refers to a certain Simon as "the noble inviter (ἀριστοκλήτωρ) of the Lord to the wedding". [21] It was also noted in Chapter 3 that Mark is identified as one of the servants at the wedding of Cana who poured the water that was turned to wine. Thus, both stories involve jars of water, both are related in the context of a festive meal, and both speak of someone named Simon as presiding over the occasion. Probably, therefore, there has been some conflation of the two stories, and it may have been the identification of Mark as one of the servants at Cana which was transmuted into his identification with the one carrying the jar of water to the house of Simon at the time of the paschal feast.

Indeed, the mention of Mark as the one carrying the water immediately follows the mention of him as one of those at the wedding of Cana in both Mawhub and Ibn Kabar. Similarly, when the proposed Petrine insertions are removed from the *Acts of Mark,* as discussed above, then the mention of the one carrying the water follows immediately after the notice that Mark accompanied Jesus into Galilee at the time of the Cana wedding. Possibly this proximity of the Cana and Passover narratives facilitated conflation.

Possibly such a conflation was also facilitated by a tradition found in the Syriac *Teaching of the Apostles* (*Didasc.* 21), which may have been misinterpreted as identifying the house in which the Passover was eaten as belonging to a certain Simon. This work, which was written in the first half of the third century, thus states: "For when our Lord and Teacher ate the Passover with us, He was betrayed by Judas after that hour; and immediately we began to be sorrowful, because He was taken from us. ...". [22] It goes on to relate how the priests and elders of the people came together on the tenth of Nisan, a few days before the Passover, to discuss how they might put him to death. It continues:

But *Jesus was* that day *in the house of Simon the leper,* and we together with Him, and He related to us that which was about to happen to Him. But Judas went out privily from us, thinking that he would evade our Lord, and went to the house of Caiaphas where the chief priests and elders were assembled, and said to them: *What will ye give me, and I will betray Him to you* when I have found an occasion?

The day spoken of by the text was the tenth of Nisan, on which the priests and elders gathered to plot against Jesus. According to Matt 26:6–16, from which this passage has derived its information, Jesus was at the house of Simon the Leper in Bethany, a few days before the Passover, and Judas, offended by the anointing of Jesus with expensive perfume, went out to the chief priests to discuss with them how he might betray Jesus. But the reference to "that day" in the *Teaching of the Apostles* could have been misinterpreted as a reference to

---

[20] Broek, *Pseudo-Cyril,* 14–15.

[21] The Greek text is cited and translated in Broek, *Pseudo-Cyril,* 30.

[22] Translation in R. Hugh Connolly, *Didascalia Apostolorum* (Oxford: Clarendon Press, 1929), 187, and so hereafter.

Passover, which was mentioned in the preceding context, perhaps because Judas also left the company during the Last Supper and went out to the chief priests and Pharisees (John 13:30; 18:2–3).

5.4. Conclusion

The *Acts of Mark* is a rich source of John/Mark traditions which are independent of the New Testament and which relate both his background and his travels in the period between Stephen's martyrdom and the famine visit of Paul and Barnabas to Jerusalem (c. 37–45).

A comparative study of the *Acts of Mark* with the Cypriot sources does not bear out the thesis that the *Acts of Mark* was dependent on either the *Acts of Barnabas* or the *Encomium of Barnabas* for its information. Rather, all of these works seem to have variously conflated the same narratives, suggesting their independent derivation from common sources.

A look at the larger picture of the relationship of Cypriot sources, the *Acts of Mark* and Coptic sources seems to suggest that they all form part of a complex web of literary interrelationship and that they were each working with a common literary tradition which has since disappeared, but which has been variously conflated with the Papian and Alexandrian depictions of Mark (and, in the case of the *Acts of Barnabas*, apparently another Markan figure associated with Iconium) to form various configurations of the Markan narrative.

Part 2

John, Who Was Also Called Mark

Chapter 6

The "Johannine" Mark

J. Edgar Bruns published two articles that drew attention to the placement, in a number of medieval sources, of John/Mark in narrative contexts drawn from the Fourth Gospel, sometimes in roles associated with the Beloved Disciple himself. [1] He also noted that John/Mark's house sometimes provides the backdrop to narratives drawn from the Fourth Gospel. [2] To these can also be added the attribution to Mark of a Gospel containing a doctrine of Christ's divinity and/or a Logos theology, which was not mentioned by Bruns. This chapter will examine these portrayals, and it will conclude that John/Mark was likely identified with John the Evangelist by some ancient writers, and that this identification was obscured by his later identification with Mark the Evangelist.

6.1. The Baptist's Disciples (John 1)

A work entitled the *Witness of Holy John the Precursor and Baptist*, which may have been composed in Syria in the fifth century, [3] provides an account of the death of John the Baptist; according to a recension of the text made in the eleventh century or earlier, the work was written by "John Mark his [John the Baptist's] disciple". [4] At the end of one manuscript of this recension (Paris 1021), the following notice is given:

I have written this, brother, I, Mark, the first disciple of the holy precursor and baptist John. After having followed him and having learned from him to believe in Our Lord Jesus Christ

---

[1] Bruns, "Confusion," 23; idem, "Riddle," 91.

[2] Bruns, "Riddle," 91; "Confusion," 23.

[3] Andrew Bernhard, "The Life and Martyrdom of John the Baptist: A New Translation and Introduction," in *New Testament Apocrypha: More Noncanonical Scriptures*, vol. 1, ed. Tony Burke and Brent Landau (Grand Rapids: Eerdmans, 2016), 253. Bruns mistakenly refers to it as an Egyptian work ("Confusion," 23).

[4] François Nau, "Histoire de saint Jean Baptiste attribuée à saint Marc l'Évangéliste," *PO* 4:526; cf. Bernhard, "John the Baptist," 251; Bruns, "Confusion," 24, John J. Gunther, "The Association of Mark and Barnabas with Egyptian Christianity (Part I)," *EvQ* 54 (1982): 233 n. 78.

who will deliver us from the wrath to come. I then attached myself to the holy leader (κορυφαῖος) of the Apostles, to Peter. [5]

Other manuscripts retain the reference to the author as a disciple (though not "first disciple" of John) but omit the mention of the name of Mark and the mention of Peter. [6]

As Bruns observes, the account found in the Paris manuscript seems to identify Mark as one of the two disciples of the Baptist who, according to the Fourth Gospel, followed Jesus after the Baptist pointed him out (John 1:35–42), thus placing Mark in the Johannine narrative. [7] Many, including Bruns, [8] would identify the unnamed disciple as the Beloved Disciple, or would at least consider the identification probable. [9] Bruns also notes that "the identification of this disciple with the Evangelist was current in Chrysostom's time" (citing Chrysostom, *Hom. John* 18.3). [10] He concludes that by being identified with this disciple, John/Mark was either confused with John or "at least assigned a role that traditionally belongs" to him. [11]

This identification of Mark with the unnamed disciple is more clearly indicated in the *Acts of Mark*, with which Bruns was not familiar. It relates that Mark was a disciple of John the Baptist and that he followed Jesus when he went from Jerusalem into Galilee (*Act. Marc.* 5). The reference is unmistakably Johannine, referring to Jesus' departure from Judea to attend the wedding at Cana in Galilee, immediately after the unnamed disciple of John 1:35 began following Jesus (John 1:43; 2:1–2).

6.2. The Wedding at Cana (John 2)

The *Acts of Mark* provides a bridge linking the claim, found in the *Witness of Holy John*, that Mark was a disciple of the Baptist who came to believe in Jesus, with the notice that Mark attended the wedding of Cana (John 2:1–10),

---

[5] Greek text in Nau, "Histoire de saint Jean," 540; translation in Bruns, "Confusion," 24.

[6] Greek text in Nau, "Histoire de saint Jean," 540; an English translation is found in Bernhard, "John the Baptist," 267.

[7] Bruns, "Confusion," 23.

[8] Bruns, "Confusion," 23.

[9] E.g. Cullmann, *Johannine Circle*, 72–73; Brown, *John*, 73; Leon Morris, *The Gospel According to John* (NICNT; Grand Rapids: Eerdmans, 1995), 136; Brian J. Capper, " 'With the Oldest Monks ...' Light from Essene History on the Career of the Beloved Disciple?" *JTS* 49 (1998): 6–8; George R. Beasley-Murray, *John* (2nd ed.; WBC 36; Dallas: Word, 2002), 26; Bauckham, *Eyewitnesses*, 127.

[10] Bruns, "Confusion," 23 n. 7, citing Chrysostom, *Hom. John* 18.3. Chrysostom refers to some who identified the unnamed disciple as the "author" of John's Gospel.

[11] Bruns, "Confusion," 24.

found in Mawhub (*Hist. Patr. Eccl. Alex.* 1.1) [12] and Ibn Kabar. [13] As discussed in Chapter 3, Mawhub claimed that Mark was one of the servants who poured forth the water that became wine at the wedding, while Ibn Kabar held that he was one of the disciples who drank from the wine.

6.3. The Healing at the Pool of Bethesda (John 5)

As noted by Bruns, the *Encomium of Barnabas* depicts Barnabas bringing Jesus to the home of Mary, the mother of John/Mark, located on the Zion Hill in Jerusalem, at the time of the healing of the man at the pool of Bethesda (192–95). [14] This account of the healing is again uniquely Johannine (John 5:1–8). [15] It adds that Jesus subsequently lodged at that house when visiting the city (217–19). [16] Possibly this is related to Eusebius' claim that the hill of Zion was where Jesus "had for the most part spent his time (or "stayed"; διατριβάς πεποίητο) and taught" (*Dem. ev.* 1.4). [17]

According to the Fourth Gospel, Jesus stayed in Bethany beyond the Jordan prior to the healing at the pool of Bethesda (John 1:28, 38–39) and did not return again to that region until near the end of his ministry, following the winter feast prior to his crucifixion (John 10:40). This tradition thus fills the gaps in the Johannine narrative concerning where Jesus lodged between these stays beyond the Jordan. Bruns concludes that in the *Encomium*, "the house of John Mark becomes the background of the fourth gospel's narrative of the Jerusalem ministry." [18]

6.5. Mark at Bethany (cf. John 11)

Mawhub uniquely records that the first place in which John/Mark preached outside of Jerusalem, after the resurrection, was Bethany near Jerusalem (*Hist. Patr. Eccl. Alex.* 1.1). Although this notice does not place Mark within a Johannine narrative as such, this village was especially prominent in the Fourth

---

[12] Cf. Bruns, "Confusion," 23. Bruns refers to Mawhub as "Severus".

[13] Hanna, *The Lamp*, 77.

[14] Bruns, "Riddle," 91.

[15] Bruns, "Riddle," 91.

[16] Cf. Bruns, "Riddle," 91.

[17] Translated from the Greek text in Ivar A. Heikel, ed., *Eusebius Werke,* vol. 7: *Die Demonstratio Evangelica* (GCS; Leipzig: Hinrichs, 1913), and so hereafter.

[18] Bruns, "Riddle," 91.

Gospel (in the Synoptics, it is mentioned in passing twice in Luke), as the home of Lazarus, Mary and Martha (John 11:1; 18; 12:1).

6.6. The Passover (cf. John 13)

Mawhub (*Hist. Patr. Eccl. Alex.* 1.1), the *Encomium of Barnabas* (229–30) and the *Acts of Mark* (6) claim that Jesus' final Passover meal was eaten at the house of Mark. This tradition is not directly associated with any uniquely Johannine account. Indeed, the Fourth Gospel does not refer to Jesus' final meal as the Passover, and the *Acts of Mark* quotes the words delivered to the master of the house as given in Matt 26:18. However, these notices seem to paint John/Mark as the host of the Last Supper, a position sometimes associated with the Beloved Disciple, based on the seating arrangements (the Beloved Disciple was to the right of Jesus, the guest of honour; John 13:23), [19] though many would identify Jesus as the host. [20] This thus represents another possible identification of John/Mark with the Beloved Disciple.

6.7. The Disciple at the Cross (John 19)

While Coptic tradition never explicitly identified John/Mark with the Beloved Disciple (nor could it, since it identified this Mark with Mark the Evangelist), it perhaps comes no closer to depicting Mark in the role of the Beloved Disciple than it does when it makes him to have been a witness of Christ's crucifixion, for in the Fourth Gospel it is the Beloved Disciple who alone of the disciples is said to have stood by Jesus at the cross (John 19:25–27). Perhaps the earliest attestation of this tradition is found in the *Acts of Peter* written by Peter, bishop of Alexandria (not to be confused with the more well-known *Acts of Peter*),

---

[19] Lewis Johnson, "Who was the Beloved Disciple?" *ExpT* 77 (1966): 157–58; Denys E. H. Whiteley, "Was John Written by a Sadducee?" *ANWR* 2.25.3 (Berlin: de Gruyter, 1985): 2481–505; J. K. Thornecroft, "The Redactor and the 'Beloved' in John," *ExpT* 98 (1986–87): 135–39; Capper, "Oldest Monks," 5, 13–15; Richard Bauckham, *The Testimony of the Beloved Disciple: Narrative, History, and Theology in the Gospel of John* (Grand Rapids: Baker, 2007), 15; Ben Witherington III, "What's in a Name? Rethinking the Historical Figure of the Beloved Disciple in the Fourth Gospel," in *John, Jesus, and History*, vol. 2, *Aspects of Historicity in the Fourth Gospel*, ed. Paul N. Anderson, Felix Just, Tom Thatcher (Atlanta: SBL, 2009), 208.

[20] E.g. Beasley-Murray, *John*, 237–38; Joseph Ratzinger, *Jesus of Nazareth: The Infancy Narratives*, trans. Philip J. Whitmore (New York: Doubleday, 2007), 66; Andreas J. Köstenberger, *A Theology of John's Gospel and Letters: The Word, the Christ, the Son of God* (BTNT; Grand Rapids: Zondervan, 2009), 77. This is disputed by Capper, "Oldest Monks," 14.

possibly in the early fourth century, in which Peter addresses Mark as follows: "you evangelist of the only-begotten Saviour, you witness of his suffering." [21] Mark continues to be referred to as "the witness to the passion" in a Coptic Doxology. [22]

A manuscript of Severus of Nastrawa's *Homily on Mark* which was not used for Bargès' edition similarly refers to Mark as "the martyr and the witness of the suffering of Christ." [23] Severus also claims that Hannah, whom he identifies as Mark's mother, "secretly joined herself to the holy women who were witnesses of the crucifixion of the Saviour and who brought perfumes to his tomb." [24] Thus, Severus seems to have been aware of traditions that placed both Mark and his mother at the cross, in what is perhaps a reminiscence of John and Mary, John's adopted mother, being at the cross. Indeed, that he knew a source that placed Mark in the role of the Beloved Disciple and identified his mother as Mary would perhaps account for why he seeks to associate John with Mark and Mary with Hannah, Mark's mother. Thus, he claims that Hannah and John (i.e. Mark) would spend time with Mary and John and were baptised by them, and that their names were thereafter changed to that of Mary and Mark. [25] Possibly Hannah was the name of Mark's biological mother; possibly it is a conflation with the Anna (the same as Hannah) who was said to have been the mother of Mary, Jesus' mother, in the *Protevangelium of James*.

6.8. Thomas' Doubting (John 20)

In another example of John/Mark's house functioning as the background for the Johannine story, the *Encomium of Barnabas* (230–31) identifies Mark's house as the place in which Jesus appeared to the disciples following the resurrection. Mawhub quotes the Johannine account, stating that it was in Mark's house that Jesus appeared "while the doors were shut" (*Hist. Patr. Eccl. Alex.* 1.1; John 20:19). [26] The Coptic homily of Ps.-Cyril, *On the Life and the Passion of Christ*, probably written in the first half of the ninth century, [27] also identifies

---

[21] Translated from the Latin translation in *PG* 18:461; cf. Gunther, "Mark and Barnabas," 233 n. 78.

[22] *The Holy Psalmody* (Lynnwood, Wash.: Saint Mary's Coptic Orthodox Church, 1997), 109.

[23] Youhanna Nessim Youssef, "The homily of Severus of Nastrāwa on saint Mark," *BSAC* 49 (2010): 147.

[24] Bargès, *Homélie sur St Marc*, 22.

[25] Bargès, *Homélie sur St Marc*, 23–24.

[26] Evetts, *Severus*, 139–40.

[27] Broek, *Pseudo-Cyril*, 70.

the house of Mary, the mother of John/Mark, as the place to which the apostles gathered, alluding to the Johannine account:

It was a dwelling place of the apostles because of the fear of the Jews, as is also written in the Acts of the Apostles. And they were hidden, together with Mary, until the whole Pentecost had passed by and the Holy Spirit came down upon them and they went through the countries and preached the resurrection of life (6–7). [28]

While Ps.-Cyril cites the book of Acts, the reference is actually found in the Fourth Gospel, in its account of the apostles being in hiding following the crucifixion (John 20:19).

6.9. The Gospel of the Divine Logos (cf. John 1; 21)

Another Johannine depiction of Mark is found in the attribution to him of a Gospel which contained either a doctrine of Christ's divinity or a Logos theology. Thus, Mark's Gospel is variously spoken of as destroying errors concerning the divinity, as declaring that Jesus is God, or as teaching the divinity and incarnation of the Logos. While these attributions seem ill-fitting for the author of Mark's Gospel, they would aptly describe the Gospel attributed to the Beloved Disciple (John 21:24), which, uniquely contains a doctrine of the divinity of the Logos (John 1:1–18). This may therefore represent another placement of John/Mark in a role associated with the Beloved Disciple.

6.9.1. The Acts of Peter *by Peter, Bishop of Alexandria*

One of the earliest such potential "Johannine" descriptions of Mark's Gospel is that of Mark as the evangelist of the "only begotten" in the possibly early fourth-century *Acts of Peter* by Peter, bishop of Alexandria, mentioned above. Only John's Gospel refers to Jesus as the "only begotten" (John 1:18).

6.9.2. Ambrose of Milan

Ambrose of Milan (c. 390) also provides a possible Johannine description of Mark's Gospel within the context of the exegetical tradition which viewed the four living creatures of Revelation, who were like a lion, a calf, a man and an eagle (Rev 4:7), as symbolizing the four Gospels. He refers to each of the four only by their ordinal number and describes the second Gospel as the lion (he follows the order of the living creatures as given in Ezek 1:10: man, lion, calf, eagle). After speaking of Matthew's Gospel, the "man", he continues:

another [Gospel] began from the expression of the divine power (*potentiae divinae*); because he has scorned death with lively courage (*vivida mortem virtute contemserit*), being king

---

[28] Broek, *Pseudo-Cyril*, 127.

from king, powerful one from powerful one, true one from true one (*ex rege rex, fortis ex forti, verus ex vero*)" (*Comm. Luc.* pref. 8). [29]

This description has often been understood as speaking of Mark, [30] though Watson, following Zahn, suggests instead that he is speaking of John's Gospel, which begins with Christ's divinity (John 1:1–3) and the statement that the life is the light that overcomes darkness (John 1:4–5), noting that "the *ex-* formulations" are "reminiscent of the Nicene Creed *(deum verum de deo vero)*". [31]

Watson argues that Ambrose, in placing this description second, was following the so-called Western Order of the Gospels (Matthew, John, Luke and Mark). [32] While plausible, Ambrose had spoken earlier in his preface of Matthew, Mark and Luke, in that order (*Comm. Luc.* pref. 3–4), suggesting the possibility that this instead represents another Johannine description of Mark's Gospel. Furthermore, his description of the writer of the Fourth Gospel, signified by an eagle, while concise, seems more appropriate for John than for Mark: "he has described the miracles of the divine resurrection more abundantly than the others". [33]

The exegetical tradition of viewing the four living creatures of Revelation (lion, a calf, a man and an eagle respectively) as symbolizing the four Gospels is first found in Irenaeus (c. 185), who interprets them of the Gospels of John, Luke, Matthew and Mark respectively (*Haer.* 3.11.8). The same correlation is later found in Juvencus (c. 330) (*Evangelicae Historiae*, pref.), [34] Victorinus (d. 303 or 304) (*Comm. Apoc.* 4:7–10), [35] (*Comm. Matt.* prolog.5), Chromatius (*Comm. Matt.* prolog. 6–7), Andrew of Caesarea (563–637) [36] and Theophylact [37] (d. c. 1107) (*Enarrat. in Evan. Marci*).

From about the turn of the fifth century, however, it is Mark who is associated with the lion and John with the eagle, as found in Epiphanius (*De mens.*

---

[29] Translated by the author from the Latin text in G. Schenkl, ed., *Ambrose: Expositio Evangelii secundum Lucam* (CSEL 32/4; Vienna: Akademie der Wissenschaften, 1902).

[30] Especially in older scholarship; e.g. Richard Trench, *The Hulsean Lectures for 1845 and 1846* (London: Macmillan, 1880), 39 n. 1; George Salmon, *A Historical Introduction to the Study of the Books of the New Testament* (London: John Murray, 1899), 33.

[31] Francis Watson, *Gospel Writing: A Canonical Perspective* (Grand Rapids: Eerdmans, 2013), 560 n. 18.

[32] Watson, *Gospel Writing*, 560 n. 18.

[33] Watson, in arguing that Ambrose if following the Western order, argues that this describes Mark 16:9–20 (*Gospel Writing*, 560 n. 18).

[34] In *PL* 19:55.

[35] William C. Weinrich, ed., *Revelation* (ACCSNT 12; Downers Grove, Ill.: IVP, 2005), 63–64. The correlations were changed in Jerome's version of Victorinus.

[36] Weinrich, *Revelation*, 63 n. 55.

[37] *PG* 123:493; for an English translation, see, *The Explanation by the Blessed Theophylact of the Holy Gospel According to St. Mark*, trans. Christopher Stade (House Springs, Mo.: Chrysostom Press, 1993), 9–10.

et pond. 35), Jerome (*Comm. Matt.* pref.) and most later writers. [38] This revised
order likely suggested to Augustine a further refinement of the imagery, for he
exchanges the symbolism of Mark (the lion) and Matthew (the man). [39] Ambrose may illustrate how it was the confusion occasioned by the attribution of
a Johannine Gospel to Mark that resulted in the misconfiguration of the imagery of the faces, so that the lion imagery, previously associated with John,
came to be associated with Mark.

6.9.3. The Monarchian Prologue to Mark

A little later, the Monarchian Prologue to Mark (late-fourth century) attributes
a Logos theology to Mark's Gospel which it then seeks to derive exegetically
from Mark's prologue. After describing Mark as a Levite who exercised the
priesthood in Israel, it claims that Mark shows in the beginning (*initio*) of his
Gospel that "the Word was made flesh" (*verbum caro factum* [40]), so that the
reader be not ignorant of "the dwelling of the God coming in flesh" (*dei
advenientis habitaculum caro*). [41] It adds that Mark's work as a bishop was "to
understand the divine nature of the Lord (*divinam domini*) in the flesh", echoing Eusebius' statement that it was reserved to John by the Spirit to declare the
doctrine of his divinity (*Hist. eccl.* 3.24.13). The prologue engages in a tortuous
exegesis of the prologue of Mark's Gospel in order to conform it to this Johannine terminology, claiming that it shows "that the body of the Lord was ani-
mated in all things by the word of the divine voice."

The prologue continues by claiming that Mark wrote these things so that the
reader "might find in himself the word of the voice (*verbum vocis*) which had
been lost in the consonants". The Irish monk Sedulius Scottus (ninth century)
suggested that the consonants referred to the other Gospels (*Comm. Marc.*). [42]
Possibly this play on words drew from the description of John as a spiritual
Gospel which taught the divinity in contrast to those which had only provided
the outward facts (σωματικά or "bodily things", found in Clement and perhaps
originating with Papias; *apud* Eusebius, *Hist. eccl.* 6.14.7). It may also be related to Origen's statement that the Gospel of John should not be understood
according to "the outward letters" (τοῖς σωματικοῖς χαρακτῆρσιν) (*Comm. Iohan.* 10.3). The prologue adds,

---

[38] Kenneth Stevenson, "Animal Rites: The Four Living Creatures in Patristic Exegesis
and Liturgy," *StP* 34 (2001): 478–80.

[39] E.g. Watson, *Gospel Writing*, 24, and n. 44.

[40] The same words are found in the prologue to John. See the text in Aland, *Synopsis*,
554.

[41] Translated from the Latin text in Aland, *Synopsis*, 555, and so hereafter.

[42] In *PL* 103:283. This view is rejected by John Chapman, *Notes on the Early History of
the Vulgate Gospels* (Oxford: Clarendon Press, 1908), 234.

indeed, both entering into the work of the perfected Gospel and commencing to proclaim God from the baptism of the Lord, he did not labour to proclaim the nativity of the flesh, which he had seen [43] in prior ones (*prioribus*).

The two claims made here, that Mark's Gospel shows in its beginning that the Word was made flesh and that Mark began with the baptism, echo the discussion of John's Gospel in Theodore of Mopsuestia (c. 350–c. 428), which similarly made the baptism of John the beginning of the account of the things said and done by Jesus, following the true beginning of the Gospel with the doctrine of the divinity (*Comm. Iohan.* Prolog.). [44]

If the refence to the "consonants" is to the former Gospels, then the reference to the "prior ones" likely refers to the prior Gospels which included accounts of Jesus' nativity (i.e. Matthew and Luke). Sedulius Scottus thus interpreted *prioribus* of, "the prior evangelists, that is, Matthew and Luke". [45] An Arabic translation of the Monarchian Prologue, dated to 946, similarly understood *prioribus* as a reference to what the "other apostles" had written. [46] The Monarchian Prologue thus seems to be claiming that Mark had before him the Gospels with the birth narratives (i.e. Matthew and Luke) when he wrote. Orchard and Riley characterise this as the "[m]ost remarkable" aspect of the prologue, [47] but it would not be so remarkable if the prologue was originally speaking of the Johannine Gospel, which was written last according to the Papian tradition (Fragment 20; cf. Clement's "elders" in Eusebius, *apud* Eusebius, *Hist. eccl.* 6.14.5–7). [48] Indeed, it echoes Eusebius' claim that John reasonably maintained silence concerning the genealogy of the Lord, since it had been written out already by Matthew and Luke (*Hist. eccl.* 3.24.3).

The prologue continues by stating that instead of the birth narratives, Mark wrote the details concerning the temptation in the wilderness, "joining together the singular points in brief, so as not to diminish the authority of the work that was done" (*singula in brevi conpingens nec auctoritatem factae rei demeret*),

---

[43] The words "had seen" (*viderat*) reflect the reading of edited texts and sizeable number of manuscripts, though the majority read *vicerat* ("had conquered"); see Jürgen Regul, *Die antimarcionitischen Evangelienprologe* (*VL* 6; Freiburg: Verlag Herder, 1969), 49.

Chapman retains *vicerat* and interprets *prioribus* of the opening paragraphs, so that Mark did not labour to tell the birth of the flesh which he had conquered in his opening paragraphs by making the divine voice the beginning of the Gospel, though he admits this is "a strange expression". See Chapman, *Notes*, 234.

[44] See Furlong, *Identity of John*, 164.

[45] *PL* 103:283. This view is shared by Orchard and Riley, *Order of the Synoptics*, 209.

[46] Karl Vollers and Ernst Von Dobschutz, "Ein spanisch-arabisches Evangelien-fragment," *ZDMG* 56 (1902): 640.

[47] Orchard and Riley, *Order of the Synoptics*, 209.

[48] The fragments of Papias are numbered according to the edition of Michael William Holmes, *The Apostolic Fathers: Greek Texts and English Translations* (Grand Rapids: Baker, 1999), and so hereafter.

where the reference to the work that was previously done again likely points to the previous Gospels. Probably the source of this account explained why John/Mark (i.e. John the Evangelist) only briefly related things which had been more fully described in the other Gospels, which the Monarchian Prologue then later explained in terms of the second Gospel's condensed account of the temptation in the wilderness.

6.9.4. Procopius the Deacon

Procopius the Deacon (early ninth century) may also preserve a Johannine-depiction of Mark's Gospel. In his *Encomium on Mark*, he relates how Mark's "eye has beheld him, whom eye has not been able to see (cf. John 1:18; 1 John 4:12), appearing in our covering (cf. John 1:14); and he left the land brought forth (by him) [i.e. heaven]" (*Encom. in Marc.*). [49] A little later, he likens Mark to

> a wise architect who carves into the vessel of his Gospel new laws, which Jeremiah had announced before in proclamation, saying: "And I will accomplish with the house of Israel and the house of Judah a new covenant, putting my laws in their hearts" (cf. Jer 31:31), so that not only by words but also by the evangelical scripture he might explain for posterity the incarnation [50] of the eternal Logos and his life among men; placing in plain view [51] the divine signs, the things suffered for us, the rising up from the tomb, and the ascension into the heavens, from whence he descended (*Encom. in Marc.*). [52]

Procopius' reference to the "new laws" may be Johannine (cf. John 13:34; 15:10?), and the mention "of the incarnation of the eternal Logos and his life among men" is undeniably so (John 1:1–3; 14). Likewise, the reference to the divine signs (θεοσημεῖαι) is likely Johannine (cf. John 2:11; 4:54, etc.), as is the mention of the ascension "from whence he descended" (cf. John 3:13; 6:62).

Addressing Mark, Procopius adds, "your voice is over the sound of the thunder; your Gospel is a light over the shafts of the sun". The reference to thunder evokes the tradition found in the *Memorial of Saint John*, of unknown date but written sometime after the mid-sixth century (perhaps no earlier than the ninth century), [53] that John received the Gospel on a mountain in Patmos, amidst

---

[49] Translated from the Greek text in *PG* 100:1189. The Greek reads: Τεθέαται γὰρ ὃν ὀφθαλμὸς ὁρᾶν οὐ δεδύνηται, τῷ ἡμετέρῳ φαινόμενον προκαλύμματι, καὶ τὴν ἐνεγκαμένην κατέλιπεν. The text is a little obscure and I have been guided by the accompanying Latin translation (1190).

[50] The word is implied by the Greek which reads τὴν τοῦ Λόγου, where ἡ οἰκονομίαν is understood.

[51] Greek: ὑπ' ὄψιν; lit. "under the eyes".

[52] Translated from the Greek text in *PG* 100:1193.

[53] Derek Krueger, *Writing and Holiness: The Practice of Authorship in the Early Christian East* (Philadelphia: University of Pennsylvania Press, 2004), 217 n. 19.

thunder and lightnings. [54] The same work relates, in a narrative similar to that found in the earlier *Acts of John by Prochorus*, [55] that Prochorus his assistant fell on his face and could not bear to dwell on such sights, and that John stood facing them, until:

At last the thunder is articulated in a certain way into a voice and responds very clearly: "In the beginning was the Word, and the Word was with God, and the Word was God." Prochorus is near the visionary sight. He clearly sees the light, but he hears no-one (the Theologian is the voice of the thunder) … [56]

The *Memorial of Saint John* continues by relating that John, having received the law, came down from the mountain, just as Moses, whom it calls ὁ θεόπτης (God-beholder), did when he received the tables. Procopius a little later also refers to Mark as ὁ θεόπτης, [57] further suggesting the possibility of some connection between the accounts.

Mark is also spoken of as "the God-beholding (θεόπτης) evangelist" in the *Acts of Mark (Act. Marc.* 1). Possibly the *Acts of Mark* preserves an allusion to the tradition of the Fourth Gospel being given by revelation on a mountain in Patmos when it writes

it was necessary that he, having been predestined for the discipleship of the only begotten Son of God and worthily called to every good work of virtue, pass to the peak (or "highest place"; εἰς ἄκρον) and so thus to receive the divine illumination of the all-holy and life-giving Spirit and to become the most clear-seeing lamp and most radiant herald of the divine discourse pertaining to the gospel (*Act. Marc.* 3).

6.9.5. An Epigram on Mark's Gospel

An epigram on Mark's Gospel found in an early-tenth-century text describes Mark as follows:

Initiated by the ineffable words of Peter, Mark, who is second among the divinely inspired authors, writes very wisely of God's reducing Himself to the nature of mortals (Τὴν τοῦ

---

[54] Greek text given in Yuko Taniguchi, François Bovon, and Athanasios Antonopoulos, "The Memorial of Saint John the Theologian (BHG 919fb)," in François Bovon, Ann G. Brock, and C. R. Matthews, eds., *The Apocryphal Acts of the Apostles* (Cambridge, Mass.: Harvard University Press, 1999), 349, 351. An English translation is also provided (344). For an explanation of why John's gospel was said to have been written on Patmos, see Furlong, *Identity of John*, 168–69.

[55] The Greek text is given in Theodor Zahn, ed., *Acta Joannis unter Benutzung von C. v. Tischendorf's Nachlass* (Erlangen: Verlag von Andreas Deichert, 1880), 155–56.

[56] Translated from the Greek text given in Taniguchi, Bovon, and Antonopoulos, "Memorial of Saint John," 351, 353.

[57] *PG* 100:1196.

Θεοῦ κένωσιν εἰς βροτῶν φύσιν), in which being at once God and man (ὤν Θεάνθωπος), He bears a double nature (διπλοῦν). [58]

The epigram alludes to the Papian tradition of Mark writing what he had heard from Peter, but its description of Mark's Gospel is clearly more fitting for the Fourth Gospel, which does speak of the divine Word becoming flesh and dwelling among humanity.

6.9.6. The Acts of Mark

The *Acts of Mark* introduces Mark as "the very great (or "greatest") herald (μέγιστος κῆρυξ) of the evangelical teaching concerning the divinity [59] (τῆς εὐαγγελικῆς θεολογίας)" (*Act. Marc.* 2). Later in the work, it similarly relates that Mark "began to explain through a prose exposition (λογογραφικῆς ἀποδείξεως), the Spirit-moved and God-breathed oracles of the evangelical teaching concerning the divinity (τῆς εὐαγγελικῆς θεολογίας)" (9). This description again seems ill-fitting for the author of the Second Gospel, but it would fittingly describe the author of the Fourth Gospel. Indeed, Eusebius describes John's Gospel similarly, stating that John began his Gospel with "the doctrine of the divinity (τῆς θεολογίας)" (*Hist. eccl.* 3.24.13).

The account in the *Acts of Mark* otherwise echoes Papias' report concerning how Mark's Gospel was written at Rome and approved of by Peter, though it depicts Mark as collaborating with Peter in writing the Gospel (9), unlike the Papian tradition, according to which Mark wrote down what he had heard Peter preach. Possibly the more important role afforded to John/Mark resulted from conflation of the Papian account with an account of John/Mark writing his own Gospel.

6.10. Refuting Errors Concerning Christ's Divinity (cf. John 1)

A number of sources also specifically relate that Mark wrote in order to refute errors concerning Christ's divinity, with some claiming that this refutation was made in the prologue to his Gospel (cf. the Monarchian Prologue to Mark).

---

[58] Greek text and translation in Robert S. Nelson, *The Iconography of Preface and Miniature in the Byzantine Gospel Book* (New York: New York University Press, 1980), 77–78.

[59] The noun θεολογία generally refers to teaching about the divinity (cf. *PGL* 627). E.g. Eusebius (*Hist. eccl.* 1.1.8), Athanasius (*Contra Arianos*, 1.18), Gregory Nazianzus (*Orat.* 38.8) and John of Damascus (*Exp. Fid.* 1.4).

6.10.1. Chromatius

The earliest such claim is found is made by Chromatius of Aquileia (d. 406 or 407) in his commentary on Matthew, in which he asserts that Mark's prologue addressed errors concerning Christ's divinity:

> Those, however, who dared to blaspheme the true divinity of the Son of God and the un-bounded nature of his eternity, denying specifically that he was born from the Father and is true God, and that he was always with the Father, saint John and Mark nevertheless imme-diately resist, condemning the faithlessness of their blasphemy, testifying in the beginning of their Gospel that the only begotten Son of God is God (*in evangelii sui principio unigenitum Dei Filium Deum esse testantes*) (*Comm. Matt.* prolog. 6). [60]

Chromatius claims that Mark's (along with John's) prologue teaches that the "one and only Son" is God, which is perhaps related to Peter of Alexandria's claim that Mark was the evangelist of the only begotten (see above). However, Chromatius' description could only be applicable to John's Gospel (John 1:1; 18). [61] Probably the source only mentioned Mark (as in the Monarchian Pro-logue), with the name of John being inserted, either by Chromatius or his source, on account of the description's better applicability to the Fourth Gos-pel.

6.10.2. Thomas Aquinas

Thomas Aquinas (1225–1274) similarly claims that Mark's prologue refuted errors concerning the divinity, though his account also mentions John, as Chro-matius does:

> For Mark and John primarily have destroyed those errors, which are concerning the divinity. Whence John in the beginning said: "in the beginning was the Word." And Mark commenced thus: "The beginning of the gospel of Jesus Christ, the Son of God." He did not say, "the son of Abraham." [62]

Aquinas thus finds an argument for the divinity in the description (in the Vul-gate, at least) of Jesus in Mark's prologue as the Son of God. However, this title is not exceptional to Mark, and Mark's prologue, unlike John's, does not especially address Jesus' divinity and can hardly be described as "destroying errors concerning the divinity". Like the Monarchian Prologue, Aquinas was likely seeking to conform the Markan prologue to the Johannine description.

---

[60] Translated from the Latin text in CCSL 9A:188.

[61] Chromatius' reading reflects the text of the Latin Vulgate, some earlier Latin writers and the majority of medieval Greek manuscripts (ὁ μονογενὴς υἱός) rather than μονογενὴς θεὸς of critical texts.

[62] Translated from the Latin text in Thomas Aquinas, *In Evangelia S. Matthaei et S. Ioannis Commentaria*, vol. 1: *Evangelium Secundum Matthaeum* (Turin: Typographia Pontificia, 1893). 7.

6.10.3. The Refutation of All Heresies

One further potential attribution to Mark of a refuting of errors with respect to
the incarnation of the Logos is found in the *Refutation of All Heresies*, written
in Rome, c. 225. This work, briefly discussed in Chapter 1, describes Mark as
"the stump-fingered" (ὁ κολοβοδάκτυλος) in a passage in which the author is
attempting to refute the teachings of the Marcionites. In this context, the author
accuses Marcion, who identified the God of the Old Testament as an evil dem-
iurge, of borrowing his teachings from the philosopher Empedocles, adding
that "neither the apostle Paul nor Mark the stump-fingered announced them"
(*Refut.* 7.30.1). The writer goes on to explain that Marcion employed the theories of Empedocles to argue that the Logos had descended to the earth independently of birth (*Refut.* 7.30.5–6).

As Black observes, "Hippolytus [sic] suggests that Marcion coated Paul's
letters and Mark's Gospel with a thick veneer of plagiarised Greek philoso-
phy", yet the idea that Marcion could put the Gospel of Mark to such a use is,
as Black notes, "puzzling". [63] It would not be puzzling, however, if the reference was to John's Gospel, with its doctrine of the descent of the Logos to
earth. [64] Possibly the author was claiming that the teachings of Paul and of
John/Mark (i.e. John) his fellow-worker (Col 4:10) refuted Marcion's Logos
doctrine.

6.10.3.1. Mark the Stump-Fingered

The origins of the epithet "the stump-fingered" (ὁ κολοβοδάκτυλος), given to
Mark by Hippolytus, are unknown. The casual way in which Mark is so described suggests that the epithet was already familiar to the author's Roman
readers. [65] Hengel thinks it may have been derived from Papias or Hegesippus. [66] The word κολοβός from which κολοβοδάκτυλος is derived can refer to
stunted growth or to mutilation. [67] The former interpretation informs the so-
called Anti-Marcionite prologue to Mark, which, though extant only in Latin,
was probably composed in Greek, [68] perhaps as early as the second century. [69]

---

[63] Black, *Apostolic Interpreter*, 93.

[64] According to the Marcionite view, Christ was the archon who made the world and
descended from the invisible Father (Epiphanius, *Pan.* 42.4.1–2).

[65] Black, *Apostolic Interpreter*, 117–18; Winn, *Purpose of Mark's Gospel*, 50; Kok, "The
Gospel on the Margins," 194.

[66] Martin Hengel, *Die vier Evangelien und das eine Evangelium von Jesus Christus:
Studien zu ihrer Sammlung und Entstehung* (WUNT 224, Tübingen: Mohr Siebeck, 2008),
144 n. 415.

[67] Swete, *St. Mark*, xxvii.

[68] Martin Hengel, *Studies in the Gospel of Mark* (Eugene, Oreg.: Wipf and Stock, 2003),
3.

[69] Guelich, *Mark 1–8:26*, xxvi.

According to this work, Mark was called the *colobodactylus* because his fingers were short in proportion to the rest of his body. [70] The other meaning likely informs the story of Mark amputating his thumb, so as not to serve in the priesthood, found in the Monarchian Prologue (though it does not use the title *colobodactylus*).

North pointed out that conscripts for the Roman army were known, even from the time of Augustus (Suetonius, *Augustus* 24.1), to have cut off their thumbs in order to be ineligible for service. [71] Thus, Ammianus Marcellinus (c. 330–c. 395), a Roman soldier and historian, praised the bravery of the Gauls by relating: "nor does anyone of them, becoming thoroughly fearful of military service, ever cut off his thumb, as those in Italy whom they locally [72] call *murci* (sing: *murcus*)" (*Hist.* 15.3). [73] North consequently notes that according to Marcellinus, the appellation of *murcus* was given to anyone who cut off a thumb to evade military service (*Hist.* 15.3). [74] *Murcus* perhaps arose as a shortened ("cut down") version of the Latin *murcidus* ("lazy" and "coward"), thus acting as a pun on the action of cutting off the thumb which was associated with shirking responsibility and cowardice

North suggests that a reader of the account of John/Mark's desertion of Paul and Barnabas, recorded in Acts, may have "fabricated this malicious pun" of *murcus* on Mark's name, and that this was later translated into Greek as κολοβοδάκτυλος. [75] Thus, Mark's desertion would have been interpreted as a demonstration of cowardice on his part, as in the *Encomium of Barnabas* and in the Coptic *Encomium on Mark the Evangelist* and *Encomium of SS. Peter and Paul*. This Greek epithet was then presumably later reinterpreted to mean that Mark's fingers were short in proportion to his body (in the Anti-Marcionite Prologue) or that he had cut off his thumb in order to be ineligible for priestly service (in the Monarchian Prologue). [76]

The epithet of Mark as the κολοβοδάκτυλος was probably given within the context of a Johannine description of this Mark's Gospel, as in the *Refutation*,

---

[70] The Latin text is in Aland, *Synopsis,* 548.

[71] North, "*ΜΑΡΚΟΣ Ο ΚΟΛΟΒΟΔΑΚΤΥΛΟΣ*," 503.

[72] Some editors amend *localiter* ("locally") to *iocaliter* ("jokingly"). See: North, "*ΜΑΡΚΟΣ Ο ΚΟΛΟΒΟΔΑΚΤΥΛΟΣ*," 503.

[73] Translated by the author from the Latin text in North, "*ΜΑΡΚΟΣ Ο ΚΟΛΟΒΟΔΑΚΤΥΛΟΣ*," 503.

[74] It is unclear whether the Gauls or the Italians give this name to those in Italy who cut off their thumbs. North takes it of the Gauls. Walter Hamilton translates it in the latter sense: "No one here ever cuts off his thumb to escape military service, as happens in Italy, where they have a special name for such malingerers (*murci*)." See Walter Hamilton, trans. *Ammianus Marcellinus: The Later Roman Empire (A.D. 354–378)* (London: Penguin, 1986), 85.

[75] North, "*ΜΑΡΚΟΣ Ο ΚΟΛΟΒΟΔΑΚΤΥΛΟΣ*," 504–5.

[76] North, "*ΜΑΡΚΟΣ Ο ΚΟΛΟΒΟΔΑΚΤΥΛΟΣ*," 506.

as this would explain why the story of Mark cutting off his thumb in the Monarchian Prologue is also accompanied by the attribution to Mark of a doctrine
of the divinity.

6.10.4. Conflation with the Acts of Peter

As discussed in Chapter 2, Isho'dad of Merv (c. 850) claimed that Mark wrote
concerning Jesus' humanity in order to counteract the teachings of Simon the
Sorcerer (*Comm. Marc.* prolog.). [77] It was also noted that according to Dionysius bar Salibi (d. 1171), Mark wrote against the teachings of "Simon" (i.e.
Simon the Sorcerer), who held that the incarnation of the Lord was not real
(*Comm. in Evang.* 40). [78] These perhaps also reflect a tradition which associated Mark's Gospel with a doctrine of the incarnation. They also perhaps reflect a conflation of the narrative, found in the *Acts of Peter* (41–54), of Peter
going to Rome to confront Simon Magus with the tradition that John the Evangelist wrote his Gospel to refute the Gnostics who denied the incarnation, found
in Irenaeus (*Haer.* 3.11.3) and Victorinus (*Comm. Apoc.* 11.1).

6.11. Conclusion

This chapter drew attention to Johannine depictions of Mark, who is sometimes
placed in narratives contexts derived from the Fourth Gospel and sometimes
placed in roles associated with the Beloved Disciple. Mark is thus identified as
one of the disciples who followed John the Baptist (cf. John 1:35–37) and is
said to have followed Jesus into Galilee (cf. John 1:43), where he attended the
wedding at Cana (cf. John 2:1–10). He is sometimes portrayed as the host of
the Last Supper, a position often associated with the Beloved Disciple (cf. John
13:23), and he is made a witness of the crucifixion, as is the Beloved Disciple
in the Fourth Gospel (cf. John 19:25–27). Furthermore, John/Mark's house is
made Jesus' lodging following the healing at the pool of Bethesda (cf. John
5:1–8) and is said to have been the location in which Jesus appeared to the
disciples after the resurrection (cf. John 20:24–29).

   This chapter also examined a number of sources which seem to reflect an
attribution to Mark of a Gospel which taught the divinity of the Son of God
and/or of the Logos. Because these sources understood the Mark in question to
refer to Mark the Evangelist, they have attempted to correct the tradition in
various ways. Chromatius and Aquinas have inserted references to John's Gospel in the descriptions, whereas the Monarchian Prologue has attempted to ex-

---

[77] Gibson, *Commentaries of Isho'dad of Merv*, 124–25.
[78] Sedlácek, *Dionysius bar Salibi*.

egetically derive a Logos theology from Mark's prologue. Others, like Procopius and an epigram on Mark's Gospel have retained the Johannine language apparently without modification, despite its obvious incongruity.

Chapter 7

Reduplicated Traditions

Theodor Zahn seems to have been the first to have suggested that John/Mark and John the Evangelist were sometimes confused in sources, pointing in support to the identification of both with the young man who fled naked in Mark's Gospel (Mark 14:51) and the association of both with the site of the Zion church in Jerusalem. [1] A little later, Francis Pritchett Badham suggested some "confluence of personality" between the two on account of depictions of both as priests wearing the sacerdotal plate (cf. Chapter 8). [2] J. Edgar Bruns, who, as discussed in the previous chapter, drew attention to the placement of John/Mark in Johannine narratives, also drew attention to the confusion of John and Mark, noting that both were said to have had a father named Aristobulus, the brother of Barnabas, which suggests that the two were "not distinguished". [3]

While scholarship has not generally furthered this avenue of research, some significant Markan and Johannine scholars have accepted as a result of Bruns's investigation that John and Mark were sometimes confused in some early Christian sources. [4] Indeed, C. Clifton Black has gone so far as to suggest that "some writers of Christian antiquity were inclined to identify John Mark with the apostle John". [5]

This chapter will survey the reduplication of these traditions and will discuss the sources identified by Bruns and others as well as other sources not previously drawn into the discussion.

---

[1] Theodor Zahn, *Introduction to the New Testament*, trans. John Moore Trout et al., vol. 2 (Edinburgh: T. & T. Clark, 1909), 447–48 n. 6, n. 7.

[2] Badham, "Martyrdom of John," 544.

[3] Bruns, "Confusion," 24.

[4] Robert Kysar, *The Fourth Evangelist and his Gospel: an Examination of Contemporary Scholarship* (Minneapolis: Augsburg, 1975), 96; Culpepper *John*, 78; Harold W. Attridge, "The Restless Quest for the Beloved Disciple," in *Early Christian Voices in Texts, Traditions, and Symbols: Essays in Honor of François Bovon*, ed. David H. Warren, Ann Graham Brock and David W. Pao (BIS 66; Leiden: Brill, 2003), 73 n. 17.

[5] Black, *Apostolic Interpreter*, 174 n. 29.

7.1. A Levitical Jerusalemite

Mark's Levitical roots are spoken of by a variety of sources. Among Coptic writers, Severus, probably in a conflation of John/Mark and the Alexandrian Mark, relates in his *Homily* that Mark's mother Hannah was of the Levitical tribe and that Mark was Egyptian by direct descent on his father's side. [6] Mark himself, according to Severus, was born and raised in Jerusalem. [7] Mawhub, while not mentioning Mark's Levitical descent, names Mark's father as a certain Aristobulus, whom he identifies as the brother of Barnabas, though he seems to distinguish this Barnabas from the one mentioned in Acts, who is said to have been the brother of Mary, Mark's mother (*Hist. Patr. Eccl. Alex.* 1.1). [8] Presumably this was because the Barnabas of Acts was a native of Cyprus (Acts 4:36) with no apparent connections with Cyrene in North Africa, where Mawhub places him. Mawhub also speaks of Mark's residence in Jerusalem, though in his version, Aristobulus and Barnabas first resided in Cyrene until they were forced to flee to Judea, where Mark was raised.

Mark's Levitical descent is also spoken of by the Greek *Acts of Mark* (2). As discussed in Chapter 2, a number of Latin sources, beginning with the Monarchian Prologue, go so far as to relate that Mark himself was once a priest who had served in Israel.

The name of Aristobulus was also associated with Mark in Greek tradition; the eighteenth-century Cypriot Archbishop Kyprianos thus speaks of Mary, Mark's mother, as the daughter of Aristobulus [9] and the Greek *Menaion* (16 March) identifies Barnabas the brother of Aristobulus with the Barnabas of Acts, recording that he was born in Cyprus and that he became bishop of the British. [10] Possibly the mention of Cyprus represents an earlier form of the tradition than that found in Mawhub, who places the two brothers in Cyrene of North Africa (cf. the possibility of confusion of Kyrenia in Cyprus with Cyrene in North Africa, discussed in Chapter 5).

All of the major claims about Mark, that he was a Levite, that his father's name was Aristobulus and that he was a priest, find correspondences in the

---

[6] Cf. Bargès, *Homélie sur St Marc*, 10, 14.

[7] Bargès, *Homélie sur St Marc*, 20.

[8] Cf. Bruns, "Confusion," 23. The seventeenth-century version attributed to Yusab (13th century) does not provide the name of Mark's father (though he does state that he was the brother of Barnabas) and mentions Aristobulus as one of his relatives. See, Ṣamu'il al-Suryani and Nabih K. Dawud, eds., *Ta'rikh al-aba' al-baṭarika li-l-anba Yusab usquf Fuwwa* (Cairo: 1987), 11. Dr Adel Sidarus, Emeritus Professor of the University of Évora kindly provided me his private French translation of the relevant section.

[9] Hackett, *History of the Orthodox Church*, 397.

[10] *Prologue from Ochrid: Lives of the Saints and Homilies for Every Day of the Year*, ed. Bishop Nikolai Velimirović, trans. Mother Maria (Birmingham, England: Lazarica Press, 1986).

Johannine tradition. Bruns thus drew attention to "the strange affirmations" of two or three Spanish ecclesiastical leaders in the seventh and ninth centuries, Julian Peter (642–690), Archdeacon of Toledo, Heleca, bishop of Saragossa (fl. 890) and possibly Braulio of Saragossa (590–651), [11] who name the father of the Apostle John as Aristobulus. As with the Greek *Menaion* mentioned above, the Aristobulus who is identified with Zebedee by Heleca is said to have been sent to England [*sic*] from Rome where he was martyred in the second year of Nero. [12]

The Greek *Synaxarion of Constantinople*, comprised of a collection of hagiographies, identifies Zebedee with Aristobulus on the authority of Sophronius of Jerusalem (seventh century), [13] who was well-travelled and had visited Rome. The conflation of Zebedee with the Levitical Aristobulus is perhaps also related to the depiction of Zebedee as a priest who served in Jerusalem before settling in Jerusalem, found in a prologue to the fifth-century *Acts of John by Prochorus*. [14]

Even the Latin tradition of Mark as a priest finds a counterpart in the Johannine tradition. Polycrates, bishop of Ephesus in the late second century, describes John the Evangelist as a priest who wore the priestly place in his letter to Victor, bishop of Rome, written around 190 (*apud* Eusebius, *Hist. eccl.* 5.24.2). The Synoptic Gospels and Acts do not relate that John the son of Zebedee was a priest, and this tradition may represent an alternative (and perhaps pre-Zebedean) identification of John the Evangelist with the priestly John/Mark.

7.2. Of Noble Birth

The *Acts of Mark* is the only work to provide any kind of detailed tradition concerning John/Mark's background and early life in Jerusalem. When recounting Mark's great generosity towards the poor, it notes that he "was allotted much wealth from his ancestors" (3). In a passing reference, Severus of Nastrawa, also makes reference to Mark's noble birth, [15] and the same tradition

---

[11] Bruns, "Confusion," 24–25; Bruns mentions three clerics, but Jean Bolland, *Acta Sanctorum Martii*, vol. 2, XV Martiis (Paris and Rome: Victorem Palme, 1865), 369, notes that the quotation attributed to Braulio by Bivarius was handed down under the name of Heleca; James Ussher also attributes it to Heleca; see *The Whole Works of the Most Rev. James Ussher, D.D.*, ed. Charles Richard Elrington, vol. 5 (Dublin: Hodges, Smith, and Co., 1864), 21.

[12] Ussher, *Works*, vol. 5, 21.

[13] Bruns, "Confusion," 24–25.

[14] Culpepper *John*, 23 n. 4.

[15] Bargès, *Homélie sur St Marc*, 30.

is also alluded to by the Greek writer Procopius the Deacon (d. 815), who relates in his *Encomium of St. Mark* that Mark

was called by the divine voice, and he spurned the affection of his near kin (ἀγχιστεύοντες); to him, the honours associated with his family descent (γένος) were nothing; possessions were a fleeting thing [16] to this one (*Encom. in Marc.*). [17]

John the Evangelist is also said to have been of noble birth. In a letter written in 417, Jerome, speaking of how those who show contempt for status (*nobilitas*) and wealth make themselves worthy of greater glory, alleges the example of John, who

was known to the high priest (cf. John 18:15) on account of the nobility of his birth (*propter generis nobilitatem*) and did not fear the plots of the Jews, to such an extent that he led Peter into the reception area [of the high priest's palace] (cf. John 18:15), and stood, alone of the apostles, before the cross, and received the Saviour's mother into his own home (cf. John 19:25–27) (*Epist.* 127.5). [18]

This description of John is exclusively drawn from the accounts of the Beloved Disciple in the Fourth Gospel, suggesting that Jerome knew a non-Zebedean portrayal of the Beloved Disciple which depicted him as an aristocratic Jerusalemite. While Jerome's depiction of John is hardly compatible with the Galilean fisherman of the Synoptic Gospels, it is consistent with the descriptions of John/Mark as an aristocrat, and with his placement in Johannine narratives, in roles reserved for the Beloved Disciple.

A description of John given the *Memorial of Saint John* (possibly ninth century) may also be related. While it states that John was by birth from Bethsaida in Galilee, reflecting the narrative of the Synoptic John, the son of Zebedee, it adds that "he partook, not in a slight way, of a Greek education" (Ἑλληνικῆς δὲ παιδείας μετεῖχεν οὐδὲ βραχύ). [19] The word παιδεία referred to a child's upbringing, training and education, and no doubt included instruction in Greek literature. [20] As with Jerome, the description is ill-fitting for the Galilean John, and inconsistent with the portrayal of this John in Acts, where he is described as "without schooling" (ἀγράμματος) and "a common man" (ἰδιώτης) (Acts 4:13). It is, however, compatible with depictions of John/Mark.

---

[16] Literally "fleeting dream," with "dream" used to denote something that is ephemeral, not, as in English, something hoped for or aspired to.

[17] Translated from the Greek text in *PG* 100:1189. The Greek text in full reads: παρ᾽ οὐδὲν αὐτῷ τοῦ γένους τὰ τίμια, ὄναρ τούτῳ ῥοώδης περιουσία.

[18] Translated from the Latin text in Isidor Hilberg, ed., *Sancti Eusebii Hieronymi Epistulae* (CSEL 56; Vienna: 1918), 149–50.

[19] Translated by the author from the Greek text given in Taniguchi, Bovon, and Antonopoulos, "Memorial of Saint John," 345.

[20] E.g. Manetho, *Fragmenta* 42; Lucian, *Dial. Mort.* 12.3.

7.3. Mark and John as the One Carrying the Jar of Water

The *Encomium of Barnabas* (2,190–225) and the *Acts of Mark* (6) among Greek works and Mawhub (*Hist. Patr. Eccl. Alex.* 1.1) and Ibn Kabar among Coptic ones claim that Mark was the one who carried the jar of water into the house in which the sacramental supper was eaten (cf. Mark 14:13; Luke 22:10). The apparent reduplication of this tradition within a Johannine context is seen in the *Life of the Virgin* (c. 1015) by Epiphanius the Monk, of Constantinople, which identifies the one carrying the jar of water as the Apostle John (*Vit. Virg.* 20). [21] This is unlikely to have arisen exegetically, since John, along with Peter, was sent to follow the one carrying the jar back to the house in which the Supper was to be held (Luke 22:8–12).

7.4. The Young Man Who Fled Naked

Mark's Gospel describes how, after the Last Supper, Jesus resorted to the Garden of Gethsemane with his disciples. A group of soldiers later arrive and arrest him; meanwhile, a "certain young man (νεανίσκος)" followed Jesus for an unspecified time, as did Peter, while the others "all forsook him, and fled" (Mark 14:50–51, 54). At some point, officers attempt to apprehend this anonymous figure, but he flees, leaving his garment in their hands (Mark 14:51).

The identity of the young man is not given. An Arabic marginal note in a Coptic manuscript dated to 1208 reports that he was identified variously as James the son of Joseph and Mark the Evangelist. [22] The identification with James probably originated with Epiphanius, who identified the youth with James the Just, the brother of Jesus (*Pan.* 78.13.3; see the discussion in Chapter 8). [23] A Greek catena of an unknown date, [24] preserved in the medieval manuscript Tolosanus, similarly states that while some held that James the Just was the young man, others said "it was the evangelist [i.e. Mark] who was present, and for this reason he purposefully passed over the name in silence." [25]

---

[21] *PG* 120:209.

[22] Rupert Allen, "Mark 14, 51–52 and Coptic Hagiography," *Bib* 89 (2008): 267.

[23] Theophylact (*PG* 123:657) and Euthymius (*PG* 129:693) also mention this view, probably based on Epiphanius (cf. Zahn, *Introduction*, vol. 2, 447 n. 6).

[24] This seems to have contained the twelfth-century history of Nikephorus Bryennios, but the manuscript is now lost. See Leonora Neville, *Heroes and Romans in Twelfth-Century Byzantium: The* Material for History *of Nikephorus Bryennios* (Cambridge: Cambridge University Press, 2012), 7–8.

[25] Greek text in Pierre Poussines (Petrus Possinus), ed., *Catena Graecorum Patrum in Evangelium Secundum Marcum* (Rome, 1673), 328; cf. Weiss, *Das älteste Evangelium*, 406.

Among Latin writers, however the young man is identified as John the Evangelist. Already in the fourth century Ambrose of Milan (c. 340–397) spoke of the John who left his father's nets as the "young man, wrapped about with a linen garment, who was following the Lord at the time of his suffering" (*Enarrat. Ps.* 36, 53). [26] A little later, Peter Chrysologus (c. 406–450), bishop of Ravenna, speaks of "Peter who had denied, Thomas who had doubted, John who had fled" (*Sermo,* 78; cf. 150, 170). [27] Gregory the Great likewise identified this person with John, stating that he returned to Jesus at the crucifixion (*Mor.* 14.57), [28] a tradition which Bede also accepts (*In Marci Evang. Exp.* 14). [29] Among non-Latin writers, the Eastern Syrian bishop Isho'dad (c. 850) claimed that this identification was found in Bar Ḥadbashaba, an Eastern Syrian ("Nestorian") bishop who was active c. 600 (*Comm. Marc.* 10). [30]

This identification of the young man with John is not one that could have been derived exegetically from the text of Mark's Gospel. [31] Possibly it resulted from an identification of the young man with the "other disciple" (i.e. the Beloved Disciple) in John's account, who followed Jesus to the courtyard of the high priest (John 18:15), as found in Bede, who seeks to reconcile the accounts by having the young man flee shortly after Jesus' arrest and before he gained entrance to Caiaphas' palace (*In Marci Evang. Exp.* 14). [32] An association of this figure with the Beloved Disciple would perhaps also explain the claim, attributed to Victor of Antioch (c. 425) in a catena, that the young man was "perhaps from that house in which they ate the Passover, and not a guest (ξένον)." [33]

The association of this figure with both Mark and with John may represent a further example of reduplication, raising the possibility that the identification of the young man with John arose as a result of his prior identification with John/Mark, who was identified as the Beloved Disciple and associated with the house in which the Last Supper was held. [34]

---

[26] *PL* 14:1040.

[27] *PL* 52:421; cf. 600, 645. Cf. Zahn, *Introduction*, vol. 2, 446 n.6; Culpepper, *John,* 170.

[28] Anon., *Morals on the Book of Job by S. Gregory the Great, the First Pope of That Name, Translated, with Notes and Indices*, vol. 2 (Oxford: John Henry Parker, 1845), 154.

[29] *PL* 92:279.

[30] Gibson, *Isho'dad of Merv,* 141.

[31] Cf. Zahn, *Introduction*, vol. 2, 447 n. 6.

[32] *PL* 92:279.

[33] Translated by the author from the Greek text in Poussines, *Catena,* 328; cf. Zahn, *Introduction*, vol. 2, 447 n. 6. The same view is found in Theophylact (*Enarrat. Mark* 14, in *PG* 123:657). Possibly this is related to the identification of the one with the jar of water as John/Mark.

[34] This was suggested by Zahn, Introduction, vol. 2, 447 n. 6.

7.4.1. John as a Young Disciple

The description of the one who ran naked as being a "young man" may be connected with the statement of Ambrose, bishop of Milan (374–397), that John referred to himself as "a young man" (*adolescens*) in his Gospel (*De offic.* 2.20.101), [35] in an evident confusion of John's Gospel with Mark's, in which the young man is mentioned.

This is perhaps also related to Jerome's claim that he had read in certain "ecclesiastical histories" (*ecclesiasticae historiae*) that John was a mere boy (*puer*), the youngest (*minimus*) among the Apostles (*Jov.* 1.26). [36] John is similarly described in an anonymous Latin work discovered among the writings of Hilarius, contained in a ninth-century Latin codex which was likely translated from Greek no later than the sixth century: [37]

John the most holy evangelist was the youngest among all the apostles, Him the Lord held (in his arms) when the apostles discussed who among them was greatest and when He said: He who is not converted as this boy, will not enter the kingdom of Heaven. It is he who reclined against the Lord's breast. It is he whom Jesus loved more than the others and to whom he gave his mother Mary, and whom he gave as son to Mary. [38]

This passage conflates two passage. The disputation in question involved the twelve apostles contending over which of them would be the greatest in the coming kingdom. Jesus is said to have set a boy (παιδίον) in their midst as an example of the humility required for entering the kingdom (Matt. 18:1–4). A παιδίον, however, was a child understood to be aged up to seven [39] and was therefore clearly not John the Evangelist.

In Matthew and Mark's account, this story occurs in Galilee, previous to Jesus' final departure to Jerusalem to be crucified (Matt 18:1–4, 19:1; cf. Mark 9:33–37, 10:1), but in Luke's account, Jesus is said to have addressed the same dispute among the apostles at the Last Supper (22:20–26). Here Jesus says that among them, the greatest would be as the younger (ὁ μείζων ἐν ὑμῖν γινέσθω ὡς ὁ νεώτερος) (Luke 22:26). It is this context of the Last Supper that seems to have associated the child who was brought to Jesus with the one who reclined on Jesus' breast, who was apparently known as the youngest (ὁ νεώτερος) of the disciples.

---

[35] Latin text in *PL* 16:130. Cf. Robert Eisler, *The Enigma of the Fourth Gospel* (London: Methuen, 1938), 50.
[36] *PL* 23:246. Cf. Cf. Eisler, *Enigma*, 50.
[37] See Eisler, *Enigma*, 46–47.
[38] Translation in Eisler, *Enigma*, 47. Eisler suggests that the author was Hippolytus.
[39] LSJ 1287.

7.5. The Virgin

Of the sources discussed in this study, Mark is only spoken of as a virgin by Severus of Nastrawa, who calls him the "virgin, holy Mark, apostle and evangelist". [40] The depiction of John as a virgin is widely attested and well-known, being first attested by Tertullian, who describes him as, "John, a certain eunuch (*spado*) of Christ" (*De. mon.* 17) [41] and by the *Acts of John* (113). The Coptic Harris fragments record that John had been an example of virginity [42] and Ephrem the Syrian in his *Hymns on Virginity* speaks of John as "the virgin young man" (ܪܕܐܗܒ ܪܕܠܟ) (*Virg.* 15.4). [43] The martyr Methodius of Olympus (d. c. 311) similarly relates that John was said to have given his body to "purity" (ἀγνεία) (*De res.* 1.59.6). [44]

Jerome gives the Evangelist's virginity as the reason he was the most beloved of Jesus and leaned upon his bosom at the Supper (*Jov.* 1.26). [45] According to Epiphanius, Jesus entrusted his mother to John and not to any other apostle for the same reason (*Pan.* 78.10.10; cf. the same tradition in Ps.-Isidore of Seville's *Concerning the Rising and Setting of the Fathers*, [46] written in perhaps the mid eighth century). [47] The Latin Monarchian Prologue to John, usually dated to the fourth or fifth century, states that John was both beloved above the others and entrusted with Mary on account of his virginity, [48] while the pious monk and cardinal Peter Damian (c. 1007–1072) in his work, *Concerning the Perfection of the Monks*, makes John's virginity the reason why he did not undergo martyrdom, "but passed on gently and quietly, as though in his sleep" (*De perf. monachorum* 7). [49]

At some point, John's virginity was also provided as the reason why he was given the epithet of "son of thunder" (Mark 3:17). Since this epithet belonged

---

[40] Bargès, *Homélie sur St Marc*, 3 ; cf. 57.

[41] Translated from the Latin text in Philip Borleffs, ed. *Quinti Septimi Florentis Tertulliani Opera Pars IV* (CSEL 76; Vienna: Tempsky, 1957), 76.

[42] See Frederick W. Weidmann, *Polycarp and John: The Harris Fragments and Their Challenge to the Literary Traditions* (Notre Dame, Ind.: University of Notre Dame Press, 1999), 43.

[43] Edmund Beck, ed. *Des heiligen Ephraem des Syrers Hymnen de Virginitate* (CSCO 224 ; Leuven : 1962), 52; cf. Eric Junod, "La virginité de l'apôtre Jean: recherché sur les origines scripturaires et patristiques de cette tradition," *CBP* 1 (Strasbourg, 1987): 119.

[44] Cited by Junod, "La virginité," 116.

[45] *PL* 23:258.

[46] *PL* 83:1288 (*De ortu et obitu patrum*); cf. Annette Volfing, *John the Evangelist and Medieval German Writing: Imitating the Inimitable* (New York: Oxford University Press, 2001), 39–40.

[47] So, Robert E. McNally, "*Christus* in the Pseudo-Isidorean 'Liber de ortu et obitu patriarchum,'" *Trad* 21 (1965): 168.

[48] See Aland, *Synopsis*, 555.

[49] Cited and translated by Volfing, *John the Evangelist*, 54.

to both of the Zebedee brothers, the virginity motif came to be associated with John's brother James also, as found in Proclus of Constantinople (d. 446) (*Hom.* 4.5). [50] This is perhaps also why Epiphanius (c. 325–403) identified both John and James as celibates (*Pan.* 58.4.6). The Latin writer known as Ambrosiaster, who wrote between 366 and 384, likely represents an earlier tradition when he maintained that all the apostles were married except John and Paul. [51]

7.6. The Theologian and Beholder of God

In the Coptic Church, Mark is given the epithet ⲑⲉⲱⲣⲓⲙⲟⲥ, which is understood to mean "the beholder of God". [52] Mark was also called "the God-beholder" (ὁ θεόπτης) in the *Acts of Mark* (*Act. Marc.* 1), in a Greek Canon of the Feast of St. Mark attributed to Theophanes (possibly eighth or ninth century) [53] and in the *Encomium of St. Mark* written by Procopius Diaconus (d. 815). [54]

Soliman asks why Mark was especially called by this epithet, since "every one of the Twelve Disciples and all of the Seventy Apostles saw Jesus Christ". [55] He suggests that it was a rebuttal against Papias, who denied that Mark had seen Jesus. [56] However, tellingly, perhaps, he notes that the epithet "is associated specifically with those few who have seen God, like Moses and Elijah". [57] According to Philo (*de mutat. nomin.* 2) and Manetho (Frag. 6), Moses was a θεόπτης because he saw God on Sinai, and the related noun θεοπτία is used by Eusebius of Daniel's vision of the throne of God (*Hist. eccl.* 1.2.24).

It was noted in the previous chapter that Procopius may have been alluding to the visionary experience of John, when he wrote his Gospel, as found in the *Acts of John by Prochorus*. These conclusions are brought into doubt, however, by the reference to Matthew as a θεόπτης in a medieval Greek prologue to the Gospels, [58] suggesting that the epithet was given to any Gospel writer believed to have seen Jesus, with no necessary connotation of a visionary.

---

[50] *PG* 65:729.

[51] *PL* 17:320.

[52] Sameh Farouk Soliman, "Two Epithets of Mark the Evangelist: Coptic ⲑⲉⲱⲣⲓⲙⲟⲥ and Byzantine Greek θεόπτης," *GRBS* 54 (2014): 499–501.

[53] Soliman, "Two Epithets," 501, citing Μηναῖα τῆς Ἀποστολικῆς Διακονίας τῆς Ἐκκλησίας τῆς Ἑλλάδος (Athens 1959–1973) Ἀπριλίου 25, 97.

[54] Soliman, "Two Epithets," 501, citing *PG* 100:1196.

[55] Soliman, "Two Epithets," 501.

[56] Soliman, "Two Epithets," 502.

[57] Soliman, "Two Epithets," 501.

[58] Minuscule 1226 (= ε 1316) (13th century). In this prologue, Mark is called a θεηγόρος ("theologian") instead. See von Soden, *Die Schriften*, 314.

Soliman himself suggests that the Coptic epithet originated as a corruption of the Greek word θεορρήμων ("divinely speaking"), used of Mark in the *Acts of Mark* (9). He approximates this to θεολόγος or "theologian", [59] the title given to John by many patristic writers [60] which is also found in the *inscriptio* of the majority of the cursive manuscripts of Revelation. [61] Soliman obviously feels the description's lack of aptness for Mark the Evangelist in comparison to John, the archetypal theologian, for he goes on to concede: "Mark was far from being a theologian in the same meaning and level of John the Evangelist". [62]

The *Acts of Mark* however does portray Mark as a skilled interpreter of the scriptures for whom such an epithet would have been fitting:

Consulting (ἐντυγχάνων) the prophetic books and devoting himself to their reading, and initiated (μυούμενος) with respect to the hidden and hard-to-understand exposition of the God-inspired predictions by divine illumination, he harmoniously explained the interpretations of those elevated divine discourses (θεηγορέων) with very great beauty and virtue, making them evident to everyone. From this, therefore, and also from his virtuous way of life, the people would call him the "speaker of mysteries" (μυστόλεκτην) and "religious herald" (ἱεροκήρυκα), as those reaping great benefit from his teaching (*Act. Marc.* 2). [63]

This Mark was thus a skilled interpreter of the scriptures who lived at the centre of Jewish intellectual and religious life.

The epithet ἱεροκήρυκα ("herald or attendant at a sacrifice" [64]), also given to Mark in this passage, is possibly related to the epithet θεοκῆρυξ ("herald of God") given to John by Chrysostom. [65]

7.7. The Zion Church

The Zion Church (the Cenacle), located on Zion Hill in Jerusalem, was one of the most important churches in Jerusalem and was associated by tradition with

---

[59] Soliman, "Two Epithets," 499.

[60] See, *PGL* 728.

[61] Robert H. Charles, *A Critical and Exegetical Commentary on the Revelation of St. John*, vol. 1 (ICC; New York: Scribner, 1920), xlvi n. 1.

[62] Soliman, "Two Epithets," 501.

[63] Author's translation.

[64] LSJ 721.

[65] Gustav Adolf Deissmann, *Light from the Ancient East: The New Testament Illustrated by Recently Discovered Texts of the Graeco-Roman World*, trans. Lionel Richard Mortimer Strachan (London: Hodder & Stoughton, 1910), 353 n. 1, citing Chrysostom, *Orat.* 36.

many events from the Gospels and Acts; it was also separately identified as the site both of the house of Mark and of John.

The antiquity of the site's importance is affirmed by Epiphanius, who speaks of it in the context of the visit of Hadrian to Jerusalem (c. 130 CE). The emperor, he relates, found the city in ruins,

except for a few houses, and the little church of God on the spot where the disciples went to the upper room on their return from the Mount of Olives after the Ascension of the Redeemer. It was built there, namely on Zion, which escaped the destruction [i.e. of 70 CE], and the houses around Zion and seven synagogues which remained isolated in Zion like huts, one of which survived into the time of bishop Maximos and of the emperor Constantine, like a shanty in a vineyard, as the Scripture says (cf. Isa 1:8) (*De mens. et pond.* 14). [66]

Murphy-O'Connor draws attention to the repetition in Epiphanius' account, with the first part claiming that only the church of God survived along with a few houses and the second claiming that a single synagogue survived. [67] He suggests that Epiphanius combined two slightly different accounts of the Zion site, and that the reference to both a synagogue and church referred to the same building; he also notes that a church was consecrated at the Zion site during the episcopate of Maximos (335–49), which he associates with the claim by the pilgrim Egeria that an earlier building (the synagogue perhaps) had "now been altered into a church". [68] One of Epiphanius' source may have been Hegesippus, who related traditions of the Jerusalem church and had lived in Palestine; he was possibly also a young man at the time of Hadrian's visit. [69]

Eusebius, while not specifically mentioning the Zion church, is also familiar with a version of the same story. Speaking of the desolate state of Jerusalem after the war, and alluding to the same prophecy of Isaiah referred to by Epiphanius, he states that

the daughter of Zion, that is, the religious service accomplished upon the mountain named Zion, is left as a tent in a vineyard and as a shanty in a cucumber garden (Isa 1:8) from the time of the coming of our Saviour Jesus" (*Demonst. evang.* 2.36). [70]

According to the *Annals* of Saʿīd ibn Baṭrīq, commonly called Eutychius (896–940), bishop of Alexandria, the Christians escaped the destruction of Jerusalem and fled across the Jordan, returning to the city after the war, in the fourth year of Vespasian (72/73), at which time they built a church and ordained Simeon,

---

[66] Translated by Jerome Murphy-O'Connor, "The Cenacle – Setting for Acts 2:44–45," in *Book of Acts*, ed. Bauckham, 307; cf. *PG* 43:261.

[67] Murphy-O'Connor, "The Cenacle," 309.

[68] Murphy-O'Connor, "The Cenacle," 309, citing Wilkinson, *Egeria's Travels* (London: SPCK, 1971), 141.

[69] Cf. Capper, "Oldest Monks," 38; cf. Brian J. Capper, "The Palestinian Cultural Context of Earliest Christian Community of Goods," in *Book of Acts*, ed. Bauckham, 346.

[70] Greek text in *PG* 22:128.

the son of Joseph's brother Clopas, as bishop. [71] His source, once again, may have been Hegesippus, who is said to have spoken both of Clopas' relationship to Joseph and of the ordination of Simeon the son of Clopas following the destruction of Jerusalem (*apud* Eusebius, *Hist. eccl.* 3.11.1).

While Eutychius relates that the Jerusalem Christians fled across the Jordan, Eusebius (*Hist. eccl.* 3.5.3) and Epiphanius (*De mens. et pond.* 15; *Pan.* 29.7.8; 30.2.7) more specifically state that they settled in the Transjordan city of Pella. Epiphanius' accounts differ with respect to some details from Eusebius', suggesting that he was not dependent upon Eusebius. Thus, where Eusebius states that the church in Jerusalem fled in response to "a certain oracle given there by revelation" (*Hist. eccl.* 3.5.3), Epiphanius states that Christ told them to depart from Jerusalem (*Pan.* 29.7.8) and that an angel of God forewarned them to leave the city (*De mens. et pond.* 15). [72]

Epiphanius' source for this tradition may have been Hegesippus, [73] though others disagree. [74] Suggestive of this dependence is Epiphanius' mention of the Syriac "Gospel of the Hebrews" a number of times in the proximity of two of his Pella passages (*Pan.* 29.9; 30.3, 6, 13, 14), since Eusebius called attention to Hegesippus' use of this document (*Hist. eccl.* 4.22.8). [75]

Archaeological evidence perhaps adds some veracity to the traditions. According to Murphy-O'Connor, it would have been difficult for the Christians to have taken possession of the Zion site after the first century, since a Roman legion was stationed in the adjoining valley in the late first century, separating the location from the city of Jerusalem. [76]

Furthermore, when Magen Broshi undertook archaeological work in the vicinity of the Cenacle, in Jerusalem's Upper City, in 1971, he found houses decorated with mosaics and frescos depicting images of birds, trees, wreaths and buildings, [77] and he noted that these excavations "leave no doubt that this quarter was occupied by the more affluent residents of Jerusalem". [78] Taylor

---

[71] *PG* 111:985; Capper, "Cultural Context," 347; Bargil Pixner, *Paths of the Messiah and Sites of the Early Christian Church from Galilee to Jerusalem* (San Francisco: Ignatius Press, 2010), 335–36.

[72] Cf. Hugh Jackson Lawlor, *Eusebiana: Essays on the Ecclesiastical History of Eusebius Pamphili, c. 264–349* (Oxford: Clarendon Press, 1912), 29–30.

[73] Lawlor, *Eusebiana*, 28–34.

[74] See the discussion in Jonathan Bourgel, "The Jewish-Christian's Move from Jerusalem as a Pragmatic Choice," in *Studies in Rabbinic Judaism and Early Christianity: Text and Context*, ed. Dan Jaffé (Leiden: Brill, 2010), 109–13.

[75] Cf. Joseph B. Lightfoot, *The Apostolic Fathers: Ignatius, and Polycarp*, part 1, vol. 1 (London: Macmillan, 1889), 331.

[76] Murphy-O'Connor, "The Cenacle," 314–15.

[77] Joan Taylor, *Christians and the Holy Places: The Myth of Jewish-Christian Origins* (Oxford: Oxford University Press, 1993), 208.

[78] M. Broshi, "Excavations on Mount Zion, 1971–72. Preliminary Report," *IEJ* 26 (1976): 86, cited by Murphy-O'Connor, "The Cenacle," 319.

suggests that this is where the priestly aristocracy of the city resided. [79] Indeed, she disputes the Zion site's authenticity on the very basis that the early Christians would not have been based in such an affluent part of the city. [80] On the contrary, however, this would be in agreement with the descriptions of John/Mark's house in Acts (cf. Chapter 2) and with the aristocratic and Levitical portrayal of him found in the *Acts of Mark* (§ 3).

7.7.1. Traditions of the Zion Church

The Zion Church is said by the pilgrim Egeria, who visited Palestine and Egypt in the period 381–384, to have been where the apostles were gathered, "when the doors were shut" following the crucifixion (*Itin.* 39.5), in an allusion to John 20:19. Epiphanius identifies the location of the church with the upper room (ὑπερῷον) in which the disciples were said to have stayed following the ascension (*De mens. et pond.* 14; cf. Acts 1:12–13). According to Hesychius of Jerusalem (d. after 451), it was the site of the Last Supper, [81] though this is perhaps presupposed already by Origen, who writes that after the disciples had taken the bread and the cup at the feast, Christ taught them to sing a hymn and "to go across from a height to a height (*de alto transire ad altum*), because the faithful one is never able to do anything in the valley; therefore, they went up to the Mount of Olives" (*Comm. Matt.* 86). [82] Finegan thinks that the mention of the mount on which the disciples sang after the Last Supper is an "unmistakable" reference to Mount Zion. [83] Epiphanius may also be interacting with the same tradition when he relates that "Jesus went out to the mountain (ἐξῆλθεν εἰς τὸ ὄρος)" to eat the Passover (*Pan.* 51.27.2), [84] and Eusebius when he claims that the new covenant began on Zion Hill (*Dem. ev.* 1.4).

---

[79] Taylor, *Christians and the Holy Places*, 208; Lee I. Levine, *Jerusalem: Portrait of the City in the Second Temple Period (538 B.C.E.–70 C.E.)* (Philadelphia: The Jewish Publication Society, 2002), 326–29.

[80] Taylor, *Christians and the Holy Places*, 208, 219.

[81] *PG* 93:1480.

[82] Translated from the Latin text of Erich Klostermann and Ernst Benz, eds., *Origenes Werke*, vol. 11 (GCS 38; Leipzig: Hinrichs, 1933), 199 (ll. 29–30)–200 (l.1).

[83] Jack Finegan, *The Archeology of the New Testament: The Life of Jesus and the Beginning of the Early Church* (rev. ed.; Princeton: Princeton University Press, 1992), 234; see also Bellarmino Bagatti, *The Church from the Gentiles in Palestine*, trans. Eugene Hoade (PSBFMi 4; Jerusalem: Franciscan Printing Press, 1971), 25; Pixner, *Paths of the Messiah*, 339–40.

[84] Pixner argues that τὸ ὄρος, with the definite article, can only point to Zion, which was the higher west hill of Jerusalem (*Paths of the Messiah*, 251).

7.7.1.1. The Zion Traditions and the Dormition of Mary

Mary's death (the dormition) is associated with Zion in the Ethiopic *Book of Mary's Repose*, which contains a narrative that dates to the fourth century at the latest. [85] In this work, an angel reveals to Mary that the death of her body was approaching and he commands her to go from where she is, in the midst of Jerusalem, to the Mount of Olives, in order to hear the angel's name (*Lib. Req* 1–2). [86] Mary's death is later said to have taken place at her home in Jerusalem (*Lib. Req* 51, 66, 70), and Shoemaker thinks that the directions given for Mary's funeral procession seem to locate her death in the vicinity of Zion. [87] He also notes similar narratives which date from the late fifth and early sixth centuries. [88] Elsewhere he mentions a Georgian fragment, which locates her death at Zion, [89] though he considers it unlikely that the text is to be dated earlier than the late sixth century on the basis of its placement of Mary's death there, even though he acknowledges that earlier texts, including the *Book of Mary's Repose*, place her death in that area of the city. [90]

Mary's death is associated with the Zion church in a number of later sources also, including Modestus, bishop of Jerusalem (632–34) (*Encomium in dorm. Virg.* 3), [91] John of Damascus (c. 700) [92] and Bernard the Monk (c. 870). [93]

7.7.1.2. The Owner of the House

The earliest extant identification of the church as the site of Mark's house is found in the work, *On the Topography of the Holy Land*, written around the turn of the sixth century by the pilgrim Theodosius (*de Situ Terrae Sanctae* 43). [94] The *Encomium of Barnabas* in the sixth century or later also identifies the site as that of Mark's house, where Jesus ate the Last Supper and appeared

---

[85] Stephen J. Shoemaker, *The Ancient Traditions of the Virgin Mary's Dormition and Assumption* (Oxford: Oxford University Press, 2006), 46. He discusses it by its shortened Latin form, *Liber Requiei*.

[86] The English translation of these sections of the work can be found in Shoemaker, *Ancient Traditions*, 290–91.

[87] Shoemaker, *Ancient Traditions* 128 n. 129.

[88] Shoemaker, *Ancient Traditions*, 128.

[89] Shoemaker, *Ancient Traditions*, 67.

[90] Shoemaker, *Ancient Traditions*, 128.

[91] *PG* 86:3288.

[92] Pixner, *Paths of the Messiah*, 401, citing *Homilia in dormitionem, PG* 96:729.

[93] Bernard the Monk, *A Journey to the Holy Places and Babylon*, 316.12, in John Wilkinson, *Jerusalem Pilgrims before the Crusades* (Warminster, UK: Aris and Phillips 1977), 144.

[94] Translated from the Latin text in Johann Gildermeister, *Theodosius de situ Terrae Sanctae im ächten Text und der Brevarius de Hierosolyma vervollstäandigt* (Bonn: Adolph Marcus, 1882), 20.

to Thomas (ll. 229–31; cf. John 20:19–26) and where the Spirit was given on the day of Pentecost (ll. 231–37; cf. Acts 2:1–13).

The Zion church was identified as the location of the Apostle John's house in the late tenth-century (?) [95] *Chronicle* of Hippolytus of Thebes (*Chron.* 4). [96] With the exception that the name "John" is found instead of "Mark," his account otherwise largely follows the familiar notices found in John/Mark sources, such as that the Passover meal was prepared at his house, that the apostles took refuge there "on account of the fear of the Jews", that the Lord appeared to the disciples there after his resurrection, "when the doors were shut", and that he later appeared to Thomas there:

This is John, whom the Lord loved, who is also the virgin, the one having written his own account of the gospel, who stayed in Jerusalem at the so-called Holy Zion, the mother of all the churches. But that was his house. There the apostles fled because of the fear of the Jews. There the Lord appear to the disciples after his resurrection from among the dead, with the doors being closed, and he gave them the Holy Spirit. There on the eight day he convinced Thomas, showing him the mark of the nails. There the Passover was prepared for eating with his disciples. For from there, having sang a hymn, they went out to the mount of Olives, into the place of Gethsemane. There the apostles performed the first sacrament (μυστήριον). There the apostles ordained James as the first bishop, not the son of Zebedee, the brother of John the Evangelist, but the brother of our Lord Jesus Christ according to the flesh, but the son of Joseph the carpenter (*Chron.* 4). [97]

He also notes that John received the God-bearer (i.e. Mary) at his house in Zion until her taking away (*Chron.* 5), after eleven years (*Chron.* 3).

The same things are also related by the church historian Nicephorus Callistus (c. 1256–c. 1335); while he knows Hippolytus' account and draws from it, he quotes this information from a certain Evodius, a "successor of the apostles", who wrote these things in his commentaries (συγγράμμασι) and in a letter entitled "The Light" (Nicephorus, *Hist. eccl.* 2.3). [98] Echle thinks the reference is to Evodius who was the bishop of Uzalum in proconsular Africa (d. after 426). [99] Probably, however, Hippolytus intended Evodius, the first bishop of Antioch, who the predecessor of Ignatius (Eusebius, *Hist. eccl.* 3.22.1), for this

---

[95] Rainer Riesner, *Paul's Early Period: Chronology, Mission Strategy, Theology*, trans. Doug Stott (Grand Rapids: Eerdmans, 1998), 59, dates this work to the seventh/eight centuries; but Francis X. Gumerlock, "Chromatius of Aquileia on John 21:22 and Rev. 10:11," in *The Book of Revelation and Its Interpreters: Short Studies and an Annotated Bibliography*, ed. Ian Boxall and Richard M. Tresley (London: Rowman, 2016), 57, places it c. 980.

[96] Summarized and translated from the Greek text in Franz Diekamp, ed., *Hippolytos von Theben: Texte und Untersuchungen* (Münster: Aschendorff, 1898).

[97] Translated from the Greek text in Diekamp, ed., *Hippolytos von Theben*.

[98] *PG* 145:757, 760.

[99] Harry A. Echle, "The Baptism of the Apostles: A Fragment of Clement of Alexandria's Lost Work Ὑποτυπώσεις in the Pratum Spirituale of John Moschus," *Trad* 3 (1945): 368.

Evodius is credited in Coptic sources with relating the story of Mary's birth to Cleopas and Anna [100] and of Mary's dormition. [101]

To account for how John came to acquire the property, Hippolytus of Thebes relates that Zebedee was one of the leading men of Galilee; following his death, John sold his inheritance and used it to buy the house at Zion; in this way, it continues, John became known to the high priest (*Chron.* 5). The same account is also related by Nicephorus, without attribution, though he goes on to draw from Hippolytus of Thebe's account (though he wrongly cites Hippolytus of Portus).

Hippolytus again mentions James, the Lord's brother, and his ordination, and he provides some additional details concerning the relatives of the Lord (*Chron.* 5). Possibly he drew his material from Hegesippus, who is known to have related traditions concerning both the episcopal succession at Jerusalem and Jesus' relatives (e.g. *Hist. eccl.* 3.11.1–12.1).

The association of Mark with the site was eventually entirely displaced by John, who continues to this day to be associated with the Cenacle. This did not, however, end the association of Mark with the Zion traditions. Instead, another site, St. Mark's Monastery in the northern section of Zion, came to be identified as the Zion church and the house of Mark and his mother Mary, as it still is today within the Coptic and Syrian Orthodox Churches. [102]

While one site was associated with John and one with Mark, both the Cenacle and St. Mark's identify themselves as the same Zion church of earlier sources; thus, St. Mark's also claims to be the site where the Passover was kept and where Jesus appeared, "when the doors were shut". [103] Similarly, a Syriac inscription at St. Mark's probably made in the 1470s [104] claims that the building is the site of the church of Zion that was erected in 73 CE "in the name of the Mother of God" (despite the association of the site with Mark's mother Mary). [105]

---

[100] Montague Rhodes James, *The Apocryphal New Testament: Being the Apocryphal Gospels, Acts, Epistles, and Apocalypses* (Oxford: Clarendon Press, 1924), 87.

[101] James, *Apocryphal New Testament*, 194–97.

[102] Pope Shenouda III, *The Beholder of God: Mark the Evangelist, Saint and Martyr*, trans. Samir F. Mikhail and Maged S. Mikhail from the 4th ed. (Santa Monica: 1995), 119–20. The origins of this church are unclear, but it may have been a church known to have been built in 1092; see Denys Pringle, *The Churches of the Crusader Kingdom of Jerusalem: A Corpus*, vol. 3, *The City of Jerusalem* (Cambridge: Cambridge University Press, 2010), 323.

[103] Cf. Shenouda III, *Beholder of God*, 119–20.

[104] Pringle, *Crusader Kingdom*, 323.

[105] Pringle, *Crusader Kingdom*, 323.

7.8. Conclusion

Both Mark and John are said to have had a Levitical father named Aristobulus and to have been born to wealth and status; both are identified as the one who carried the jar of water at the time of the Last Supper and as the young man who fled naked after the supper; both are said to have been virgins and both are presented as exceptional theologians. Both are also associated with the Church of Holy Mount Zion in Jerusalem.

These reduplications do not suggest that one figure was simply identified with the other. Thus, the tradition of wealth and Levitical heritage and close kinship with Barnabas would suggest that John has been identified with John/Mark, whereas the motifs of virginity and theological insight would suggest the opposite. Perhaps, instead, both John/Mark and John the Evangelist reflect traditions relating to the same figure, though obscured by the later identifications of John/Mark with Mark the Evangelist and John the Evangelist with the Zebedean John.

Chapter 8

The Priest Wearing the Sacerdotal Plate

The late second-century bishop of Ephesus, Polycrates, described John the Evangelist as a priest who wore the sacerdotal plate or πέταλον in his letter to Victor, bishop of Rome, written in around the year 190 in response to a dispute between Asian and Roman Christians over the correct day for celebrating Easter (*apud* Eusebius, *Hist. eccl.* 5.24.2). Mark too is said to have been a priest who wore the sacerdotal plate or *petalum* in a fragment from an otherwise lost Latin work of unknown date and provenance, suggesting that this is yet another example of the reduplication of traditions related to John and Mark. Indeed, the possibility of some literary relationship between Polycrates and the Valois fragment was noted by Badham, who draws attention to the "curious coincidence" of the two statements; anticipating the work of Bruns, he adds that it is "somewhat suggestive of a confluence of personality" between John and Mark in the tradition. [1]

A third figure, James the brother of Jesus, is also said to have been a priest and is described as wearing the πέταλον by Epiphanius in the late fourth century, in a passage for which he is thought by many to have been dependent on Hegesippus' lost *Memoirs*. He also identifies James with as the young man who fled naked, a tradition associated with John in other sources (cf. Chapter 7), and he describes James as a virgin who died in old age, which also echoes the Johannine tradition; Benjamin Wisner Bacon consequently proposed that Epiphanius' James had been conflated with John the Evangelist. [2] This chapter will consider Bacon's theory and will posit the possibility that all three depictions of a potentially Johannine figure wearing the sacerdotal plate were drawn from the same source, to be identified as Hegesippus' *Memoirs*.

---

[1] Badham, "Martyrdom of John," 544.

[2] Benjamin W. Bacon, *The Fourth Gospel in Research and Debate: A Series of Essays on Problems Concerning the Origin and Value of the Anonymous Writings Attributed to the Apostle John* (New York: Moffat, 1910), 148–49.

8.1. Mark as a Priest Wearing the Sacerdotal Plate

Mark is described as a priest who bore "the sacerdotal plate of the high-priestly crown (*pontificalis apicis petalum*) among the Jewish people" [3] in the now lost work entitled the *Passion of Mark*, which was quoted by Valois in a marginal note to an edition of Eusebius' *History*, as discussed in Chapter 2.

A more well-known description of John as a priest wearing the sacerdotal plate (πέταλον) is found in the letter to Victor, bishop of Rome, written in the late second century by Polycrates, bishop of Ephesus, in which he defends the Asian reckoning for keeping Easter against the Roman one by appealing to the practice of the "great lights" of Asia who had fallen asleep, among whom he places John the Evangelist:

> ... there is also John, who reclined on the Lord's bosom, who was a priest wearing the sacerdotal plate (τὸ πέταλον), and a witness (μάρτυς) and teacher. He sleeps in Ephesus (*apud* Eusebius, *Hist. eccl.* 5.24.2). [4]

The reference to this John as the one who reclined on the Lord's bosom alludes to the "disciple whom Jesus loved" (John 13:23) who was identified as the author of John's Gospel (John 21:20–24).

Polycrates also describes John as a "witness" (μάρτυς) and teacher, and Bacon suggested that the combination of priest, witness and teacher in Polycrates' description may recall the traditions of Hegesippus. [5] According to the fragments preserved by Eusebius, Hegesippus described James as a priest (*apud* Eusebius, *Hist. eccl.* 2.23.5–8) and he spoke of the descendants of Jude as presiding over the churches as "witnesses" until Trajan's reign (*apud* Eusebius, *Hist. eccl.* 3.20.6), possibly denoting that they were eyewitness disciples of Jesus. A little later, he mentions "false teachers" who troubled the Christians at that time (*apud* Eusebius, *Hist. eccl.* 3.32.8).

The reference to John wearing the sacerdotal plate (πέταλον) is puzzling. Originally the word πέταλον denoted a leaf or petal (which is etymologically derived from πέταλον), and it was used in older Greek with the meaning of "wreath," e.g. the *Epinicians* of the fifth-century BC Lyric poet Bacchylides, which speaks of the olive-branch "victory wreath" (εὐδαιμονίας πέταλον) used to crown the victor in the ancient Olympics (*Epin.* 5), though this meaning came to be taken over by the word στέφανος. The fifth-century tragedian Euripides employs the word to describe "yellow flowers" (κρόκεα πέταλα) (*Ion* 889); from its meaning of a leaf or petal, it was used of any kind of metal beaten

---

[3] Translated from the Latin text in Badham, "Martyrdom of John," 544 n.16. Cf. *PG* 5:1360.

[4] Translated by the author.

[5] Bacon, *The Fourth Gospel*, 263–64.

into thin (i.e. leaf-like) sheets, from the second century BCE onwards, and it is used in this sense as a Greek loanword in Syriac[6] and Aramaic.[7]

The Septuagint thus renders the high priest's "golden plate" (ציץ זהב) in Exod 28:36 and other texts with χρυσοῦν πέταλον, and the *Letter of Aristeas* (98) and Philo (*Migr.* 103; *Moses* 2.114) show the same usage, though Josephus translates ציץ with κάλυξ, referring to it as "a calyx of gold" (*Ant.* 3.172). Polycrates' reference to the πέταλον has consequently often been taken as in some way identifying John as a high-priestly figure.[8] Indeed, this interpretation is found as early as Jerome, who states that John was Jesus' "high priest" (*pontifex eius*) and that he wore "the golden plate (*aurea lamina*) on his brow" (*de script. eccl.* 45).[9] Rufinus similarly described John as "a high priest" (*summus sacerdos*), stating that he wore "the high-priestly plate" (*pontificale petalum*) (Eusebius-Rufinus, *Hist. eccl.* 5.24.3–4).[10] Such a conception seems to inform Epiphanius' depiction of James also, for he speaks of him as a priest wearing the πέταλον in the context of relating how he alone was allowed to enter the temple, where he would make intercession for the people.

8.2. James as a Priest Wearing the Sacerdotal Plate

Epiphanius (c. 315–403) speaks of another figure, James the Just, as a priest who wore the πέταλον in his *Panarion*, a work addressing heresies, which he wrote around 375. He describes James as a priestly and ascetic figure who would spend long periods praying in the temple:

He died, being ninety-six, a virgin, on whose head no razor came, who did not use the baths, who did not eat anything living, who did not put on a second tunic and wore only a linen cloak, just as it says in the Gospel: "the young man fled, and discarded the linen garment

---

[6] R. Payne Smith, ed. J. Payne Smith, *A Compendious Syriac Dictionary: Founded upon the Thesaurus Syriacus of R. Payne Smith* (Oxford: Oxford University Press, 1902), 442.

[7] See CALP, under פיטלון. Cf. TgLamWT 4:1.

[8] Heinrich Delff, *Das vierte Evangelium: Ein authentischer Bericht über Jesus von Nazaret* (Husum: Delff, 1890), 8; H. Latimer Jackson, *The Problem of the Fourth Gospel* (Cambridge: Cambridge University Press, 1918), 26; Hengel, *Johannine Question*, 144 n. 29; Craig L. Blomberg, *The Historical Reliability of John's Gospel: Issues & Commentary* (Downers Grove, Ill.: IVP, 2001), 25; Daniel Stökl Ben Ezra, *The Impact of Yom Kippur on Early Christianity* (WUNT 163; Tübingen: Mohr Siebeck, 2003), 256; Bauckham, *Testimony*, 49; J. Ramsey Michaels, *The Gospel of John* (NICNT; Grand Rapids: Eerdmans, 2010), 9.

[9] Translated from the Latin text in Martin Joseph Routh, *Reliquiae Sacrae, sive, Auctorum fere iam Perditorum Secundi Tertiique Saeculi post Christum Natum quae Supersunt*, vol. 1 (Oxford: Cooke, 1814), 381. Cf. John H. Bernard, *A Critical and Exegetical Commentary on the Gospel According to St. John* (ICC; New York: Scribner, 1929), 596.

[10] Translated from the Latin text in Routh, *Reliquiae Sacrae*, vol. 1, 381.

with which he was clothed" [Mark 14:52]. For John and James and James, these three all had the same way of life (ταύτην τὴν πολιτείαν ἐσχήκασιν), the two sons of Zebedee on the one hand, and James the child of Joseph on the other, the brother of the Lord because he lived with him, and was brought up with him, and had the status of a brother ... Only to this James was it permitted to enter once a year into the holy of holies (τὰ ἅγια τῶν ἁγίων), because he was a Nazirite (Ναζιραῖον), and belonged to the priesthood (ἡ ἱερωσύνη) (*Pan.* 78.13.2–5). [11]

Epiphanius adds that James "wore a πέταλον on his head" and once lifted up his hands to heaven during a drought and prayed with the result that it immediately rained (*Pan.* 78.14.1). Furthermore, "he never wore a woollen garment; his knees hardened like camels, from his always kneeling before the Lord on account of his reverence." Because of these things, he continues, he was called "the Just". He adds that he never used the public baths and did not eat meat (while noting that this had been mentioned before) or wear sandals (*Pan.* 78.14.1–2).

Bauckham doubts that any direct literary borrowing is responsible for the depictions of John and James as priests wearing the πέταλον; instead, he suggests, they arose as a result of the independent employment of an "evidently stereotyped" description of the "exercise of the high priest's office in the temple". [12] But independent employment of high-priestly language would not account for why the young man who fled naked, spoken of by Epiphanius within the same context, also happens to have been associated with, and only with, the same three figures of John, James and Mark.

Furthermore, while Bauckham characterises the descriptions as "evidently stereotyped", there is no evidence of any such stereotypical representation of the high priest exercising his office as a priest who wore the πέταλον. Where the exercise of the high-priestly office is spoken of in other sources, the actor is referred to as the "high priest", not simply as a priest, and the πέταλον is accompanied by the adjective "golden"; [13] where the sacerdotal plate is mentioned, it is done so only alongside the other regalia of the high priest. The description of a figure as a priest wearing the πέταλον is unique to the descriptions of Mark, John and James.

Bauckham is aware of the depiction of Mark as a priest wearing the sacerdotal plate, and he suggests that it was borrowed from Polycrates' description of John and applied to Mark in order to "elaborate the existing tradition that

---

[11] Translated by the author from the Greek text in Holl, *Epiphanius*, vol. 3: *Panarion haer. 65–80* (GCS 37; Leipzig: Hinrichs, 1933), and so hereafter.

[12] Bauckham, *Testimony*, 46–47.

[13] E.g. Exod 28:36; Lev 8:9; Philo, *Migr.* 103, *Mos* 2.22. *T. Levi* 8.1 is an exception, speaking of the "πέταλον of faithfulness" in its list of high-priestly items, but this is not a simple description of the exercise of the high-priestly role but rather an exegetically-expanded account.

Mark was a Levite." [14] But a claim that Mark served as a high priest seems to venture a considerable distance beyond mere elaboration.

Since no such stereotypical description is attested, it is preferable to posit that there is some form of literary interrelationship connecting the three depictions, perhaps related to the pattern of the reduplication in the traditions pertaining to Mark and John. Epiphanius' description of James, moreover, may provide the clue to uncovering this source, for his account parallels a similar account of James in Eusebius, which, according to the historian, was drawn from Hegesippus' *Memoirs*.

8.2.1. Epiphanius, Eusebius and the Memoirs of Hegesippus

Eusebius' parallel account of James, for which he was dependent upon Hegesippus' *Memoirs* (*Hist. eccl.* 2.23.4–7), depicts James in a similar manner to Epiphanius, but it does not refer to him as a priest or mention the πέταλον:

> The charge of the Church passed to James the brother of the Lord, together with the Apostles. [4] He was called the 'Just' by all men from the Lord's time to ours, since many are called James, but he was holy from his mother's womb. [5] He drank no wine or strong drink, nor did he eat flesh; no razor went upon his head; he did not anoint himself with oil, and he did not go to the baths. [6] He alone was allowed to enter into the sanctuary, for he did not wear wool but linen, and he used to enter alone into the temple and be found kneeling and praying for forgiveness for the people, so that his knees grew hard like a camel's because of his constant worship of God, kneeling and asking forgiveness for the people. [7] So from his excessive righteousness he was called the Just and Oblias, that is in Greek, 'Rampart of the people and righteousness,' as the prophets declare concerning him (Lake [LCL]).

While it is clear that Epiphanius and Eusebius have provided interrelated accounts, and that Eusebius' version is said to have come from Hegesippus, opinion on the question of which one more closely follows Hegesippus is divided. Lawlor has argued at length that Epiphanius better reflects Hegesippus' original text [15] while Pratscher favours Eusebius as likely better representing it. [16] Ropes [17] and Colson [18] are more cautious, allowing the possibility that Epiphanius' reference to the πέταλον may have been either his own contribution or independently derived from Hegesippus. Bauckham, however, however, characterises Epiphanius' version as an "interpretative rewriting", [19] and Lambers-

---

[14] Bauckham, *Testimony*, 47 n. 45.

[15] Lawlor, *Eusebiana*, 4–9.

[16] Wilhelm Pratscher, *Der Herrenbruder Jakobus und die Jakobustraditionen* (FRLANT 139; Göttingen: Vandenhoeck & Ruprecht, 1987), 103–4.

[17] James H. Ropes, *A Critical and Exegetical Commentary on the Epistle of St. James* (ICC; New York: Scribner, 1916), 72.

[18] Colson, *L'énigme*, 37.

[19] Bauckham, *Testimony*, 46.

Petry similarly attributes Epiphanius' depiction of James to his "pious enthusiasm". [20]

A third opinion is given by Eisler, who proposes that Epiphanius faithfully reproduces Eusebius' original text, [21] and that the latter's text was later edited, noting in support that the Syriac and Latin versions of Eusebius depict James as entering the holy of holies, as in Epiphanius. [22] But it can be noted against this theory that these sources do not record that James wore the πέταλον.

Daniel Stökl Ben Ezra observes that both Epiphanius and Eusebius independently demonstrate knowledge of ancient Jewish customs, so that they include in their accounts differing yet complementary details, [23] which he attributes to their likely independent use of the same account of James (i.e. in Hegesippus). [24] This proposal is consistent with Eusebius' claim that Hegesippus was familiar with unwritten Jewish traditions and that he quoted Hebrew (possibly Aramaic) and Syriac documents (*Hist. eccl.* 4.22.8). [25] Thus, both writers attribute ascetic practices to James which seem to presuppose familiarity with the list of six prohibitions for the Day of Atonement found in the Mishnah. [26] These are as follows: "On the Day of Atonement it is forbidden to (1) eat, (2) drink, (3) bathe, (4) put on any sort of oil, (5) put on a sandal, (6) or engage in sexual relations" (*m. Kippurim* 8:1 A). [27]

Stökl Ben Ezra further observes that the prohibition on drinking is mentioned by Eusebius and not by Epiphanius, whereas the prohibition on wearing sandals is mentioned by Epiphanius and not by Eusebius. [28] He points out that a prohibition on frequenting public bathhouses is mentioned elsewhere in the Mishnah in connection with days of mourning. [29] Moreover, it is Epiphanius,

---

[20] Doris Lambers-Petry, "How to become a Christian Martyr: Reflections on the Death of James as Described by Josephus and in Early Christian Literature," in *Internationales Josephus-Kolloquium Paris 2001*, ed. Folker Siegert, Jürgen U. Kalms (MJS 12; Münster, 2002), 113 n. 47.

[21] Robert Eisler, *The Messiah Jesus and John the Baptist*, trans. Alexander Haggerty Krappe (London: Methuen, 1931), 541.

[22] Eisler, *The Messiah Jesus*, 541; cf. Daniel Stökl Ben Ezra, *The Impact of Yom Kippur on Early Christianity* (WUNT 163; Tübingen: Mohr Siebeck, 2003), 247.

[23] Stökl Ben Ezra, *Yom Kippur*, 249.

[24] Stökl Ben Ezra, *Yom Kippur*, 249.

[25] William Telfer, in his widely referenced article, "Was Hegesippus a Jew?," *HTR* 53 (1960): 143–53, argues that since Eusebius was not competent to ascertain Hegesippus' abilities in Aramaic, Eusebius' testimony on this point ought to be dismissed. However, Eusebius could have ascertained that Hegesippus referenced Hebrew and Syriac documents without having to have known the languages himself.

[26] Stökl Ben Ezra, *Yom Kippur*, 249.

[27] Jacob Neusner, trans., *The Mishnah: A New Translation* (New Haven, Conn.: Yale University Press, 1988), 277.

[28] Stökl Ben Ezra, *Yom Kippur*, 249.

[29] Stökl Ben Ezra, *Yom Kippur*, 249, citing *mTa'an* 1:6.

not Eusebius, who associates James' intercession with the coming of rain during a drought, and – as Stökl Ben Ezra notes – one of the duties of the high
priest on the Day of Atonement according to a Babylonian tradition was to pray
for rain for the coming year. [30]

Even though Epiphanius and Eusebius probably both drew independently
from Hegesippus, Epiphanius does not appear to have had direct access to
Hegesippus' work, for he names his sources for the depiction of James as the
writings of "Eusebius, Clement, and others" (*Pan.* 29.4.4). He adds that they
spoke of James wearing the πέταλον "in the memoirs [written] by them" (ἐν
τοῖς ὑπ' αὐτῶν ὑπομνηματισμοῖς)" (*Pan.* 29.4.4), [31] although Eusebius does not
record this. Presumably Epiphanius used Eusebius' work but also gleaned additional details from other writers which he conflated into a single account.

8.2.1.1. Epiphanius' Unique Material

The arrangement of material in Eusebius and Epiphanius differs; in Eusebius'
version, which is said (unlike Epiphanius') to have been taken from Hegesippus, James is introduced by the statement that he "succeeds to the government
(διαδέχεται) of the church, together with the apostles" (*Hist. eccl.* 2.23.4). In
Epiphanius' version, however, James is introduced within the context of his
argument for Mary's perpetual virginity, one of the arguments for which was
that Joseph and James were not at the cross. It is after mentioning James in this
context that he goes on to state that "he [i.e. James] died, being ninety-six, a
virgin", which is not found in Eusebius, adding that no razor came on James'
head and that he did not use the baths or eat anything living, both of which are
included among the ascetic practices listed by Eusebius. He also adds that
James did not wear a second tunic but only a linen coat, and he proceeds to
identify James as the young man dressed in linen who fled naked. Eusebius,
however, makes no mention of the second tunic or linen cloak, nor of the young
man who fled naked.

The passages then converge with the account of James being permitted to
enter the temple, though the explanations differ. According to Eusebius, James
was allowed to enter into the holy place because he wore linen and not wool.
Epiphanius, however, who has already added James' wearing of linen to the
list of ascetic practices in order to introduce the story of the young man, makes
James to have been allowed to enter the holy of holies (not holy place, as in
Eusebius) because he was a Nazirite and a member of the priesthood, though
he does note a little further on that James did not wear wool, which he places
between his account of James' prayers for rain and his comment that James'

---

[30] Stökl Ben Ezra, *Yom Kippur*, 248, citing *bYom* 53b, *bTaan* 24b.
[31] This is taken as a reference to Hegesippus' *Memoirs* (Ὑπομνήματα) by Lightfoot, *Apostolic Fathers*, part 1, vol. 1, 330.

knees grew calloused through constant prayer, both of which Eusebius also mentions.

It is in this temple context that Epiphanius also relates that James wore the πέταλον, which is not mentioned by Eusebius. Both accounts go on to relate that James was known as "the Just", with Eusebius adding, "as the prophets reveal concerning him". [32]

Table 8.2.1.1: The Arrangement of Material in Eusebius and Epiphanius

Eusebius	*Epiphanius*
Charge of church passed on to James	Died, aged 96
Called the Just	
No wine	No razor
No meat	No baths
No razor	No meat
No anointing with oil	No second garment
No baths	
	He wore only linen cloak
	Young man who fled naked
James alone allowed in the holy place; for he wore linen and not wool	James alone allowed in holy of holies because he was a Nazirite and priest
	Wore a πέταλον
Kneeling and praying for forgiveness of the people	Prayed and it rained
	Never wore woollen garment
Knees hardened	Knees hardened
Called the Just	Called the Just

Epiphanius seems to have transposed the mention of the linen to the end of the list of ascetic practices as it enabled him to introduce the story of the young man. With Eusebius' material removed, Epiphanius' account would read as follows:

Mary Magdalene stood by the cross, and Mary the wife of Clopas, and Mary the mother of Rufus, and the other Mary, and Salome and other women. And it did not say Joseph was there, or James the Lord's brother. He died, being ninety-six, a virgin, who did not put on a second tunic and wore only a linen cloak, just as it says in the Gospel: "the young man fled and discarded the linen garment with which he was clothed" [Mark 14:52]. For John and James and James, these three all had the same way of life (*Pan.* 78.13.2–4a).

---

[32] Possibly this is related to Hegesippus' account of James' martyrdom, in which he states that James' murderers fulfilled the prophecy of Isaiah (cf. Isa 3:10; 51:1), "Let us take away the just one, for he is unmanageable for us" (*apud* Eusebius, *Hist. eccl.* 2.23.15).

Epiphanius then adds the description of James as a Nazirite and a priest who wore the πέταλον to Eusebius' description of James as a quasi -priestly ascetic who used to enter the temple.

As Bacon observes, the features that are unique to Epiphanius' description of James (his virginity and his identification as the young man who fled naked and as a priest wearing the πέταλον) are attributed in other sources to John (cf. Chapter 7). [33] The claim that James died at ninety-six years can also be added, since John the Evangelist's death in old age is spoken of by Irenaeus (*Haer.* 2.22.5) and Jerome (*Comm. Gal.* 6.10), and likely by Papias (Fragment 19). Noting some of these things, Bacon suggested the possibility that Epiphanius conflated descriptions of John and James. [34]

Epiphanius does name John immediately after mentioning the young man who fled naked (indeed, some scholars think he was thus named because Epiphanius identified him as the young man and was likening James' wearing of linen to John's [35]); John was also mentioned a little earlier by Epiphanius, where he claims that Mary was entrusted to him at the cross on account of his virginity. This occurs within the larger context of his argument for the perpetual virginity of Mary; within the immediate context, he argues that Joseph had died when Jesus was young (*Pan.* 78.10.5–8), and one of his arguments for this was that had he been alive, Mary would not have been entrusted to John:

[9] Then, at the completion itself, when the Saviour was on the cross, having turned, as the Gospel according to John has it: "the Lord saw the disciple whom he loved and he said to him concerning Mary: 'Behold, your mother' And to her he says: 'Behold, your son.'" [10] If Mary had children and if her husband still lived, for what reason was he entrusting Mary to John and John to Mary? Why does he not rather entrust her to Peter? Or why not to Andrew, Matthew, and Bartholomew? But it is clear that she is entrusted to John because of his virginity (διὰ τὴν παρθενίαν). (*Pan.* 78.10.9–10) [36]

Epiphanius then briefly diverges from his topic (discussing, among other things, speculations concerning the manner of Mary's death), but he resumes discussion of the subject again, noting how Joseph was also absent from the wedding at Cana (*Pan.* 78.13.1). It is at this juncture that the passage under discussion begins, in which Epiphanius introduces James by noting that Mary Magdalene and other women were at the cross, while Joseph and James were not. Here too he seems be continuing his earlier argument that Joseph must have already died since he was not present at the crucifixion. This time, however, he mentions James as not being at the cross also, and this segues into his

---

[33] Cf. Bacon, *The Fourth Gospel*, 148. However, Bacon thinks that Epiphanius was identifying the young man with John, not James.

[34] Cf. Bacon, *The Fourth Gospel*, 149.

[35] E.g. Zahn, *Introduction to the New Testament*, vol. 2, 446–47 n. 6; Bacon, *The Fourth Gospel*, 148.

[36] My translation from the Greek text in Holl, *Epiphanius*, vol. 3.

ascetic and priestly description of James. This differs markedly from Eusebius' passage, which introduces James, not in the context of the cross, but by speaking of how James "succeeds to the government of the church, together with the apostles" (*Hist. eccl.* 2.23.4).

The earlier mention of John at the cross was likely related in his source to the later reference to Joseph and James as not being at the cross; possibly Epiphanius applied to James descriptions belonging to John. Indeed, even in Epiphanius' account of John at the cross, his virginity was spoken of. Possibly a conflation arose from a misunderstood antecedent; thus, after relating that Mary was entrusted to John on account of his virginity, Epiphanius' source might have noted that Joseph and James were not at the cross, adding that "he" (meaning John, not James) died at ninety-six, a virgin. This is only a suggestion, but such things can and indeed do happen, and it is illustrative that scholars have not been agreed concerning the identity of Epiphanius' antecedent in his account of the young man who fled naked, with some understanding him as referring to James [37] and others (as noted above) holding that he intended John. [38]

8.3. Conclusion

Attention was drawn to sources which describe either John, Mark or James as a priest wearing the πέταλον. It was suggested that the depiction of John and Mark reflects the pattern of reduplications observed in previous chapters. The additional mention of James, however, required further explanation.

First, evidence was provided suggesting that the depictions of John and James may have ultimately derived from Hegesippus. Attention was then drawn to the Johannine nature of the non-Eusebian depiction of James in Epiphanius, and it was suggested that Epiphanius may have conflated a description of a Johannine figure as a priest wearing the πέταλον with the description of James found in Eusebius. Thus, all the traditions of John, Mark and James as priests wearing the πέταλον may have all been derived from a single depiction of a Johannine figure that was found in Hegesippus' *Memoirs*.

---

[37] E.g. James A. Brooks, Mark (NAC 23; Nashville: Broadman & Holman Publishers, 1991), 238; Allen, "Mark 14, 51–52," 265; Abraham Kuruvilla, "The Naked Runaway and the Enrobed Reporter of Mark 14 and 16: What Is the Author Doing with What He Is Saying?," *JETS* 54 (2011): 530; Dean B. Deppe, *The Theological Intentions of Mark's Literary Devices: Markan Intercalations, Frames, Allusionary Repetitions, Narrative Surprises, and Three Types of Mirroring* (Eugene, Oreg.: Wipf and Stock, 2015), 249.

[38] E.g. Zahn, *Introduction to the New Testament*, vol. 2, 446–47 n. 6; Bacon, *The Fourth Gospel*, 148.

Chapter 9

The Origins of the Πέταλον Motif

The Syriac scholars Rendel Harris and Alphonse Mingana suggested that the source of Polycrates' statement that John was a priest wearing the πέταλον was to be found in the Syriac version of the *Odes of Solomon*, in which the Odist is depicted as an apparently prominent Christian leader and as a priest wearing a crown or wreath (ܟܠܝܠܐ). [1] This chapter will examine this theory and will consider features of the *Odes* that might have suggested to an ancient reader the identification of the Odist as a Johannine figure. [2]

This chapter will further consider the potential light that this theory sheds on the proposal of Chapter 8 that the πέταλον motif common to John, James and Mark had its source in Hegesippus' *Memoirs*. Here it will be suggested that Hegesippus, who employed Aramaic and Syriac sources for his Greek *Memoirs* (cf. *Hist. eccl.* 4.22.8), knew of the passage in the Odes and deliberately translated ܟܠܝܠܐ with the Geek πέταλον rather than στέφανος, used of crowns or wreaths, in order to evoke high-priestly imagery. His reason for doing so, it will be argued, was on account of his casting of the episcopal office in terms of the Israelite high-priesthood.

Lastly, this chapter will draw attention to a possible association of John/Mark with a Johannine Odist in a depiction of John/Mark leading the brothers in hymn singing to the divine Christ in the Jerusalem temple, found in the *Acts of Mark*.

9.1. Polycrates and the Πέταλον: Proposed Solutions

Polycrates' description of John as a priest wearing the πέταλον has long puzzled scholarship. As noted in the previous chapter, the word is used of the "golden plate" (χρυσοῦν πέταλον) which the high priest wore on the Day of Atonement (Exod 28:36, LXX), and the reference to John as a priest who wore

---

[1] Rendel Harris and Alfonse Mingana, *The Odes and Psalms of Solomon*, vol. 2, *Translation with Introduction and Notes* (Manchester: Manchester University Press, 1920), 318–19.

[2] The author independently developed the same theory before becoming aware of their work on the matter.

the πέταλον seems to denote some high-priestly connotation. Proposed solutions for this difficulty have varied. Eisler went so far as to argue that John was the historical high priest Theophilus ben Ananus (37–41). [3] Delff more plausibly thought that John might have served as a substitute for the high priest, since the Mishnah relates that a substitute was appointed every year in case the high priest could not officiate (*Yoma* 1.1). [4] As Delff notes, Josephus records an instance of this actually happening (*Ant.* 17.165–67). [5] But even if it were allowed that John was believed to have functioned in this way, it would be surprising, as Bauckham notes, that no other reference to this "remarkable fact" about John has been preserved elsewhere. [6]

Bernard holds out the possibility that golden plate of the high priest "was (even occasionally) worn by the ordinary Jewish priest in N.T. times"; in this way, it might have been worn by John, James and Mark, giving rise to the separate notices concerning them. [7] Colson similarly suggests the possibility that the plate was worn by priests within the priestly aristocracy, though he concedes that evidence for this is lacking. [8]

Bruce thinks that Polycrates was speaking figuratively; he argues that just as the similar depiction of James in Epiphanius denotes his "intercessory ministry which he exercised on behalf of the people", so the same might have been true of John. [9] Braun similarly suggests it was a rhetorical way of signifying that John was head of the Asian churches. [10] But it is difficult to see what purpose this would have served; the reference to the high priesthood is likely connected to the dispute over the keeping of Passover, and while the exact connection is unclear, the reference to John as a priest wearing the πέταλον likely served to heighten the authority of John for rightly determining the correct observation of the Paschal feast. [11] A metaphorical reference to John's apostolic or episcopal authority would not have accomplished this purpose.

More recently, Bauckham has explained the reference as an exegetical expansion of Acts 4:6, in which a figure named John is spoken of as a relative of the high priest. According to Bauckham, this John was identified with the Evangelist, [12] though quite how this metamorphosised into an exegetical claim that he wore the πέταλον is unclear, for this John is not spoken of as a high

---

[3] Eisler, *Enigma*, 39.

[4] Delff, *Das vierte Evangelium*, 9–10.

[5] Delff, *Das vierte Evangelium*, 9–10.

[6] Bauckham, *Eyewitnesses*, 449–50.

[7] Bernard, *St. John*, 596.

[8] Colson, *L'énigme*, 37.

[9] Frederick F. Bruce, "St John at Ephesus," *BJRL* 60 (1978): 343.

[10] François-Marie Braun, *Jean le Théologien et son évangile dans l'Église ancienne*, vol. 1 (EtB; Paris: Gabalda, 1959), 340.

[11] Stökl Ben Ezra, *Yom Kippur*, 256–57.

[12] Bauckham, *Eyewitnesses*, 451–52; *Testimony*, 49–50.

priest and there is no mention of the sacerdotal plate. Furthermore, Polycrates' apologetic purpose in appealing to John as a priest wearing the πέταλον would have carried little weight unless he was appealing to a tradition that was known and accepted at Rome; a tenuous exegetical inference whose chain of deduction was unfamiliar to its readers would not have constituted a persuasive argument.

Another exegetical interpretation is offered by Behr; he argues that John was being identified by Polycrates as the high priest of the paschal mystery, as he had been present at the crucifixion of Jesus, who was identified in the Johannine Gospel as the Lamb of God and the true temple of God, and because he had initiated the paschal celebration. [13] But again, this is not an obvious solution and inferences of this kind probably would have failed in their appeal to the Roman readership, especially one so discordant with the universal association of Jesus himself as the new high priest. In any case, the Beloved Disciple does not seem to assume any obvious priestly function in John's Gospel; it is Jesus who makes the offering of his own life (c.f. John 10:11).

9.1.1. The Proposal of Harris and Mingana

A century ago, Rendel Harris, who discovered most of the Syriac Odes, and his co-editor Alphonse Mingana cautiously suggested the possibility that the source of Polycrates' statement that John was a priest wearing the πέταλον was the *Odes of Solomon*, [14] in which a possibly Johannine figure is depicted as a priest wearing a crown or wreath.

The *Odes of Solomon* was written early enough to allow this possibility, for it is usually dated between 100 and 125 CE. [15] Some allow that the *Odes* may have even been composed in the late first century; Charlesworth places it in the late first to early second century [16] and Aune between the last quarter of the first century and first quarter of the second. [17] Though their provenance is unknown, the Odes are usually thought to have originated in Syria, [18] perhaps in

---

[13] John Behr, *John the Theologian and his Paschal Gospel: A Prologue to Theology* (Oxford: University Press, 2019), 97.

[14] Harris and Mingana, *The Odes*, vol. 2, 318–19.

[15] Lee Martin McDonald, "The *Odes of Solomon* in Ancient Christianity: Reflections on Scripture and Canon," in *Sacra Scriptura: How "Non-Canonical" Texts Functioned in Early Judaism and Early Christianity*, ed. James H. Charlesworth and Lee Martin McDonald (London: Bloomsbury, 2012), 119; cf. Simon Gathercole, *The Composition of the Gospel of Thomas: Original Language and Influences* (Cambridge: Cambridge University Press, 2012), 38. Michael Lattke, *The Odes of Solomon: A Commentary*, trans. Marianne Ehrhardt (Hermeneia; Minneapolis: Fortress, 2009), 7–10, places them in the early second century.

[16] James H. Charlesworth, "Odes of Solomon," *OTP* 2:725.

[17] David E. Aune, "The Odes of Solomon and Early Christian Prophecy," *NTS* 28 (1982): 436.

[18] Lattke argues that the links between the Odes and the epistles of Ignatius "strongly suggest Syria" (*The Odes*, 11).

Antioch or Edessa. [19] Scholarship favours either a Syriac [20] or Greek [21] original, though Qumran Hebrew has also been suggested. [22]

The *Odes of Solomon* was an important work within early Christianity and was widely disseminated, with fragments surviving in Syriac, Greek, Coptic and Latin. [23] It may have been considered canonical by some; Lactantius, at least, in the early fourth century, quoted Ode 19 as a canonical work which he attributed to Solomon (*Epist.* 39.2; cf. *Div. inst.* 4.12). [24] The name of Solomon may have been attached to the Odes as a result of their placement alongside the older *Psalms of Solomon* in early collections, and the inclusion of his name in the title may have been unknown to Montanus in the second half of the second century, who cited a passage simply as "from the Odes" (ἐκ τῶν ᾠδῶν). [25]

Harris and Mingana suggested that the twentieth Ode, which depicts a priestly figure wearing a ܟܠܝܠܐ, might have been source of Polycrates' reference to John as a priest wearing the πέταλον. [26] It reads:

I am a priest of the Lord, [27]
and to him I serve as a priest;
[...]
But put on the grace of the Lord generously,
and come into his Paradise,
and make for yourself a crown (ܟܠܝܠܐ) from his tree (Ode 20.1, 7; trans. *OTP* 2:753).

A similar depiction of a priestly figure wearing a crown is found in the extant Coptic fragment of the first Ode, which was not available at the time Harris and Mingana wrote, in which the Odist declares: "The Lord is on my head like a crown [or "wreath"]" (trans. *OTP* 2:734). [28]

---

[19] Aune, "The Odes of Solomon," 436; McDonald, "The *Odes of Solomon*," 119.

[20] E.g. Arthur Vööbus, "Neues Licht zur Frage der Originalsprache der Oden Salomos," *Mus* 75 (1962), 275–90; John A. Emerton, "Some Problems of Text and Language in the Odes of Solomon," *JTS* 18 (1967): 372–406; Aune, "The Odes of Solomon," 456 n. 5; Charlesworth, "Odes of Solomon," 726.

[21] Lattke, *The Odes*, 10–11.

[22] Jean Carmignac, "Les Affinités qumrâniennes de la onzième Ode de Salomon," *RevQ* 3 (1961): 71–102.

[23] Cf. Lattke, *The Odes*, 11.

[24] Cf. Lattke, *The Odes*, 2.

[25] See Lattke, *The Odes*, 8.

[26] Harris and Mingana, *The Odes*, vol. 2, 318–19.

[27] Harris and Mingana (*The Odes*, vol. 2, 319) suggest that Jerome's *pontifex eius* ("his high priest"; see Chapter 8), if representative of Polycrates' original text, would "make an excellent parallel" to the Odist's words here.

[28] The Coptic text is given in Majella Franzmann, *The Odes of Solomon: An Analysis of the Poetical Structure and Form* (NTOA 20; Göttingen: Vandenhoeck & Ruprecht, 1991), 15.

The word ܚܠܬܐ employed by the Odist is also used of the high priest's plate in the Syriac Peshitta. Thus, speaking of the golden plate (צ'ץ) of the high-priestly crown, the Syriac reads: "make a ܚܠܬܐ of pure gold" (Exod 28:36), where the Septuagint speaks of a πέταλον. The related Aramaic word כלילא is likewise used in Targum Onkelos to denote the high priest's crown (*Targ. Onk.* Exod 29:6, where the LXX has τὸ πέταλον), as well as the golden plate upon which the holy name was inscribed (*Targ. Onk.* Exod 39:30; this text is not part of the LXX).

Harris and Mingana are cautious in their proposal. Acknowledging the difficulties involved in interpreting the twentieth Ode, they suggest it speaks of spiritual priesthood, [29] and they tentatively propose the possibility of a connection with John. [30] However, they caution that even if Polycrates' depiction of John did originate with the Odes, it would not follow that "John is himself the Odist, or the person of whom the Odist is thinking." Rather, "Polycrates might have applied the language of the Odes about 'priesthood' and πέταλον to his great predecessor." [31]

9.2. The Johannine Odist

In support of their proposal, it can be noted that the Odist is described, as is John in Polycrates, as a priest rather than as the high priest, and the adjectival qualification "golden" is not employed as it usually is when the sacerdotal plate is mentioned. Furthermore, as in Polycrates, only the ܚܠܬܐ of the priestly figure is spoken of rather than any of the other regalia associated with the high priest.

There is also much in the Odes that might have suggested the Johannine identity of the Odist to an ancient reader. Indeed, the Johannine flavour of the Odes has long been recognised within scholarship, to the extent that authorship has often been sought within the context of the putative Johannine community, [32] or even attributed to a disciple of John. [33] The Orientalist James Montgomery, who belonged to the first generation of scholars who discussed the Odes, went so far as to suggest that "this Johannine atmosphere with its unique

---

[29] Harris and Mingana, *The Odes*, vol. 2, 318.

[30] Harris and Mingana, *The Odes*, vol. 2, 318–19.

[31] Harris and Mingana, *The Odes*, vol. 2, 319.

[32] Carmignac, "Les affinités qumrâniennes," 98; Titus Nagel, *Die Rezeption des Johannesevangeliums im 2. Jahrhundert: Studien zur vorirenäischen Aneignung und Auslegung des vierten Evangeliums in christlicher und christlich-gnostischer Literatur* (Leipzig: Evangelische Verlagsanstalt, 2000), 190; James H. Charlesworth, "A Study in Shared Symbolism and Usage: The Qumran Community and the Johannine Community," in *The Bible and the Dead Sea Scrolls*, vol. 3: *The Scrolls and Christian Origins*, ed. James H. Charlesworth (Waco, Tex.: Baylor University Press, 2006), 150.

[33] McDonald, "The *Odes of Solomon*," 109.

terminology" may have sprung from "out of the Beloved Disciple's experience". [34] Perhaps an ancient reader thought so too.

Johannine features include a play on the words wind and spirit in *Ode* 6.1–
2 (cf. John 3:8) [35] and possible allusions to John's Gospel in the call to the
thirsty to drink living waters (*Ode* 30.1–2; cf. John 7:2, 37). Robinson points
out that the stretching out of hands as a representation of crucifixion occurs in
John's Gospel (21:18) and the Odes (27.1–3; 41.1–3). [36] Some have also noted
that the third Ode shares the theme of love with the Gospel and 1 John: "He
loves me. For I should not have known how to love the Lord, if He had not
continuously loved me" (*Ode* 3.3; trans. *OTP* 2:735; cf. John 14:21; 15:16 and
1 John 4:10, 19). [37]

The Odes also contain a pronounced Logos doctrine, which Pollard refers to
as its "key Christological concept". [38] As he notes, [39] the *Odes* present the
Logos as the mediator of creation, echoing the Johannine doctrine of the Logos
who was in the beginning, through whom the worlds were made (Ode 16.18–
19; John 1:2). The twelfth Ode similarly echoes the Johannine prologue, stating: "the dwelling place of the Word is man" (Ode 12.12, trans. *OTP* 2:747; cf.
John 1:14). But perhaps the most elevated expression of this Logos doctrine
comes in Ode 41, in which Christ speaks of the Father who "possessed me from
the beginning" (Ode 41.9, trans. *OTP* 2:770; cf. Prov 8:22), adding, "For his
riches begat me" (Ode 41.10, trans. *OTP* 2:770 cf. Prov 8:23). It further equates
the "Word that was before time in him" (Ode 41.14, trans. *OTP* 2:770) with
"The Man who humbled himself" and was raised (Ode 41.11–12; trans. *OTP*
2:770; cf. Phil 2:6–11). Such statements strongly evoke the Johannine works,
and the prologue of John's Gospel in particular.

An association with John might have also been suggested by the Odist's
claims of having experienced paradise, with its trees, fruits and river (11.16),
as well as heaven (36.1–2), evocative of the experiences of the apocalyptic

---

[34] James A. Montgomery, "The recently discovered Odes of Solomon," *BW* 36 (1910):
99.

[35] Aune, "The Odes of Solomon," 437.

[36] John A. T. Robinson, *The Priority of John* (London: SCM, 1985), 71 n. 164.

[37] Cf. J. H. Charlesworth and R. A. Culpepper, "The Odes of Solomon and the Gospel of
John," *CBQ* 35 (1973): 300.

[38] Thomas Evan Pollard, *Johannine Christology and the Early Church* (Cambridge: Cambridge University Press, 1970), 34.

[39] Pollard, *Johannine Christology*, 34.

seer. Indeed, both the *Odes* and Revelation speak of a crown and of being in-scribed in a book (Ode 9:11; Rev 3:5, 11; 2:10),[40] and both mention a dragon with seven heads (Ode 22:5; Rev 13:1).[41]

Ode 29 might have especially lent itself to being understood as identifying the Odist as an apostle and as John. First, the Odist speaks of taking the rod of the Messiah's power to rule over the thoughts of the Gentiles, indicating some early Christian leader involved in the expansion of Christianity to the nations. Indeed, on the basis of this description, Spitta argues that lines 7–9 can only refer to "an apostle of Christ" (whom he identifies with Paul, the apostle to the Gentiles).[42]

A little later, the Odist writes: "And I gave praise to the Most High, because he has magnified his servant and the son of his maidservant" (Ode 29.11; trans. *OTP* 2:761), where the speaker is likely describing himself as the son of the handmaid of God.[43] This seems to be an allusion to the psalmist, who refers to himself as a servant and as the son of God's maidservant (Ps 86:16; 116:16),[44] unless it is an allusion to a similar passage in the Wisdom of Solomon (Wis 9:5).[45] But there may also be an allusion to Luke's prologue (1:38),[46] in which God is likewise referred to as "Most High" (Luke 1:32; 35), unlike in the other passages, and in which Mary is spoken of as God's maidservant[47] (Luke 1:38; 48). If so, this would suggest that the Odist was claiming to be the son of Mary, and such a claim would have been applicable to the Beloved Disciple, to whom Jesus' mother was entrusted at the crucifixion (John 19:25–27).

9.2.1. Πέταλον *as a Mistranslation*

While the word πέταλον was used specifically of the sacerdotal plate, the word ܟܠܝܠܐ could denote any crown in general,[48] including a wreath, for which Greek would use στέφανος. Thus, where Paul speaks of the athlete's wreath

---

[40] Pierre Prigent, *Commentary on the Apocalypse of St. John*, trans. Wendy Pradels (Tü-bingen: Mohr Siebeck, 2004), 194; cf. David E. Aune, *Revelation 1–5* (WBC 52A; Dallas: Word, 1998), 223.

[41] Cf. Preserved Smith, "The Disciples of John and the Odes of Solomon," *Mon* 25 (1915): 174.

[42] Cited by Lattke, *The Odes*, 403.

[43] Lattke, *The Odes*, 413.

[44] Lattke, *The Odes*, 413–14.

[45] Harris and Mingana, *The Odes*, vol. 2, 70; cf. Lattke, *The Odes*, 414.

[46] E.g. Craig A. Evans, *Word and Glory: On the Exegetical and Theological Background of John's Prologue* (JSNTSup 89; Sheffield: Sheffield Academic Press, 1993), 71.

[47] Pace Lattke, who claims that ܐܡܬܐ does not represent δούλη, used of Mary in Luke's prologue, but παιδίσκης, citing Ps 85:16 (LXX) and Wis 9:5 (*The Odes*, 414). However, the Peshitta of Luke 1:38 does employ ܐܡܬܐ of Mary, representing the Greek δούλη.

[48] E.g. 2 Kgdms 1:10; 4 Kgdms 11:12; Ps 20:4; Zech 6:11; 1 Macc 13:37; 2 Macc 14:4; Rev 14:14.

(στέφανος) (1 Cor 9:25), the Peshitta employs ܟܠܝܠܐ. In the *Martyrdom of Ig-natius*, the martyr is similarly said to have striven for the στέφανος in Greek [49] but for the ܟܠܝܠܐ in the Syriac version (*Mart. Ign.* 5). [50]

Thus, a Greek speaker familiar with Syriac and/or Aramaic might have translated ܟܠܝܠܐ with πέταλον if it was understood as the high-priestly crown, or with στέφανος if a wreath was understood. While the priestly context may have suggested the sacerdotal plate, the crown in question in the Odes is said to have been taken from a tree (Ode 20.7), denoting a wreath. [51]

Ordinary Israelite priests do appear to have worn wreaths on their heads; thus, where the Hebrew Bible has, "you shall be for me a holy nation and a kingdom of priests" (Exod 19:6), Targum Pseudo-Jonathan reads: "You shall be before me as kings knotted with the wreath (כלילא, which is the equivalent of the Syriac ܟܠܝܠܐ)". [52] The Roman historian Tacitus in his *Histories* (5.5) also notes that the Israelite priests were bound with (wreaths of) ivy (*hedera*). [53] Daniélou, who thinks that the wearing of wreaths by priests might have been associated with the feast of tabernacles, [54] draws attention to an image of a priest within the setting of this feast whose hair is decorated with what appears to be leaves or flowers, found among the Dura Europos synagogue frescoes. [55]

9.2.1.1. The Exegetical Origins of the Πέταλον Motif

If Polycrates derived the depiction of John as a priest wearing the πέταλον from Hegesippus, as argued in the previous chapter, it may be that Hegesippus appropriated the imagery in turn from the Syriac Odes. His use of Hebrew (probably Aramaic) and Syriac sources is attested by Eusebius (cf. *Hist. eccl.* 4.22.8), and the preference for πέταλον over στέφανος could be accounted for on the basis of his apparent interest in interpreting the episcopal office in high-priestly terms, as demonstrated by Epiphanius' discussion of James the Just, for which, as discussed above, he was likely dependent upon Hegesippus. Thus, speaking of Christ's kingdom, Epiphanius remarks that it has both a kingly and priestly aspect to it: kingly, because, "he in himself is a greater king, from

---

[49] Ignatius of Antioch, *Corpus Ignatianum: A Complete Collection of the Ignatian Epistles, Genuine, Interpolated, and Spurious*, ed. William Cureton (Berlin: Asher, 1849), 193.

[50] William Wright, "Syriac Remains of S. Ignatius," in *The Apostolic Fathers, Part II: S. Ignatius, S. Polycarp: Revised Texts*, vol. 3 (2nd ed.; London: Macmillan, 1889), 120. Cf. Jdt 15:13; 3 Macc 4:8; 4 Macc 9:6; 1 Cor 9:25.

[51] Cf. Lattke, *The Odes*, 294–95.

[52] Translated by the author from the Aramaic text in the *Targum Pseudo-Jonathan to the Pentateuch* (CALP; Hebrew Union College, 2005), Exod 19:6.

[53] Cf. Jean Daniélou, *Primitive Christian Symbols*, trans. Donald Attwater (Baltimore: Helicon Press, 1964), 15.

[54] Daniélou, *Symbols*, 14–23.

[55] Daniélou, *Symbols*, 16, citing Carl H. Kraeling, *The Excavations of Dura-Europos: Final Report*, VIII, I (New Haven, Conn.: 1956), 114.

eternity, according to his divine nature (κατὰ τὴν θεότητα)", and priestly, because Christ "is the high priest, and leader of high priests (ἀρχιερέων πρύτανις),
with James being appointed the first bishop, who is called the brother of Jesus
and an apostle" (*Pan.* 29.3.8–9). Thus, for Epiphanius, and perhaps for
Hegesippus, bishops were high priests. The mention of James' ordination in
this context is also suggestive of Epiphanius' use of Hegesippus, for according
to Eusebius, Hegesippus related how James "succeeds to the government of the
church, together with the apostles" (*Hist. eccl.* 2.23.4).

Perhaps Epiphanius, or rather Hegesippus, was answering an objection,
raised from the Hebrew text of Jer 33:17–18 (this text is not found in the LXX),
that the Levitical priesthood was to be perpetual and that there would always
be a king upon the throne of David. If so, the objection would have been answered by elevating Christ's kingship into a heavenly one, and by interpreting
the continuance of the priesthood in terms of Christ's high priestly office and
by the succession of bishops in the church, beginning with James. Such an exegetical interest on Hegesippus' part would also explain his interest in drawing
up episcopal succession records (*apud* Eusebius, *Hist. eccl.* 4.22.3).

This exegetical framework may be related to the conception of James as
chief bishop of the church underlying the Clementine literature and other second-century works. [56] It may also inform the high-priestly interpretation of the
episcopal office found in texts written around the turn of the third century.
Thus, Tertullian states that the right of giving baptism belongs, "to the high
priest (*summus sacerdos*), who is the bishop". [57] Tertullian's use of Hegesippus' work is not directly attested, though he likely was familiar with it and
followed it for his account of the persecution of Christians under Domitian
(Tertullian, *Apol.* 5.4). [58]

The early third-century Roman work, the *Refutation of All Heresies*, which
is sometimes ascribed to Hippolytus, similarly describes the episcopacy in
high-priestly language, claiming: "we, being the successors (διάδοχοι)" of the

---

[56] For discussion of the conception of James in this period, see Martin Hengel, "Jakobus
der Herrenbruder – der erste 'Papst'?," in *Glaube und Eschatologie: Festschrift für Werner
Georg Kümmel zum 80. Geburtstag*, ed. Erich Grässer, Otto Merk (Tübingen: J.C.B. Mohr
[Paul Siebeck], 1985), 71–104; cf. Oskar Skarsaune, "Fragments of Jewish Christian Literature Quoted in Some Greek and Latin Fathers," in *Jewish Believers in the Jesus: The Early
Centuries*, ed. Oskar Skarsaune and Reidar Hvalvik (Peabody, Mass.: Hendrickson, 2007),
347.

[57] Translated from the Latin text in Allen Brent, "Tertullian on the Role of the Bishop,"
in *Tertullian and Paul*, ed. Todd D. Still and David E. Wilhite (New York: Bloomsbury,
2013), 176.

[58] Marta Sordi, The Christians and the Roman Empire, trans. Annabel Bedini (London:
Routledge, 1994), 40; cf. Ekkehard W. Stegemann and Wolfgang Stegemann, *The Jesus
Movement: A Social History of its First Century*, trans. O. C. Dean (Edinburgh: T. & T.
Clark, 1999), 453–54; Ramelli, "John the Evangelist's Work," 43.

apostles, share "in the same grace of high priesthood (ἀρχιερατεία) and teaching" (*Refut.* pref. 6). The third-century *Apostolic Tradition* (likewise sometimes attributed to Hippolytus) speaks of the bishop "exercising the high-priestly office (ἀρχιερατεύειν)" in "your sanctuary" (*Ap. Trad.* 3.2,3) and interprets this in terms of his "ministering night and day without ceasing, to placate your face and to offer to you the gifts of your holy church" (*Ap. Trad.* 3.3–4). It adds that the bishop is "to have authority to forgive sins by the high-priestly spirit (τῷ πνεύματι τῷ ἀρχιερατικῷ)" (*Ap. Trad.* 3.5; cf. John's promise to pray and find forgiveness for the robber captain in *Quis div.* 42). [59]

According to Eisler, Hippolytus, in a fragment from a lost work entitled *Odes on all the Scriptures*, refers to John as "the Ephesian high priest" (ἀρχιερεὺς Ἐφέσιος), [60] echoing Polycrates' description of John as a priest wearing the πέταλον. Bauckham thinks that Hippolytus' reference was "certainly" dependent upon Polycrates' description of John, [61] but, unlike Polycrates, Hippolytus localises John's high-priestly status at Ephesus, presumably in reference to John's episcopal office, agreeing with Epiphanius' claim that Christ was the head of an episcopal line of high priests. Probably both Polycrates and Hippolytus were interacting with the same high-priestly interpretation of the episcopal office which Epiphanius' work would suggest originated with Hegesippus, whose *Memoirs* would likely have been available to Hippolytus in Rome, where they were written some decades previously.

9.3. Epiphanius' Construction of James as Literal High Priest

While a rendering of ܐܠܠܐ with πέταλον on Hegesippus' part would have been conducive for an episcopal interpretation, this need not mean that Hegesippus was unaware of the contextual connotation of the priestly wreath in the *Odes*. Possibly he took advantage of the ambiguity of the meanings to portray John as a high-priestly figure in what was only intended as a poetic and hyperbolic description of John. This might explain why his account, as preserved by Eusebius, does not depict James as entering the holy of holies in Jerusalem in the fashion of a quasi-High Priest, as Epiphanius' does. His account only states that James "alone was allowed to enter into the sanctuary, for he did not wear wool but linen". Possibly Hegesippus conflated James the Just with another, priestly James, who was, alone of the disciples, able to enter the temple. James the son of Alphaeus would be the obvious candidate, for he was one of the

---

[59] Translated by the author from the Greek text given in Allen Brent, *Hippolytus and the Roman Church in the Third Century: Communities in Tension Before the Emergence of a Monarch-Bishop* (Leiden: Brill, 1995), 473.

[60] Eisler, *Enigma*, 55, citing the Parisian Codex Coislin 195.

[61] Bauckham, *Eyewitnesses*, 448 n. 38.

twelve and may have been a Levite. [62] Furthermore, James the Just was often identified with James the son of Alphaeus [63] and was likely so identified by Hegesippus. [64]

In any case, Epiphanius seems to have misunderstood Hegesippus' exegesis by transforming James into a literal high priest who entered the physical holy of holies every year, where Hegesippus seems to have rather interpreted the episcopal office in terms of a spiritual high priesthood derived from Christ. Presumably, this idea was evoked by Hegesippus' depiction of James (as found in Eusebius) as being alone allowed to enter the holy place [65] and by the description of a priestly figure who wore the πέταλον, as the high priest had.

9.4. Hymns to the Divine Christ

Perhaps these Odes, with their strong Logos theology, are among those referred to by an anonymous writer (c. 230), thought by Lightfoot to have been Hippolytus, [66] quoted by Eusebius, who spoke of those "psalms and odes" (ψαλμοὶ ... καὶ ᾠδαὶ) written by brothers "from the beginning", which were "praising Christ, the Word of God, as God [67]" (τὸν λόγον τοῦ θεοῦ τὸν Χριστὸν ὑμνοῦσι θεολογοῦντες)" (*apud* Eusebius, *Hist. eccl.* 5.28.6). [68]

The existence of such hymns might in turn be related to the notice of Pliny the Younger, who speaks in his letter to Trajan (c. 111 CE) of the Christians rising early "to sing antiphonally a hymn to Christ as to a god (*Christo quasi*

---

[62] Some infer that this James was a Levite on the basis that Matthew/Levi appears to have been his brother, e.g. Marcus, *Mark 1–8*, 225.

[63] Broek, *Pseudo-Cyril* 18; 28.

[64] See, Furlong, *Identity of John*, 29–31.

[65] Some scholars still read high-priestly language into Eusebius' account for this reason; thus, John Painter, *Just James: The Brother of Jesus in History and Tradition* (Edinburgh: Fortress, 1999), 126, thus states that, "The stress on the exclusive role of James implies that the sanctuary alluded to is the Holy of Holies"; similarly, Skarsaune, "Fragments of Jewish Christian Literature," 140–41. Stökl Ben Ezra also argues that James was originally depicted as a high-priestly figure (*Yom Kippur*, 246). This view is rejected by Ernst Zuckschwerdt, "Das Naziraat des Herrenbruders Jakobus nach Hegesippus," *ZNW* 68 (1977): 276–87, who denies any priestly allusion, arguing that the Nazarite aspect of the portrayal is an anti-priestly motif. However, as Painter points out, the two aspects are not necessarily contradictory (*Just James*, 126).

[66] Lightfoot states that this writer has, for "excellent reasons", been identified with Hippolytus, though he does not elaborate (*Apostolic Fathers,* part 1, vol. 2, 407).

[67] To the author's knowledge, all the standard translations of Eusebius understand θεολογοῦντες in the sense that they were ascribing divinity to Christ. For various uses of the verb, see *PGL* 626–27.

[68] Preserved Smith suggests a connection between the statement of the anonymous writer and the Odes ("The Disciples of John," 181). See also Bernard, *St. John*, vol. 1, cxlvi.

Deo)" (Epist., 10.96). [69] Indeed, the Odes do contain antiphonal responses in the words of Christ. [70]

Possibly these notices are also connected with the *Acts of Mark*, which presents Mark as gathering the brothers together at the Jerusalem temple for the purpose of "laudatory hymn singing (δοξολογικὴν ὑμνῳδίαν) to the master of all things, to Christ the God (τῷ δεσπότῃ τῶν ὅλων Χριστῷ τῷ θεῷ)" (9), where the reference echoes the anonymous writer's description of the brothers who praised "Christ, the Word of God, as God" and Pliny's reference to those singing "to Christ as to a god". Possibly also in depicting Mark as leading the brothers in singing, the *Acts of Mark* preserves a reminiscence of an identification of John/Mark as the Odist.

While ecclesiastical sources do not associate John with hymns to Christ, they call him the θεολόγος, which may have originated in such a context. Thus, an inscription found in Athens refers to a hymn written by Ofellius Laetus, a travelling philosopher who visited Ephesus, probably during Domitian's reign, reads: "Hearing the sublime hymn of Laetus, the theologian (θεολόγος), I saw heaven open for people", [71] which Van Tilborg explains in terms of the classical meaning of the word θεολόγος as "one who makes hymns of the gods". [72]

Two inscriptions describing officials in the imperial cult of Asia Minor also associate the epithet θεολόγος with hymn singing. The first, an early second-century inscription from Smyrna, refers to the same individual as both "hymnodist and theologian" (ὑμνῳδὸς καὶ θεολόγος); the second, from Ephesus, reads: καὶ τοῖς θεολόγοις καὶ ὑμνῳδοῖς; as Deissmann notes, the article is not repeated, rendering it, "theologians who were also hymnodists". [73]

As noted above, Eusebius' anonymous author speaks of those who were "theologising" (θεολογοῦντες), by "praising Christ, the Word of God (τὸν Λόγον τοῦ Θεοῦ τὸν Χριστὸν ὑμνοῦσι) (*apud* Eusebius, *Hist. eccl.* 5.28.6), using the participial form of the related verb. Furthermore, the earliest reference to John as the θεολόγος occurs in Origen, in the third century, where he

---

[69] Latin text in Betty Radice, ed., *Pliny. Letters and Panegyricus*, 2 vols (LCL; Cambridge, Mass.: Harvard University Press, 1969).

[70] Cf. David E. Aune, *Prophecy in Early Christianity and the Ancient Mediterranean World* (Grand Rapids: Eerdmans, 1983), 296.

[71] Cited and translated by Sjef van Tilborg, *Reading John in Ephesus* (Leiden: Brill, 1996), 127.

[72] Van Tilborg, *Reading John in Ephesus*, 127.

[73] Gustav Adolf Deissmann, *Bible Studies: Contributions Chiefly from Papyri and Inscriptions to the History of the Language, the Literature and the Religion of Hellenistic Judaism and Primitive Christianity*, trans. Alexander Grieve (Edinburgh: T. & T. Clark, 1901), 231–32.

speaks of John as the author of the Johannine prologue, [74] which was itself likely based on a hymn. [75]

9.5. Conclusion

Mingana and Harris posited that the motif of John wearing a πέταλον found in Polycrates originated in the depiction of the Odist as a priest wearing a ܟܠܝܠܐ, a word which can refer both to a wreath (στέφανος) and to the sacerdotal plate (πέταλον). There are features in the Odes that could have led an ancient reader to identify the Odist as a Johannine figure, including allusions to the Johannine writings and a Logos doctrine, as well as language which could lend itself to understanding the Odist as an apostle and son of Mary. But there does not appear to be any reason for thinking that Polycrates was versatile in Syriac or that he would have so obviously mistranslated the word ܟܠܝܠܐ in support of his position in his letter to Victor.

Hegesippus, on the other hand, is said to have made use of Hebrew and Syriac documents for his *Memoirs*, written at Rome in Greek. He also likely had an exegetical interest in interpreting the Christian episcopacy in high-priestly terms; a rendering of the ܟܠܝܠܐ of the Syriac Odes with the Greek πέταλον, which was used by the high priest, would have facilitated this interpretation.

Lastly, there is the account of John/Mark leading hymns to "Christ the God" in the temple, which evokes the similar notices found in early sources which speak of the singing of hymns to the divine Christ. Possibly the association of Mark with such hymns to "Christ the God" in the *Acts of Mark* represents a vestige of an identification of the Odist as the Johannine John/Mark.

---

[74] GCS 10, 483.

[75] Ernst Käsemann, "Aufbau und Anliegen des johanneischen Prologs," in *Liberias Christiana Friedrich Delekat zum fünfundsechzigsten Geburtstag*, ed. Walter Matthias and Ernst Wolf (BEvT 26; Munich: Kaiser, 1957), 75–99; Brown, *John*, 19–23; Evans, *Word and Glory*.

Chapter 10

John's Life and Travels

The following two chapters will examine evidence for the reduplication of traditions at the narrative level. That is, they will attempt to show that the narratives of the lives and journeys of John the Evangelist and John/Mark correlate, though this correlation has been obscured by the identification and conflation John/Mark with Mark the Evangelist. A further circumstance also works to obscure the correlation: while narratives of John/Mark are mostly silent concerning his life after c. 65, the earliest and most reliable Johannine tradition says little about John's early travels, primarily addressing his later Ephesian ministry.

An exception to the emphasis on John's later ministry is found in a number of medieval texts, many of Syriac origin, which purport to fill in the gaps in the Johannine narrative. However, on account of their late date, narratives found in these texts contain significant conflation with other traditions. The most significant of these conflations appear to have arisen as a result of the inclusion of John the Evangelist in the tradition according to which the twelve apostles were sent into their fields of labour soon after the resurrection. This narrative, arising in part as a result of the identification of the Evangelist with John the son of Zebedee, conflicted with an arguably earlier tradition according to which John the Evangelist did not leave Jerusalem until the death of Mary, many years later.

Nevertheless, the main contours of the earlier travels of the Evangelist can still be delineated and will be laid out in this chapter. In the next chapter an attempt will be made at correlating the Johannine narrative with that of John/Mark. It will be concluded that the significant correlations and general complementarity of the narratives of John the Evangelist and John/Mark likely indicate that both are derived from a single template, suggesting that the two figures might have once been undifferentiated.

10.1. Early Johannine Traditions

The earliest and most reliable traditions concerning John the Evangelist speak of the latter part of his life. Thus, one of the earliest extant writers, Irenaeus, states that he died in Ephesus, in the reign of Trajan (98–117) (*apud* Eusebius,

Hist. eccl. 3.23.4 = Irenaeus, *Haer.* 2.22.5). Tertullian is one of the oldest witnesses to John's exile; in his *Prescription against Heretics*, written sometime between 198 and 203, he speaks of Rome as the place "where Peter attains to the suffering of the Lord, where Paul is crowned with the departure of John [i.e. beheading], where the apostle John, after he was plunged into boiling oil, having suffered nothing, is exiled to an island" (*Praescr.* 36). Tertullian juxtaposes the sufferings of Peter, Paul and John at Rome in a way that suggests that he placed John's plunging in oil at around the same time as the martyrdoms of the two apostles (c. 65–67).

Jerome also draws attention to the tradition of John the Evangelist being placed in burning oil; he relates that according to Tertullian, John, "having been cast into an earthenware vessel full of burning oil by Nero, came out more refined and invigorated than when he entered" (*Jov.* 1.26). [1] This account seems too dissimilar to the one quoted by Tertullian for it to have been Jerome's source, [2] and Jerome may have quoted from one of Tertullian's lost works. [3] The context for the oil immersion and for John's subsequent exile, was according to Tertullian (as related by Jerome), the reign of Nero.

Elsewhere, Jerome connects this incident with John's banishment, relating that according to "ecclesiastical histories", John,

was thrown into an earthenware jar of boiling oil for the purpose of martyrdom, and proceeded from there for the purpose of taking up his crown as an athlete of Christ, and from there he was immediately sent into the island of Patmos" (*Comm. Matt.* 20.23). [4]

While the source of the tradition is not given, his "ecclesiastical histories (*ecclesiasticae historiae*) may have referred to the *Memoirs* written by Hegesippus, whom he elsewhere describes as "weaving together all the histories of ecclesiastical deeds from the passion of the Lord until his own time" (*omnes ecclesiasticorum actuum texens historias*) (*Vir.* 22). [5] The tradition that John was banished to Patmos from Rome was also found in Hippolytus, though he does not relate when it took place (*Antichr.* 36).

The dominant view within scholarship is that the early sources placed John's exile late in Domitian's reign, even though this claim is never unambiguously

---

[1] Latin text given by Ramelli, "John the Evangelist's Work," 43. See also Francis Gumerlock, *Revelation and the First Century: Preterist Interpretations of the Apocalypse in Early Christianity* (Powder Springs, Ga.: American Vision, 2012), 42 n. 17.

[2] See Ramelli, "John the Evangelist's Work," 42–43. See also the brief discussion below.

[3] William. H. Simcox, *The Revelation of S. John the Divine* (CGTSC; Cambridge: Cambridge University Press, 1909), xliv.

[4] Translated by the author from the Latin text in CCSL 77: 178.

[5] Translated from the Latin text in *PL* 23:674.

made before Eusebius. [6] The basis for this confidence is a potentially misinterpreted statement by Irenaeus that was understood by Eusebius as claiming that the apocalyptic vision of Revelation was seen late in Domitian's reign. A full discussion of this has been given elsewhere and cannot be repeated here, [7] but it can be noted that the Latin translator of Irenaeus, sometime between the late second century and the fourth century, [8] did not understand the vision as the thing seen, as Eusebius did, and likely understood it as referring to John, whom the elders mentioned in the context are said to have seen face to face, using a subject accusative (the participle *visum*) with the passive verb, as is well attested for passive constructions in the Latin of the period. [9] This interpretation of Irenaeus' words would be in agreement with the (apparently Papian) tradition that the elders saw John late in Domitian's reign and persuaded him to write his Gospel at that time, with which Irenaeus and other sources of Papian material seem to be familiar. [10]

This interpretation of Irenaeus also agrees with the logic of his argument, that John would have revealed the name of antichrist to those who saw him face to face, had the fulfilment been imminent at the time when Irenaeus was writing, as "he was seen" – by the elders – late in Domitian's reign, which was nearly in Irenaeus' own time (*Haer.* 5.30.1). The argument is predicated on when John could have declared the meaning to the elders, not on when the apocalyptic vision was seen. [11]

Furthermore, in another place Irenaeus seems to have placed the apocalyptic vision a long time before the writing of John's Gospel at the end of the first century. This Gospel, he relates, was written to remove the heresies then being sown by the Valentinians, and that which was sown "a long time previously" (*multo prius*) by the Nicolaitans (*Haer.* 3.11.1). Elsewhere, however, he states that the activities of the Nicolaitans were addressed in Revelation (*Haer.* 1.26.3), suggesting that he placed the writing of Revelation "a long time previously" to the Gospel of John. [12]

Eusebius also sought evidence for John's late Domitianic exile in Clement of Alexandria's claim that John returned to Ephesus from exile "after the death of the tyrant" (*apud* Eusebius, *Hist. eccl.* 3.23.6–19 = Clement, *Quis div.* 42). However, while the tyrant is not named, it is unlikely to have been Domitian, for

---

[6] Victorinus places John's exile in Domitian's reign, but he seems to have placed its commencement early in his reign; see: Furlong, *Identity of John*, 62–63.

[7] See Chapter 6 in Furlong, *Identity of John*; a summary of the arguments can be found in Behr, *Paschal Gospel*, 68.

[8] Dominic J. Unger, trans., *St. Irenaeus of Lyons Against the Heresies, Book 1* (ACW 55; New York: Newman Press, 1992), 14–15.

[9] See: Furlong, *Identity of John*, 100–101, and the sources cited there.

[10] See Chapter 8 in Furlong, *Identity of John*.

[11] Furlong, *Identity of John*, 98–99; cf. Behr, *Paschal Gospel*, 68.

[12] Furlong, *Identity of John*, 109–10; cf. Behr, *Paschal Gospel*, 67.

Clement speaks of John travelling in Asia Minor afterwards for what appears to have been many years. During this time, John is said to have left a young man in the care of a bishop of another city, who instructed and later baptised him; by degrees, however, the young man was led astray by others of his own age. They encouraged him to more and more wicked deeds, until he began accompanying them on raids. Eventually the young man cast off all restraint and formed his own band of robbers. John happened to be visiting this city, and upon enquiring of the bishop concerning the young man, he learned what had transpired. John presented himself to the band of robbers and is brought to the young man; entreating him, he brought him back to the church and remained with him until he was fully restored.

The account seems to leave insufficient space for the events of John's later travels to have unfolded in the few short years between a release from Patmos in 96 CE and John's death in extreme old age a few years later, c. 100 CE. Moreover, Clement seems to share the same narrative framework as the *Acts of John* (see below), [13] which relates how John ministered in Asia Minor over the course of many years, if not decades, culminating in his death. The extant text of the *Acts of John* does not mention John's exile, but if it did relate anything concerning it, it would have had to have done so in the lost beginning of the work (the extant beginning commences with John sailing away from Miletus, which could have been a stopping point on a journey from Patmos to Ephesus). [14]

The references by Irenaeus and Clement amounted to Eusebius' sole evidence for the placement of John's exile late in Domitian's reign. It is perhaps noteworthy that he could appeal to no clear tradition of this late exile, nor to any unambiguous writers. Just as telling is Eusebius' manufacture of a late-Domitianic persecution of Christians within which he contextualises John's exile. Certainly, Domitian did target the upper classes in Rome during the 90s, executing some and banishing others on whatever convenient pretext he could find, for the purpose of seizing their property and replenishing the imperial coffers (Suetonius, *Domit.* 12.1–2), and one of those pretexts may well have been the profession of Christianity. But Domitian did not specifically target Christians as Christians, and in any case, John was not a member of the Roman aristocracy with property in Rome, and he therefore would not have been directly affected by the persecution.

---

[13] Cf. Theodor Zahn, *Forschungen zur Geschichte des neutestamentlichen Kanons und der altkirchlichen Literatur*, vol. 6: *Apostel und Apostelschüler in der Provinz Asien* (Leipzig: Deichert, 1900), 16–17 .

[14] Cf. Pieter J. Lalleman, *The Acts of John: A Two-stage Initiation into Johannine Gnosticism* (Leuven: Peeters, 1998), 16.

10.1.1. *The* Acts of John

The oldest collection of apocryphal traditions pertaining to John the Evangelist is found in the second- or third-century [15] *Acts of John*, which purports to give an account of John's ministry in Asia Minor, culminating in his death, known as the Metastasis. Its provenance is unknown, with scholars favouring Egypt, [16] Syria [17] or Asia Minor. [18] It is one of five apocryphal Acts, the others being the *Acts of Peter*, the *Acts of Paul*, the *Acts of Andrew* and the *Acts of Philip*; Eusebius refers to these as writings that "Acts such as those of Andrew and John and the other apostles" which were "put forward by heretics under the name of the apostles" (*Hist. eccl.* 3.25.6 [Lake]).

The original text of the *Acts of John* has not survived, but about two-thirds of it has been reconstructed. The beginning of the work, however, is lost, and the reconstructed text begins with John sailing to Ephesus from Miletus (18). [19] The account narrates a number of stories set during John's stay in Ephesus, including the raising of a woman named Cleopatra, the subsequent conversion of her and her husband, Lycomedes (19–25), the healing of aged women in the theatre of Ephesus (30–36), the collapse of the temple of Artemis at John's prayer (37–45) and the raising of a father to life (48–54). It then relates John's plans to journey to Smyrna (55), where (according to one manuscript) he spends four years, and where he raised the sons of Antipatros, a leading citizen of the city, and ordained Polycarp. [20] The extant text resumes with John preparing to leave Laodicea and return to Ephesus (58). In relating the journey back, the *Acts of John* tells the humorous story of John being bothered by bedbugs at an inn and commanding them to find another home for the night (59–60). After relating John's return to Ephesus, it tells the story of the raising of Drusiana to life (63–86).

The order of the cities John visited, Ephesus, Smyrna and Laodicea, corresponds with the first, second and last of the seven churches of Revelation, and the original text may have recorded a journey to all seven churches of Revelation in order. [21] A vestige of this narrative perhaps survives in the request of the church at Smyrna to John that he come "to Smyrna and to the other cities" (εἰς

---

[15] Cf. Bauckham, *Eyewitnesses*, 463.

[16] E. Junod and Jean-Daniel Kaestli, *Acta Iohannis*, vol. 2 (CCSA; Turnhout: Brepols, 1983), 692–700.

[17] Knut Schäferdiek "Herkunft und Interesse der alten Johannesakten." *ZNW* 74 (1983): 255.

[18] Lalleman, *The Acts of John*, 244–70.

[19] From the Greek text in Richard. A. Lipsius and Max Bonnet, eds., *Acta Apostolorum Apocrypha*, vol. 1/2, *Passio Andreae. Acta Andreae et Matthiae. Acta Petri et Andreae. Passio Bartholomaei. Acta Ioannis. Martyrium Matthaei* (Leipzig: 1898).

[20] James, *Apocryphal New Testament*, 239.

[21] Lalleman doubts this (*The Acts of John*, 18–19).

τὴν Σμύρναν καὶ εἰς τὰς λοιπὰς πόλεις) (55), where the definite article presupposes that a distinct group of cities is in view.

The final major event related in the work is the *Metastasis* or death of John (106–115). It relates that on the Lord's Day, John gathered all the brethren who were in Ephesus and broke bread with them. When they had finished, he took a disciple named Verus and some others, instructing them to bring shovels, and he brought them to the tomb of a certain brother, where they dug. At last, John laid down in the hole and expired. Some versions record the disciples coming back the next day to find that John's body was gone.

10.1.1.1. The Lost Beginning

While the extant text of the *Acts of John* does not mention the exile to Patmos, Lalleman has proposed that it may have been related in the lost beginning of the work. [22] In agreement with this, it can be noted that the extant text commences with John sailing to Ephesus from Miletus (18), which would have been a natural stopping point for anyone travelling from there to Ephesus. [23]

Another possibility, and the two are not necessarily mutually exclusive, is that the lost beginning related an account of John being allotted Asia Minor as his field of labour. Evidence for this is possibly indirectly provided by Origen in his lost *Commentary on Genesis*. He writes:

the holy Apostles and disciples of our Saviour were scattered throughout the whole world. Thomas, as tradition relates, obtained by lot Parthia, Andrew Scythia, John Asia (and he stayed there and died in Ephesus), but Peter seems to have preached to the Jews of the Dispersion in Pontus and Galatia and Bithynia, Cappadocia, and Asia, and at the end he came to Rome and was crucified head downwards, for so he had demanded to suffer. What need be said of Paul, who fulfilled the gospel of Christ from Jerusalem to Illyria and afterward was martyred in Rome under Nero? (*apud* Eusebius, *Hist. eccl.* 3.1.1–3 [Lake])

Origen's source for his statement about John may have been the *Acts of John*, since the five apostles mentioned by Origen (Thomas, Andrew, John, Peter and Paul) correspond to the five ancient apocryphal Acts; [24] furthermore, the story of Peter being crucified upside down is found in the *Acts of Peter* and the story of Paul's beheading, while a common Christian tradition, was related in the *Acts of Paul*. [25]

As with the *Acts of John*, the beginnings of the *Acts of Peter* and the *Acts of Paul* are not extant. The *Acts of Thomas*, however, begins with an account of the allotting of labours to the twelve apostles, with Thomas being allotted India

---

[22] Lalleman, *The Acts of John*, 16.
[23] Lalleman, *The Acts of John*, 16.
[24] MacDonald, "Legends" 177.
[25] MacDonald, "Legends," 177.

(parts of which belonged to the Parthian empire) (*Act. Thom.* 1). [26] The beginning of the *Acts of Andrew* is only incompletely preserved, but it gives an account of the allotment to Andrew and Matthew. Possibly the *Acts of Peter* began with a similar account of the allotment of labours. [27]

The dispersion of the apostles may have been placed twelve years after the ascension. Apollonius (fl. c. 180–210), an anti-Montanist writer who probably resided in Asia Minor, related in his now lost works that the twelve apostles were commanded by the Saviour to remain in Jerusalem for twelve years (*apud* Eusebius, *Hist. eccl.* 5.18.13). Some connection between the traditions known to Apollonius and the *Acts of John* is suggested by the reference of both to a man who was raised to life by John in Ephesus (Apollonius, *apud* Eusebius, *Hist. eccl.* 5.18.14; *Act. Johan.* §§ 45–47). Furthermore, the *Acts of Peter* also seems to allude to the tradition of the twelve years, for it claims that Peter did not leave Jerusalem for Rome until the twelve years were fulfilled which had been enjoined upon him by the Lord Christ (*Act. Petr.* 5). The *Acts of Andrew* places its account after the ascension, while the *Acts of Thomas* only states that it took place while the apostles were at Jerusalem.

Possibly the *Martyrdom of Andrew* preserves the version of the allotment tradition originally associated with the Apostle John when it claims: "And Peter was allotted the west; James and John the east (τὴν ἀνατολὴν); Philip the cities of Samaria, and Asia". [28] The identification of John the Evangelist with the Apostle John, however, found already in the *Acts of John* (*Act. Johan.* 88), may have resulted in the introduction of Asia, associated with the Evangelist, as the place to which the Apostle John was allotted.

10.2. Later Sources of Johannine Traditions

A number of sources of Johannine traditions seem to recycle narratives known to the *Acts of John*. These will be summarised here, but the importance of some of these works for the reconstruction of the Johannine narrative will be discussed later in the study.

10.2.1. *The* Suffering of John *and the* Virtues of John

Both the the *Suffering of John* (often referred to by its Latin name, *Passio Iohannis*) of Ps.-Melito, which was originally written in Greek in the fifth or

---

[26] Probably the inclusion in this motif of secondary figures arose later. Thus, the *Preaching of James* claims that James' lot was Jerusalem (Lewis, *Mythological Acts*, 140) while the *Martyrdom of Mark* identifies Mark's lot as Egypt (*Mart. Marc.* 1).

[27] MacDonald, "Legends," 177–78.

[28] Author's translation from the Greek given by Jackson, *Problem*, 146.

sixth century, [29] and the related *Virtues of John* (often referred to as the *Virtutes Iohannis*) of Ps.-Abdias, which was possibly written in Gaul in the late sixth century, [30] recycle narratives otherwise found in the *Acts of John*, namely the resurrection of Drusiana, the collapse of the temple of Artemis and the tradition of John lying down in his grave. [31] They both also relate the story of two young men in Pergamum who regretted giving away their wealth, which is not found in the extant text of the *Acts of John* but which may have been derived from it. In addition, the *Virtues of John* tells the story of the young man restored to repentance by John, given by Clement of Alexandria (*Quis div.* 42), which was possibly related in the *Acts of John*. [32]

Both works also speak of John's exile during Domitian's reign, no doubt on account of the influence of Eusebius' *History*, from which the *Suffering of John* quotes (*Hist. eccl.* 3.17.1; cf. *Virt. Ioh.* 2; Eusebius, *Hist. eccl.* 3.20.8–9). [33] This then likely necessitated that the exile be placed within the context of the Asian ministry, unlike in the *Acts of John*, which likely placed the exile prior to the commencement of the Asian ministry, before Domitian's reign.

10.2.2. The History of John

The *History of John* is a Syriac work preserved in two manuscripts belonging to the sixth and ninth centuries, but perhaps written at the end of the fourth century or earlier. [34] There is also a version of this account found in the *Story of John, Son of Zebedee*, [35] preserved in an Arabic manuscript said to be from the sixteenth-century. [36]

The account begins with the story of the apostles entering into their different fields of labour. In this version of the tradition, however, the allotment takes place sometime after Pentecost, and the work does not mention the tradition of the apostles remaining in Jerusalem for twelve years. Thus, the apostles gather together, and Peter addresses them, reminding them of Jesus' instructions for them to go forth and teach and baptise the nations. [37] The account continues:

---

[29] Junod and Kaestli, Acta Iohannis, vol. 2, 769.

[30] Volfing, *John the Evangelist*, 17.

[31] Summarized from the Latin texts of the *Passio Iohannis* in *PG* 5:1239–50 and the *Virtutes Iohannis* in Johann Albert Fabricius, ed., *Codex Apocryphus Novi Testamenti*, vol. 2 (Hamburg: 1703), 531–90.

[32] Cf. Zahn, *Forschungen zur Geschichte*, vol. 6, 16–17.

[33] *PG* 5:1241.

[34] Junod and Kaestli, *Acta Iohannis*, vol. 2, 705.

[35] Lewis, *Mythological Acts*, 167.

[36] Lewis, *Mythological Acts*, x.

[37] William Wright, *Apocryphal Acts of the Apostles: Edited from Syriac Manuscripts in the British Museum and Other Libraries*, vol. 2 (London: Williams and Norgate, 1871), 3–4.

Each of them then went to such country and region as he was charged by the grace (of God). And it happened that when this holy virgin, namely John, the son of Zebedee, went forth, the grace (of God) accompanied him, through the Spirit of holiness, that it might lead him to the country of the Ephesians, where the head and power of idolatry was dominant. [38]

John travels to Ephesus by foot, preaching in the cities and villages on the way, for forty-eight days. When he finally reaches Ephesus, he finds a certain Secundus, who kept the public bath house, with whom John begins to work. [39] Later, the procurator arrests John but releases him after John restores his son, Menelaus, to life. [40]

Three months later, many of the followers of Artemis turn to the faith preached by John and pull down her image. [41] Nero, hearing of these things, imprisons the procurator, exiles John and decrees that the city be laid waste. [42] Nero, however, having been struck by an angel, commanded that John be released back to Ephesus. [43]

Later, Peter and Paul visit Ephesus and urge John to write a Gospel, after which they returned to Jerusalem, to James, before journeying to Antioch. [44] The account concludes by stating that John lived to a hundred and twenty years of age and was buried at his hut in Ephesus. [45]

The chronology of this work is confused. As in the *Prochorus Acts* (see below) John seems to have journeyed to Ephesus soon after the resurrection, but the account also states that John's arrival in Ephesus can be "found in the books, which are written on paper, in the archives of Nero, the wicked emperor", [46] suggesting John's arrival in Nero's reign (as in the *Acts of Timothy*; see discussion below); it also places John's exile during Nero's reign. But upon John's return to Ephesus, he is visited by Peter and Paul, who then afterwards go first to James in Jerusalem and then to Antioch. No reason is given for the visit to James, but the narrative may reflect a tradition which placed the writing of John's Gospel at the time of the Syrian mission, at which time Peter and Paul were active in Antioch (cf. Acts 11:25–27; Gal 2:11–13) and in which James and those in Jerusalem were overseeing the work in Antioch (cf. Acts 11:22; 12:17).

---

[38] Wright, *Apocryphal Acts*, vol. 2, 5.
[39] Wright, *Apocryphal Acts*, vol. 2, 12.
[40] Wright, *Apocryphal Acts*, vol. 2, 19–23.
[41] Wright, *Apocryphal Acts*, vol. 2, 44–46.
[42] Wright, *Apocryphal Acts*, vol. 2, 55.
[43] Wright, *Apocryphal Acts*, vol. 2, 56.
[44] Wright, *Apocryphal Acts*, vol. 2, 59.
[45] Wright, *Apocryphal Acts*, vol. 2, 59.
[46] Wright, *Apocryphal Acts*, vol. 2, 9.

10.2.3. The Acts of John by Prochorus

The *Acts of John by Prochorus*, a Greek work variously dated from as early as the fourth century to as late as the seventh, [47] opens with an account of the twelve apostles being allotted the territories in which they were to preach, with John being allotted Asia, as in the *History of John*. It thus relates that "after a certain time after the ascension of our Lord Jesus Christ to heaven all the apostles gathered together at Gethsemane" (3). [48] As in the *History of John*, the account does not relate the tradition of the apostles remaining in Jerusalem for twelve years prior to their dispersion, speaking only generically of the apostles leaving Jerusalem after the resurrection.

At Gethsemane, Peter addresses the disciples, reminding them that they are to take Christ commands to all nations and baptise them, as in the *History of John*, and he makes reference to Mary, "the mother of us all", who had "departed from this life" (3–4). They cast the lots, and James' lot was to remain in the city of Jerusalem, and not to depart; for John, however,

the lot fell for Asia, and he bore this with difficulty, and having groaned and wept he fell on his face three times and bowed before all the apostles, and taking him, Peter raised him by the hand and said to him: we all hold you as a father and your patience is a foundation for all of us. And why have you done this and disturbed our hearts? And John, having answered with tears and bitter groanings, he said: "I have sinned in this hour, my father Peter, and I am about to experience dangers on the sea" (5–6).

The apostles then left Jerusalem to enter into their respective fields, and lots were cast for each of the seventy-two disciples; the lot of Prochorus (cf. Acts 6:5), the purported author of the book, was to follow John (7). The two of them left Jerusalem and came to Joppa, where they stayed for three days. They found a ship from Egypt, headed for western lands, which they boarded. It then adds:

John began to cry out and said to me that tribulation and dangers of the sea await me, and my spirit will be punished, but God has not revealed to me concerning death or life. If, child, you survive the sea, go to Asia and enter Ephesus and remain there three months, and if I come to you in the third month, we will complete our service " But if I do not arrive the third month and do not come to you, turn, child, to Jerusalem, to James, the Lord's brother, and whatever he instructs you, do (7–8).

A storm arose, and the crew is shipwrecked off the coast of Seleucia, the port city of Antioch; Prochorus is washed ashore in Seleucia with the rest of the crew, where he is brought to the magistrate on the accusation that he and John had caused the shipwreck through sorcery. After he explains their mission, he

---

[47] See Culpepper, *John*, 206. Junod and Kaestli place it in the fifth century (*Acta Iohannis*, vol. 2, 748–49).

[48] References are to the page numbers in the Greek text in Zahn, *Acta Joannis*, 3–165, and so hereafter. Zahn did not organize the text into chapters.

is released and makes his way by land to a placed called Marmareon near Ephesus; there he witnesses John being washed ashore by a huge wave, and the two of them then journey by road to Ephesus (8–14).

After the two of them arrive in Ephesus, John finds employment as a stoker of the fires at the local bath owned by Dioscorides, the chief magistrate of the city. Various miracles are related, including the resurrection of Dioscorides' son and the destruction of the temple of Artemis at John's prayer. John and Prochorus are said to have been apprehended on the false charge of being runaway slaves, but they were released after three days and were sent out of the city. They came to Marmareon, but John was instructed in a vision to return to Ephesus, and he was informed that after three months he would be sent into exile. Upon their return, the people complained to Trajan [49] that the worship of idols was being neglected, and Trajan ordered that John and Prochorus be exiled to Patmos for dishonouring the gods (44–46).

While sailing to Patmos under an imperial guard, the crew were caught up in a storm, which John is said to have calmed by his prayers (50–51). In Patmos John again did many wonders, including causing the destruction of the temple of Apollo (81). Finally, another king arose who allowed John to return to Ephesus from exile; his disciples urged him to stay, but when he could not be persuaded, they instead asked that he leave them a writing, since he had seen the signs done by the Son of God and heard his words (151–52). He went up to a mountain and after some days there arose thunder and lightning, and Prochorus fell down as dead; John lifted him up and began dictating to him the words of the Gospel of John, as Prochorus sat and wrote the words on papyrus (154–56). Later, John directed Prochorus to transcribe the Gospel onto parchments (μεμβράναι); these were to be kept in Patmos, while the papyri were to be sent to Ephesus (156–58). The account ends with the familiar tradition of John's disciples digging a grave and John lying in it, with his disciples being unable to find his body the following day (162–65).

10.2.4. The Acts of John in Rome

Brief mention can be made of the work sometimes known as the *Acts of John in Rome*. [50] This work, likely written between the fourth and sixth century, [51] begins with Domitian summoning John to Rome to account for why he was preaching that the seat of the Roman Empire was to be removed and given to

---

[49] On the origin of the placement of John's exile in Trajan's reign, see Furlong, *Identity of John*, 67–85.

[50] Keith Elliott, *The Apocryphal New Testament: A Collection of Apocryphal Christian Literature in an English Translation* (Oxford: Clarendon Press, 1993), 347. An English translation can be found (under a different title) in ANF 8.560–64.

[51] Elliott dates it to the sixth century (*Apocryphal New Testament*, 347); Junod and Kaestli to the fourth or fifth century (*Acta Iohannis*, vol. 2, 857).

another. John explains that the coming king he preaches was an eternal one, who will come from heaven. Domitian nevertheless must uphold his own rules and banishes John to Patmos.

10.3. The Dormition Tradition

Some sources know a tradition according to which John remained with Mary, the mother of Jesus, until her death in Jerusalem. One of the earliest writers to speak of Mary's death (the dormition) is Epiphanius; while he states that no-one knew how Mary died, he nevertheless provides three suggestions: that she fell asleep and was buried; that she was martyred, for which he quotes Luke 2:35 ("a sword will pierce your own soul also"); or that she remained alive, since God can do anything (*Pan.* 78.11.2–5). Whether he is repeating three traditions that he knew or whether he was just speculating concerning possibilities is unclear, though the former is suggested by the independent attestation of these views elsewhere. Thus, the fourth-century or earlier Ethiopic *Book of Mary's Repose* places Mary's death in her home in Jerusalem and her burial outside of the city (*Lib. Req* 51, 66, 70), corresponding to the first suggestion. Ambrose, Epiphanius' contemporary, seems to have known (though he does not accept) the claim that Mary was martyred, for he claims when discussing Luke 2:35 that neither "scripture nor history" teaches that Mary would be pierced with a literal sword (*Comm. Luc.* 2.61). [52] While there is no extant source contemporaneous with Epiphanius that claims that Mary did not die, the so-called *Tübingen Theosophy*, perhaps written around 500, just over a century after Epiphanius wrote, spoke of "the birth and assumption of our undefiled lady the God-bearer (Theotokos)" [53] which may reflect such a view.

Dates for Mary's dormition vary greatly, but it was often placed between ten and fifteen years after the ascension, corresponding to the early part of Claudius' reign (41–54). [54] Thus, the Syriac *Book of the Bee* claims that Mary was received into John's house for twelve years after the ascension, with one manuscript reading that it was thirteen years (44). [55]

---

[52] Translated by the author from the Latin text in Schenkl, *Ambrose*. Cf. Shoemaker, *Ancient Traditions*, 12.

[53] Translated by the author from the Greek text in Shoemaker, *Ancient Traditions*, 28.

[54] Latin sources, however, exhibit great variation, placing it between two and twenty years after the ascension, though these seem to be secondary in nature; see Mary Clayton, *The Apocryphal Gospels of Mary in Anglo-Saxon England* (Cambridge: Cambridge University Press, 1998), 89–90.

[55] Budge, *Book of the Bee*, 97.

Among Coptic sources, Severus of Nastrawa states that Mary lived with John, the Beloved Disciple, for fifteen years after the crucifixion, [56] while the Coptic homily on the dormition by Ps.-Cyril, which may have been written in the early ninth century, relates that Mary shared a house with John in Jerusalem until the time of her death, ten (or, according to some texts, fifteen) years after the resurrection, which it attributes to Josephus and Irenaeus, who are both said to be from among the Hebrews (*On the Virgin Mary* 39). [57] The mention of Irenaeus in this text is clearly erroneous, but the name of Josephus may have been a mistake for Hegesippus, since the two names were sometimes confused. [58] Ps.-Cyril also claims that Josephus and Irenaeus related information on Mary's genealogy, and he provides the names of her mother and father as Anna and Joachim, as they appear in the *Protevangelium of James*. [59]

Among Greek writers, Arethas of Caesarea places Mary's death fourteen years after the crucifixion, [60] while the *Chronicle* of Hippolytus of Thebes places it eleven years afterwards (*Chron.* 3; 5; see discussion below).

10.3.1. The Dormition and John's Departure from Jerusalem

In the account given by the tenth-century Byzantine exegete Arethas of Caesarea, it is related that John the Evangelist remained in Jerusalem with the mother of the Lord for fourteen years before journeying to Asia. Interpreting the 144,000 of Revelation as those who believed in Christ from among the Jews, Arethas continues:

For there were many and above number who had believed in Christ from among the Jews. And these are witnesses to the divine Paul when he was in Jerusalem, saying: "Do you see, brother, how many multitudes there are of Jews who have believed? [Acts 21:20]" The one who gave the divine revelations [χρηματίζων] to the Evangelist says that these will not partake of the destruction by the Romans. For the ruin by the Romans had not yet overtaken the Jews when the Evangelist was prophesying these things. And he was not in Jerusalem, but in Ionia, near Ephesus, for after the suffering of the Lord he was waiting [προσεδρεύω] in Jerusalem only fourteen years, for as long as also the God-assuming tabernacle of the Lord's mother was preserved in this temporal life after the suffering and resurrection of her incorruptible child. And he stayed with her, seeing that she was a mother entrusted to him by the

---

[56] Bargès, *Homélie sur St Marc*, 23.

[57] James, *Apocryphal New Testament*, 197; Broek, *Pseudo-Cyril*, 94.

[58] Kirsopp Lake, ed. and trans., *Eusebius: The Ecclesiastical History*, vol. 1 (LCL; London: Heinemann; 1926), xlvi; Herbert J. Bardsley, *Reconstructions of Early Christian Documents*, vol. 1 (London: SPCK, 1935), 216–17; Riesner, *Paul's Early Period*, 185–86. See also Geoffrey W. H. Lampe, "A.D. 70 in Christian Reflection," in *Jesus and the Politics of his Day*, ed. E. Bammel and C. F. D. Moule (Cambridge: Cambridge University Press, 1984), 168, and by Daniel C. Harlow, *The Greek Apocalypse of Baruch (3 Baruch) in Hellenistic Judaism and Early Christianity* (SVTP 7; Leiden: Brill, 1996), 107 n. 105.

[59] Broek, *Pseudo-Cyril*, 94, 118.

[60] *PG* 106:605.

Lord. For after her death, the report is that he no longer dwelt in Judea but moved to Ephesus, regarding which, as has been said, the apocalyptic revelation (or "Revelation") under discussion was brought about. [61]

Arethas thus specifically cites Mary's being entrusted to John as the reason he remained with her and he has emphasised that he waited in Jerusalem until after her death before leaving. It adds that after that time, he moved to Ephesus.

The (tenth-century?) historian Hippolytus of Thebes places Mary's dormition eleven years after the crucifixion:

And she lived from the incarnation of our Lord thirty-three years. And from the ascension of the Lord she lived with the disciples in the house of John the Evangelist for eleven years. Altogether she lived fifty-nine years (Hippolytus, *Chron.* 3). [62]

Hippolytus seems to assume that John went to Ephesus following her death, for a little later he adds that "after her ascension, having preached the word in Ephesus of Asia, John was there taken up" (Hippolytus, *Chron.* 5). The same things are also related by the fourteenth-century historian Nicephorus Callistus (Nicephorus, *Hist. eccl.* 2.3).

Lastly, the Greek *Menologium* (1.7), said to be written in Constantinople in 980, likewise places John's departure from Jerusalem after Mary's dormition. It reads for September 26:

The great apostle and evangelist John, after the ascension of the Lord and the death of the Mother of God, went to Ephesus preaching the Christ. And having been charged by Domitian the Roman king, he was banished to Patmos, the island, where also the saint wrote the Gospel. But after the death of Domitian, having been called back again, he returned to Ephesus. And after having taught the multitude and having led them to Christ through baptism, he foresaw his death. And when the Lord's day came, when he had taught the brethren the great things of God, and having charged them to keep all that he had taught them, he ordered his disciple to take men, secure the implements needed for digging, and follow him. And when they had come to the place, he commanded them to dig a deep trench in the shape of a cross. And after he had prayed and said, "Peace be with you, brothers," he reclined in the trench. Then, when the disciples had covered him, they withdrew. And after this, when they came to see him, they could not find him. [63]

As with Arethas, the *Menologium* seems to envision John journeying to Ephesus following Mary's death. Here, however, the account reflects the dominant view of Eusebius that the exile occurred in Domitian's reign. The account of John's death reflects the Metastasis tradition found in the *Acts of John* and related texts.

---

[61] Translated by the author from the Greek text in *PG* 106:605.

[62] Translated from the Greek text in Diekamp, ed., *Hippolytos von Theben*, 3–4.

[63] Culpepper's translation, *John*, 235 n. 4. Greek text in *PG* 117:73.

10.4. The Dormition and the Allotment Tradition

In Arethas of Caesarea, Hippolytus of Thebes and in the Greek *Menologium*, the departure of John from Jerusalem is associated with the death of Mary. There is no mention of the tradition of the twelve apostles being allotted their labours.

The allotment is mentioned, however, in the *History of John* and the *Prochorus Acts*, though neither work demonstrates any awareness of the tradition that the apostles remained in Jerusalem for twelve years. Instead, the *History of John* relates that the apostles went into their fields of labour "some days" after Pentecost while the *Prochorus Acts* states that they did so "after the ascension of our Lord Jesus Christ to heaven".

This separation of the allotment tradition from the twelve years seems to have influenced these works' retelling of the Johannine narrative in important ways. Thus, for the *History of John*, the tradition of the apostles leaving Jerusalem soon after Pentecost has displaced the tradition of John's leaving Jerusalem upon Mary's death. Indeed, this work does not even mention the dormition, possibly because it was generally placed towards the beginning of the reign of Claudius (41–54), a decade after Pentecost and therefore after John's departure from Jerusalem.

The *Prochorus Acts* on the other hand, apparently without regard for the original chronological setting of the dormition tradition, has merged the two commission narratives. Consequently, it places the scene of the allotment tradition at Gethsemane, the site associated with Mary's tomb from at least the fifth century, [64] and it presumably places the narrative shortly after Mary's death, which is mentioned in the context. Indeed, an Ethiopic version of the *Prochorus Acts* reads "grave of Mary" instead of Gethsemane for the place to which the apostles gathered. [65] Thus the identification of John the Evangelist, who remained in Jerusalem until Mary's death, with John the son of Zebedee, who featured in the allotment tradition, has produced a conflated commission narrative in the *Prochorus Acts*.

10.4.1. Book of John Concerning the Falling Asleep of Mary

Another conflation of the allotment and dormition traditions is possibly represented by the work entitled the *Book of John Concerning the Falling Asleep of Mary*. [66] This work, which is related to the *Book of Mary's Repose*, was written in Greek perhaps no later than the fourth century. [67] It tells of how the angel

---

[64] Shoemaker, *Ancient Traditions*, 102.

[65] Budge, *Contendings*, 222.

[66] A translation of this work can be found in ANF 8.587–91.

[67] See discussion in Culpepper, *John*, 232–33.

Gabriel appeared to Mary near the Lord's sepulchre, where Mary was praying that she might return to Christ, and how he announced to her that she would soon die. She then returns to her second home in Bethlehem [68] and prays that the Lord would send John and the other apostles to her. After this, John is snatched up in a cloud and brought from Ephesus to Mary's house in Bethlehem, to witness Mary death. [69] The Spirit then brought the other living apostles by a cloud to Bethlehem, and even temporarily raised up those who had died so that they might witness Mary's death.

The entire dormition narrative is set in the time of Tiberius (14–37), which is consistent with the tradition of the early departure of John from Jerusalem, found in the *Prochorus Acts* and other works. However, it seems to have conflated the narratives at the expense of maintaining the connection between the dormition and John's departure from the city. Since it places Mary's death after John's departure, it could presumably have still placed it ten to fifteen years after the ascension; possibly Ps.-Melito entitled the *Departure of Mary* provides a clue as to why it did not do so (see below).

10.4.2. Ps.-Melito's Departure of Mary

Another version of the narrative of John being translated to Judea to witness Mary's death is found in the Latin work of Ps.-Melito entitled the *Departure of Mary*, written in the sixth or seventh century. [70] It commences by relating, like the *Acts of John by Prochorus*, that the apostles went out into the world following the ascension, preaching according to their lots (*Trans. Mariae* 1). Mary, however, remains in Jerusalem, where she dies in the second year following Christ's ascension (*Trans. Mariae* 2), again in Tiberius' reign, as in the *Book of John Concerning the Falling Asleep of Mary*.

The mention of two years may provide a clue as to the origin of the Tiberian placement of Mary's death, for the chronological reconstruction to be laid out in the following chapter would suggest that Mary died about two years after the dispersal of the apostles (which, in its pre-conflated form, took place twelve years after the ascension), which possibly accounts for Mary's death two years after the dispersal of the apostles in this account.

In this version, however, unlike in the *Book of John Concerning the Falling Asleep of Mary* which places Mary's death in Bethlehem, Mary is said to have taken up residence at the house of John's parents, adjacent to the Mount of

---

[68] The association of Mary's death with Bethlehem instead of Zion is perhaps on account of the association of the Zion site with Mark, who was increasingly being identified with Mark the Evangelist and the Alexandrian Mark.

[69] The same tradition is found in the dormition account of the later Ethiopic *Six Books* (Shoemaker, *Ancient Traditions*, 379).

[70] Clayton, *Apocryphal Gospels*, 85. Cf. Note 71 below.

Olives (*Trans. Mariae* 1).[71] It presumably did so in order to keep Mary under John's care after his departure from the city, even if indirectly.[72]

10.5. The Syriac Narrative of John in Ephesus

A number of Syriac sources exhibit a common narrative of John's preaching in Asia, founding of the church in Ephesus and burial near the city. Some of these claim that Mary accompanied John to Asia and that she was later buried near Ephesus, and this too may have arisen from the conflation of the allotment tradition, which placed John's preaching in Ephesus shortly after the resurrection, with the dormition narrative, which is usually placed ten to fifteen years after the resurrection. The *Prochorus Acts* privileged Mary's death in Jerusalem at the expense of its chronological setting, whereas Syriac sources seem to have maintained John's early departure from Jerusalem and Mary's later death, as well as the tradition of John caring for Mary until her death, at the expense of the geographical placement of Mary's death in Jerusalem.

Already by the late fourth century, Epiphanius, in his *Panarion* (c. 375 CE) speculates as to whether Mary had been in Asia with John. When addressing those who were teaching that it was permissible for an unmarried man and woman to live in the same house as "beloved friends", he remarks that John and Mary dwelled together as a special dispensation (*Pan.* 78.11.1)[73]; he adds:

let them search through the scriptures and neither find Mary's death, nor whether or not she died, nor whether or not she was buried – even though John surely traveled throughout Asia. And yet, nowhere does he say that he took the holy Virgin with him. Scripture simply kept silence because of the overwhelming wonder, not to throw men's minds into consternation (*Pan.* 78.11.2).[74]

Epiphanius may have been interacting with a claim that Mary had accompanied John into Asia, as found in later sources. Such a tradition seems to be attested some decades later, in 431, by Cyril of Alexandria, who spoke of Ephesus as

---

[71] The Latin text is in Clayton, *Apocryphal Gospels*, 334–43.

[72] Shoemaker dates this work early, to the fifth century, on the supposition that the unique placement of Mary at the Mount of Olives predates the Zion tradition (see Shoemaker, *The Ancient Traditions*, 35). The probable conflation of the dormition and allotment traditions exhibited by this work make an early date unlikely, however. The placement of Mary at the Mount of Olives, far from being evidence for the source's antiquity, is nothing more than a gloss designed to account for how John continued to care for Mary after his earlier departure from the city.

[73] Translation in Frank Williams, *The Panarion of Epiphanius of Salamis*, vol. 2, *Books II and III. De Fide* (2nd rev. ed.; NHMS 79; Leiden: Brill, 2013), 624.

[74] Translation in Williams, *Panarion*, 624.

the place "where John the Theologian and Mary are", [75] which Shoemaker suggests may presuppose "a local tradition that Mary had accompanied John to Ephesus". [76]

10.5.1. Moses Bar Kepha

A tradition of Mary's residence with John in Asia is also attested some centuries later in the writings of Moses Bar Kepha (c. 815–c. 903), the Jacobite bishop of Mosul, Beth Raman and Beth Kiyonaya:

John left Jerusalem and took with him the mother of God, because it is written in the Gospel: Child, behold your mother, etc. She went up with him into Asia, and Ignatius of Antioch and Polycarp of Smyrna served them, and when she died, John, as well as Papias and Polycarp, buried her in her clothing and they interred her in the land of Ephesus, in Mount Ankllos (or Aikllos), and John received the order not to reveal the tomb to anyone, as Ignatius makes it known in his letter to Timothy. [77]

Presumably the claim that Mary had wished for the location of the tomb to be kept a secret was employed to account for the lack of any physical tomb associated with Mary in Ephesus.

The mention of Ignatius, Polycarp and Papias as John's disciple has likely been influenced by Eusebius' claim, in his *Chronicle* (as preserved in Jerome's version), [78] that these three were hearers of John.

10.5.2. Mingana 540

While Bar Kepha does not explicitly place John's residence in Asia during the reign of Tiberius (14–37), further evidence that the Syriac tradition is interacting with this form of the allotment tradition is found in a similar version of the narrative (though without the mention of Mary) found in the Peshitta manuscript Mingana Syriac 540. This manuscript, written in 1749, was copied from

---

[75] Stephen J. Shoemaker, *Mary in Early Christian Faith and Devotion* (New Haven, Conn.: Yale University Press, 2016), 224.

[76] Shoemaker, *Mary*, 224.

[77] Translated by the author from the French translation in Filbert de la Chaise, "A l'origine des récits apocryphes du 'Transitus Mariae.'" *EphMariol* 29 (1979): 82.

[78] August Helm, *Die Chronik des Hieronymus.* (Berlin: Akademie-Verlag, 1956), 193–94.

an exemplar possibly dating to around 750 CE; [79] the same account is also given by Solomon of Basra in the early thirteenth century. [80] Mingana 540 relates:

[John] preached in Asia at first, and afterwards was banished by Tiberius Caesar to the isle of Patmos. Then he went to Ephesus and built up the church in it. Three of his disciples went thither with him, and there he died and was buried. [These three were] Ignatius, who was afterwards bishop in Antioch and was thrown to the beasts at Rome; Polycarp, who was afterwards bishop in Smyrna and was crowned [as a martyr] in the fire; John, to whom he committed the priesthood and the episcopal see after him. [81]

Once again Ignatius and Polycarp are mentioned, though instead of Papias, Mingana 540 speaks of a second John as one of John's disciples. It goes on to associate this John with the second memorial to John in Ephesus and with the authorship of "the Revelations", [82] using information which was no doubt derived from Eusebius and his (indirect) attribution of Revelation to John the Elder (*Hist. eccl.* 3.39.6). [83]

This account also speaks of John's exile as taking place prior to his residence in Ephesus, which may have been informed by Eusebius' statement that John took up residence in the city after he left Patmos (*Hist. eccl.* 3.23.6), so that the early placement of John's residence in Ephesus has also resulted in an early placement of the exile which preceded it.

The same manuscript also contains what Bruce refers to as a "prefatory note" [84] before the Gospel of John, which perhaps reflects the attribution of the Gospel to a second John. It reads: "The holy Gospel of our Lord Jesus Christ – the preaching of John the younger". [85] Bruce suggests that this second John is being distinguished from the Apostle and is possibly to be identified with Papias' John the Elder. [86] The designation of "John the Younger" is also found in the late fifth- or early sixth-century Syrian fragments of the Six Books,

---

[79] Alphonse Mingana, "The Authorship of the Fourth Gospel," *BJRL* 14 (1930): 333–39. Other Syriacists, however, do not necessarily share the confidence in the precision with which Mingana dated manuscripts; see James Farwell Coakley, "A Catalogue of the Syriac Manuscripts in the John Rylands Library," *BJRL* 75 (1993): 115 n. 27.

[80] A French translation of this passage is provided by Esbroeck, "Deux listes d'apôtres," 21.

[81] Translated by Bruce, "St John at Ephesus," 356–57.

[82] Bruce, "St John at Ephesus," 357.

[83] Bruce, "St John at Ephesus," 357.

[84] Bruce, "St John at Ephesus," 357.

[85] Bruce, "St John at Ephesus," 357; Mingana, "Authorship of the Fourth Gospel," 333.

[86] Bruce, "St John at Ephesus," 358. Leon Morris, *Studies in the Fourth Gospel* (Grand Rapids: Eerdmans, 1969), 283, dismisses this: "'John the younger' is a curious description of 'John the elder.'" SBut it may have distinguished him from the older John, the son of Zebedee (so Eisler, *Enigma*, 24).

which purport to relate traditions about Mary's dormition written by James, [87] though in these he is identified (perhaps by conflation) with John the son of Zebedee. [88]

10.5.3. Codex 825

The narrative found in the Syriac codex 825 (date?), housed in the British Museum, is also consistent with a presupposition of John's early preaching in Ephesus, for it too relates that Mary accompanied John into Asia, and it places Mary's death in the late 40s:

Mary remained with John seventeen years. When John was sent into exile to the island of Patmos, the saintly one was also with him. Ignatius his disciple served her. According to the book, after the return of John from exile, on the 25th December, a Thursday, at the ninth hour, this saintly one fell ill until Friday morning. She crossed over from this life to the blessed abodes of the Father. John buried her with her own clothing, and he buried her at Mount Ilinus in the territory of Ephesus. He received an order from her not to tell anyone of the apostles how they had buried and interred her holy body. [89]

The period of seventeen years would place Mary's death between 47 and 49 CE, depending on how the work calculated dates. As in Mingana 540, John's exile is mentioned; here, however, Mary is said to have been exiled along with John. While the name of the emperor is not mentioned, its occurrence prior to Mary's death would be consistent with the Tiberian narrative of Mingana 540.

10.5.4. Syriac Manuscript 16401

A Syriac manuscript dated to the year 874 and housed at the British Museum (numbered 16401) relates like codex 825 that Mary was exiled with John, but it also emphasises John's duty of caring for Mary until her death, as in Bar Kepha:

John the Evangelist departed from Jerusalem, him and the virgin Mary, because the Saviour had entrusted her to him when he was hanging at the cross, and she arrived with him in Asia. And when he was exiled in Patmos, she was with him. He preached the gospel of the Messiah to the barbarian people who were found there on Patmos. He taught them and baptised them. And when he went out from exile, he preached in the whole of Asia, and in all the islands next to Asia. He taught and baptised and built the church of Ephesus, and there he founded the apostolic seat. They served him – Ignatius, he who was the patriarch of Antioch and who was delivered to the beasts at the order of Trajan; Polycarp, he who became the bishop of Smyrna and was crowned the martyr of fire. Such were the disciples of John at Ephesus. The seventh year of Domitian (i.e. 87 C.E.), the blessed Mary left this world, the 23 Iyar, [90] Friday

---

[87] Shoemaker, *Ancient Traditions*, 370–71. Clayton notes that fifth-century fragments of this work are extant (*The Apocryphal Gospels*, 31).

[88] Shoemaker, *Ancient Traditions*, 374.

[89] Chaise, "A l'origine des récits apocryphes," 82.

[90] This month, the eighth of the Hebrew year, usually falls in April-June.

at the third hour. And she counselled John not to reveal where her body would be placed, and John consented, and interred her in the land of Ephesus. And when John had gone through all the islands by the sea, he gave the laying on of priestly hands, the last of all the apostles, and he himself also left the world. He had indeed lived a long time in the world. He preached the gospel from the first year in which Claudius reigned [41 CE] until the sixth year of Trajan [103 CE]. [91]

It goes on to relate that John had ordained Timothy, Paul's disciple, as bishop of Ephesus, and he adds (loosely following Eusebius, as in Mingana 540) that there were two tombs in Ephesus named for a John: one belonging to the Evangelist and one belonging to "John the Elder, the disciple of the Evangelist, who wrote Revelation". [92]

This account differs from codex 825 in placing Mary's death in the seventh year of Domitian, or 87 CE, rather than seventeen years after the crucifixion, for reasons which are unclear.

A perhaps summarised form of this narrative is found a century later in a work of the Jacobite bishop Bar Hebraeus (thirteenth century), though he also mentions Polycarp as one of John's disciples:

> Now he went down from Jerusalem, and Mary the mother of the Lord, with him, and together they were banished to the island of Patmos. And when he returned from banishment he preached in Asia, and founded a church in Ephesus, and Ignatius, the fiery, and Polycarp ministered to him; and he interred the blessed Mary, and no man knows where he laid her (*Comm. Matt.* 10). [93]

10.5.5. Dionysius bar Salibi

The version of the story found in the writings of the Jacobite bishop Dionysius bar Salibi (twelfth century) contains the unique claim that John came to Ephesus after a prior period of preaching in Antioch:

> John preached at Antioch; he went away to Ephesus and the mother of our Lord accompanied him. Immediately, they were exiled to the island of Patmos. On returning from exile, he preached at Ephesus and built a church. Ignatius and Polycarp served him. He buried the blessed Mary. He lived 73 years and died after all the other apostles; he was buried at Ephesus. [94]

The reference to John preaching in Antioch is perhaps related to the tradition attested in a note found at the end of the fifth-century Armenian translation of the Syriac commentary on the *Diatessaron* of Ephrem the Syrian (306–373),

---

[91] Translated by the author from the French translation in Esbroeck, "Deux listes d'apôtres," 22.

[92] Summarized by the author from the French translation in Esbroeck, "Deux listes d'apôtres," 22.

[93] Carr, *Bar-Hebraeus*, 27, with minor changes.

[94] Translated in Culpepper, *John*, 235.

preserved in a manuscript dated to 1195,[95] which claims: "John wrote that
[Gospel] in Greek, at Antioch, for he remained in the land until the time of
Trajan."[96] Culpepper notes this as "a curious departure from the tradition that
John worked at Ephesus."[97]

10.6. John's Preaching in Antioch

The mention of John's preaching in Antioch found in bar Salibi and Ephrem's
commentary on the *Diatessaron* may represent another narrative which was
chronologically displaced by the early placement of John's residence in Asia,
as the Zion version of the dormition narrative appears to have been. Evidence
for this is furnished by other sources which appear to have conflated the same
two narratives of John's early stay in Asia with his preaching in Antioch, as
bar Salibi appears to have, though in independent ways.

10.6.1. The Geez Commentary

John's preaching in Antioch is also mentioned in a Geez commentary on Revelation, which was written by a Jacobite, perhaps from Egypt or Jerusalem, no
earlier than the late thirteenth century (Cowley suggests it was written in the
late sixteenth century).[98] Whoever wrote it was learned, for it cites a wide
range of Coptic, Latin, Greek and Syriac authors (though probably via Arabic
translations).[99]

   The commentary begins by attributing the founding of the churches in Asia,
addressed in Revelation, to John, claiming that he was the one who turned the
inhabitants of Asia away from the worship of Artemis,[100] perhaps in allusion to
the story of the destruction of Artemis' temple and the conversion of her followers found in the *Acts of John*. The commentary goes on to recount the story of
the apostles being allocated their fields of labour, as in the *Prochorus Acts*:

When the apostles apportioned the countries of the world, in order that they should preach
the holy proclamation, namely the gospel, the lot fell to this honoured disciple that he should
go to the country of Asia, which we mentioned previously, and bring them to the correct
faith, which is found in our Lord Jesus Christ. He appointed bishops for them ... [101]

---

[95] For information on the manuscript, see Conybeare, "Ein Zeugnis Ephräms," 192.

[96] Translated by the author from the Latin translation of the text given in Conybeare,
"Ein Zeugnis Ephräms," 193.

[97] Culpepper, *John,* 157.

[98] Roger W. Cowley, *The Traditional Interpretation of the Apocalypse of St John in the
Ethiopian Orthodox Church* (Cambridge: Cambridge University Press, 1983), 73–74.

[99] Cowley, *Traditional Interpretation,* 72–73.

[100] Cowley, *Traditional Interpretation,* 79.

[101] Cowley, *Traditional Interpretation,* 81.

It adds that John appointed bishops in the seven churches of Asia, though the account only names three, those of Ephesus, Smyrna and Pergamum, stating concerning the other four: "we do not know their names". [102]

It then relates that John left that region, intending to travel to Antioch, but was shipwrecked and came to an island, where he saw the vision:

When he left that country in order to go to the country of Antioch, he embarked on a boat, a wind arose against him, the boat was broken, and he sank in the sea. By the will of God the sea brought him up and put him on this island which we mentioned previously. He lived on it for forty days and forty nights, and saw there all this vision [103]

The writer had spoken of the island a little earlier as the place in which John had seen his apocalyptic vision:

The island on which he saw this vision is Fəṭmo, one of the islands of Sälagya of Antioch. This happened in the ninth year after the ascension of our Saviour – to whom be praise – in the second year of the reign of Claudius Caesar, son of Tiberius. [104]

Sälagya is probably rightly identified as Seleucia, the port city of Syrian Antioch, [105] which would locate the apocalyptic vision off of the Syrian coast. This is perhaps related to the statement of Richard of St. Victor (c. 1150) that Patmos was "in the Syrian sea" (*in mari syrico*). [106] There are no such islands near Seleucia, however, and the nearest one, the large island of Cyprus, is eighty miles distant, though it would confront anyone sailing away from the port towards the open Mediterranean, and it was in the Syrian Sea. Possibly this Sälagya tradition is related to the claim that John wrote his Gospel "in Patmos of Cyprus" (ἐν τῇ Πάτμῳ τῆς Κύπρου) found in a medieval Greek prologue to the Gospels. [107]

The commentary places John's vision in this island in both the ninth year after the ascension (i.e. between 38 and 40 C.E) and the second year of Claudius (i.e. 42 CE) (one recension simultaneously places it in the second year after Stephen's death), [108] which suggests that it too, like the *Prochorus Acts* and the Syriac tradition, might have placed the commencement of John's Ephesian ministry (which took place earlier than the exile in this version) in Tiberius' reign. The Geez Commentary does note, however, that according to some, John was exiled

---

[102] Cowley, *Traditional Interpretation*, 81.

[103] Cowley, *Traditional Interpretation*, 81.

[104] Cowley, *Traditional Interpretation*, 81.

[105] Ian Boxall, *Patmos in the Reception History of the Apocalypse* (OTRM; Oxford: Oxford University Press, 2013), 125–26.

[106] Boxall, *Patmos*, 76; cf. *PL* 196:684.

[107] See von Soden, *Die Schriften*, 304.

[108] Cowley, *Traditional Interpretation*, 81.

instead in the ninth year of Domitian, to the island of "Bäṭmus", [109] which is distinguished from Fəṭmo and presumably refers to the Aegean Patmos. [110]

Whereas bar Salibi worked an Antioch mission into his account before John's preaching in Asia, the Geez Commentary has John sail to Antioch from Ephesus. It has also woven the exile tradition into this journey, claiming that before John could reach Antioch, he was shipwrecked on the way at Fəṭmo (apparently a corruption of Patmos), where he saw the vision early in Claudius' reign. A conflation of a Tiberian residence in Asia with a Claudian mission in Antioch perhaps accounts for the mistaken reference to Claudius as the son of Tiberius.

10.6.2. The Apocalypse Andəmta

The Apocalypse *Andəmta*, a collection of various oral traditions on Geez texts written in Amharic, also contains a version of the narrative known to the Geez Commentary, with a few variations. It relates:

> After this, they knew that Jesus had said to them, "Go and teach", and at the time when they went out to teach, having divided up the world by lots, the land of Greece fell to St John. They told him to go and teach. He said, "I will not go to a land where many idols are worshipped; I was always afraid." St Peter encouraged him, saying, "But you, the beloved of the Lord, if we say to you that you will be an example of bravery, will you be an example of cowardice? If we say to you that you will be an example for good, will you be an example for evil? By what will the world be fulfilled for us which says, 'Do not fear those who kill you flesh'?", and he took John, went with him, and returned. [111]

John's expression of fear seems to be related to the claim in the *Prochorus Acts* that John groaned and cried when he learned that his lot was Asia (5). It is probably also related to the account in the Syriac *History of John* in which Jesus appears to John on the third day of his journey to Asia, instructing him not to be afraid (6–7).

The story continues by relating that after John had turned the inhabitants away from worshipping idols, "he went to take teaching to places it had not reached, he went having appointed for them, in place of the seven stars, seven spiritual stars, namely bishops." [112]

This account weaves its story of the shipwreck and the apocalyptic vision into the narrative by placing them during this time in which John was teaching in Syria:

---

[109] Cowley, *Traditional Interpretation*, 82.
[110] Boxall, *Patmos*, 126.
[111] Cowley, *Traditional Interpretation*, 176.
[112] Cowley, *Traditional Interpretation*, 176.

When he was going to and fro, to Syria having taught in Antioch, and to Antioch having taught in Syria [113] he was shipwrecked in the sea of Seleucia. He was on one bit of wreckage and his disciple Prochorus on another, and they entered the island called Patmos. [114]

Thus, this work also speaks of John's preaching in Antioch, and like the Geez Commentary it places it after the Ephesian ministry and associates John's travels to Antioch with a shipwreck near Patmos. A little later, it also dates the writing of Revelation to the ninth year after the ascension, [115] as in the Geez Commentary.

But whereas the Geez Commentary places the shipwreck and apocalyptic vision during John's journey to Antioch, the Apocalypse *Andəmta* places it during a time in which John is already "going to and fro, to Syria having taught in Antioch, and to Antioch having taught in Syria". [116] Both, however, likely represent attempts at harmonizing the early Ephesian ministry with a tradition of John's preaching in Antioch.

10.6.3. The Original Context of the Shipwreck Narrative

A shipwreck tradition is also found in the probably fifth-century [117] *Acts of Timothy*, which relates that John arrived in Ephesus after being shipwrecked on the shore:

For when Nero was raging for the martyrdom of the chief apostles Peter and Paul, and with them their illustrious fellow disciples in different ways, John the great theologian happened to arrive in this radiant metropolis [i.e. Ephesus] after being cast ashore from a shipwreck, as it is possible to learn for those who wish from the things written about him by Irenaeus, bishop of Lugdunum (7). [118]

Unfortunately, the *Acts of Timothy* does not relate where John was when he was shipwrecked, though it was probably near Ephesus. A story from a twelfth- or thirteenth-century codex [119] relates that John and Prochorus sailed in a small boat of cork from Patmos to the shore of a village located eight miles from Miletus, before arriving in Ephesus; [120] possibly this was where the shipwreck

---

[113] Presumably John is envisioned as sailing from the port city Seleucia of Antioch to other cities along the Syrian coast, unless the author has no knowledge of Syrian geography and does not realize that Antioch is in Syria.

[114] Cowley, *Traditional Interpretation*, 177.

[115] Cowley, *Traditional Interpretation*, 178.

[116] Cowley, *Traditional Interpretation*, 177.

[117] Cavan W. Concannon, "The Acts of Timothy: A New Translation and Introduction," in *New Testament Apocrypha: More Noncanonical Scriptures*, vol. 1, ed. Tony Burke and Brent Landau (Grand Rapids: Eerdmans, 2016), 396–97.

[118] Translation in Concannon, "The Acts of Timothy," 403. The Greek text can be found in Hermann Usener, ed., *Acta S. Timothei* (Bonn: Caroli Georgi Universitas, 1877)

[119] Lipsius and Bonnet, *Acta Ioannis*, xxvii.

[120] From the Greek text in Lipsius and Bonnet, *Acta Ioannis*, 159–60.

was held to have taken place. As noted above, the *Acts of John* begins its narrative in Miletus and it may have related that John sailed there (or was shipwrecked near there) from Patmos.

The *Prochorus Acts* possibly still reflects knowledge of this landing near Miletus in its claim that John was washed ashore at Marmareon, near Ephesus. While there is no obvious link between Marmareon and Miletus, besides their proximity to Ephesus, Marmareon seems to be related to the Greek word for marble, μάρμαρον, and Miletus was an important shipment point for the marble trade in Roman times. [121]

There may therefore have been an original Patmos setting for the story of the shipwreck, which has been variously conflated with an Antioch narrative by the *Prochorus Acts* and the Ethiopic texts, the need for which was probably occasioned by a chronological placement of John's Ephesian ministry and the exile which preceded it at the same time as John's Antioch mission. The *Prochorus Acts* has combined the narratives by placing the shipwreck before this early Ephesian ministry while the Ethiopic texts have placed it after it.

The Geez Commentary has maintained the association of the shipwreck with Patmos but has moved the site of the revelations from Patmos to an island near Seleucia. John is said to have seen apocalyptic vision over the course of forty days following the shipwreck. A variant found in a manuscript of the Apocalypse *Andəmta*, which omits any mention of John drifting on the wreckage, records instead that the ship "was driven around for forty days". [122] The time period was no doubt inspired by the account of Moses spending forty days and nights on Sinai (Exod 34:28) and was probably originally associated with the Patmos vision, suggesting that the Geez Commentary has maintained a more original form of the tradition.

In the *Prochorus Acts*, John is said to have been cast adrift for forty days and nights before being washed ashore at Marmareon near Ephesus. However, it employs the Sinai motif of the thunder and lightning on a mountain of Patmos later in its account, when it speaks of the writing of the Gospel, again suggesting that the Sinaitic imagery had originally been associated with John receiving a revelatory experience in Patmos. Presumably this long period of time in which John was cast adrift conveniently enabled the *Prochorus Acts* to account for how John could have been washed ashore so far away from the shipwreck near Seleucia.

Possibly the lost beginning of the *Acts of John* couched John's vision on Patmos in motifs drawn from Moses' experience on Sinai; possibly too it spoke of a shipwreck during John's journeys from Patmos to Ephesus. These motifs were then independently conflated by the *Prochorus Acts* and the Ethiopic texts with

---

[121] Dora P. Crouch, Geology and Settlement: Greco-Roman Patterns (Oxford: Oxford University Press, 2003), 192; Michael Greenhalgh, *Marble Past, Monumental Present: Building With Antiquities in the Mediaeval Mediterranean* (Leiden: Brill, 2009), 118.
[122] Cowley, *Traditional Interpretation*, 177.

an Antioch mission of John, which was contextualised either at around the time of Stephen's death or early in Claudius' reign (see the next chapter for a discussion of the chronological discrepancy). Presumably they did so because of their adoption of a chronology which brought John to Ephesus during Tiberius' reign.

10.7. Ephesus and Beyond

As discussed above, Tertullian is said to have spoken of John being exiled to Patmos from Rome, during Nero's reign, and Irenaeus and Clement of Alexandria spoke of him living in Ephesus in the latter part of the first century, with Irenaeus adding that John remained there until the reign of Trajan. While John's stay in Ephesus is well attested, no extant earlier source addresses the question of when John settled in Ephesus. [123] According to the *Acts of John by Prochorus* (162) and one recension of Ps.-Dorotheus, [124] John was fifty years old and seven months when he settled in Ephesus, which perhaps reflects a tradition which placed John's arrival in the city in the fifties or early sixties. The Syriac *History of John*, mentioned above, makes John to have settled in Ephesus (following an earlier stay in the city) from Jerusalem during the reign of Nero (54–68), [125] and it adds that John was exiled to Patmos in his reign. [126]

10.8. Conclusion

The earliest version of the Johannine tradition seems to have viewed John as ordinarily resident in Jerusalem until Mary's death, probably in the mid–40s, though there may have been tradition of John preaching in Antioch earlier than this. He then laboured in Ephesus, probably in the fifties or early sixties.

This narrative appears to have undergone significant revision as a result of John's identification with the Zebedean John and his subsequent inclusion in

---

[123] Clement of Alexandria (*apud* Eusebius, *Hist. eccl.* 3.23.6–19 = Clement, *Quis div.* 42) only records that John returned to Ephesus after the death of the tyrant.

The conjecture that John arrived in Ephesus during or after the Jewish War lacks any support in the sources. Carson and Moo (*Introduction*, 254) cite Eusebius, *Hist. eccl.* 3.1.1–3, in support of this view, but this passage does not state that John moved to Ephesus after the Jewish War any more than it places Peter's sojourn in Rome or Paul's ministry in Illyricum, also mentioned in the context, at that time. Rather, it speaks generally of the movements of the apostles after the ascension.

[124] Schermann, *Vitae Fabulosae*, 154.

[125] Wright, *Apocryphal Acts*, vol. 2, 9.

[126] Wright, *Apocryphal Acts*, vol. 2, 55.

the tradition of the apostles being sent out after the ascension into their respective fields of labour, which resulted in the placement of John's Ephesian residence, and the Patmos exile which preceded it, in the reign of Tiberius.

Attempts were made to reconcile this with the tradition that Mary remained with John until her death in Jerusalem. Some sources have made Mary to have accompanied John into Asia, where she died and was buried; others have had John miraculously transported back to Jerusalem to witness her death, while others still have brought Mary's death forward chronologically, to the time of the allotment of labours.

Lastly, it was argued that the Tiberian narrative displaced another narrative, according to which John had preached in Antioch. Various different versions of the Antioch tradition were explained as independent attempts at conflating the Asian and Antioch narratives. Thus, bar Salibi placed the Antioch mission prior to John's Asian residence, and the *Prochorus Acts* placed John's shipwreck, which took place *en route* to Ephesus, near Seleucia of Antioch. The Ethiopic texts, on the other hand, have John first go to Ephesus and then later to Syria, though they have conflated the Syrian narrative with the Patmos exile.

Chapter 11

The Parallel Lives of John and Mark

The general outline of John's movements, including an Antioch mission shortly after Stephen's death, a short stay in Seleucia, a journey to Cyprus, a final departure from Judea in the 40s and a residence in Ephesus and Asia Minor in the 50s, yield a number of correlations with the John/Mark narrative. Indeed, sometimes the John/Mark narrative seems to throw light on the otherwise confused and conflated traditions found in the Johannine sources of the previous chapter. This chapter will identify these various correlations, and it will conclude that the complementarity of the narratives suggests that John/Mark and John the Evangelist may have once been identified.

11.1. The Preaching in Antioch

The *Acts of Mark* relates that Mark journeyed with Barnabas to Antioch, where together they preached the gospel. It adds that after spending some time in Antioch, John/Mark journeyed to Seleucia, where he preached the gospel and where he was eventually imprisoned (*Act. Marc.* 6).

As discussed in the previous chapter, the *Prochorus Acts* and the two Ethiopic texts seem to represent differing attempts at conflating John's stay in Ephesus with an early ministry in Antioch and Seleucia, such as is found in the *Acts of Mark*. Thus, while the *Acts of Mark* records that Mark was arrested and imprisoned in Seleucia, the *Prochorus Acts* relates that Prochorus is arrested and imprisoned in Seleucia, while John is cast adrift for forty day and nights until he is washed ashore at Marmareon.

The Ethiopic texts have instead placed John's ministry in Antioch after his residence in Ephesus. The account of John's being cast adrift onto the (non-existent) island of Fəṭmo near Seleucia, at this time, as told by Geez Commentary, or to an island in the Sea of Seleucia, in the Apocalypse *Andəmta*, may represent additional conflations of Mark's imprisonment in Seleucia with the Johannine exile and shipwreck tradition.

As discussed in Chapter 5, the *Acts of Mark* seems to place the journeys of Mark during the time in which the Hellenist Christians travelled "as far as Phoenicia, Cyprus and Antioch" (Acts 11:19). The first of the two dates for John's shipwreck given in one recension of the Geez Commentary, the second year after Stephen's death (sometime in the period c. 36–39), may correspond to the time that Mark arrived in Seleucia according to the *Acts of Mark*.

The *Acts of Mark* continues by relating that Mark then spent much time in Caesarea of Palestine (*Act. Marc.* 6) before sailing to Cyprus, where he is said to have travelled around the island, performing great miracles. Possibly it is this narrative that underlies the claim of the Ethiopic texts that John was cast adrift to an island near Seleucia, since there are no other islands in the vicinity. Conflation of the Cypriot ministry with the Patmos tradition is perhaps also reflected in the curious claim that John wrote his Gospel "in Patmos of Cyprus" (ἐν τῇ Πάτμῳ τῆς Κύπρου), which is found in a medieval Greek prologue to the Gospels. [1]

11.2. John/Mark's Return to Antioch from Pamphylia

The *Acts of Mark* continues by relating that Mark, after preaching throughout the island of Cyprus, sailed to Pamphylia in Asia. There he wished, according to the *Acts of Barnabas* (5) and the *Acts of Mark* (8), to travel west but was prevented by the Spirit. Possibly this was responsible for the claim that John and Prochorus boarded an Egyptian ship at Joppa headed for "western lands", found in the *Prochorus Acts* (7).

From Pamphylia, Mark returned to Antioch, as he heard that Paul and Barnabas were there (*Act. Marc.*7), before returning to Jerusalem (*Act. Marc.* 8), whence he departed to Rome with Peter (*Act. Marc.* 9). The journey to Pamphylia and Cyprus is perhaps reflected in the claim of Syriac manuscript 16401, discussed in the previous chapter, that when John "went out from exile, he preached in the whole of Asia, and in all the islands next to Asia".

This manuscript also claims that John, after his exile, "preached the gospel from the first year in which Claudius reigned [41 CE] until the sixth year of Trajan [103 CE]." [2] The date given for John's release from exile, the first year of Claudius, possibly correlates to John/Mark's departure from Cyprus. The *Acts of Mark* does not provide any specific details as to when Mark travelled through the island, but it does correlate Mark's later return to Jerusalem with Peter's departure from Jerusalem to Rome (*Act. Marc.* 9), which, as was argued earlier in the study, was informed by the tradition in the *Acts of Peter* of Peter's departure to Rome in the twelfth year after the ascension (cf. Jerome's placement of Peter's departure in the second year of Claudius, or 42 CE, in *Vir.* 1).

---

[1] See von Soden, *Die Schriften*, 304.

[2] Translated by the author from the French translation in Esbroeck, "Deux listes d'apôtres," 22.

The Geez Commentary's placement of the shipwreck, which occurs on the journey to Antioch, in the second year of Claudius possibly corresponds with the date of Mark's return to Antioch from Pamphylia in the *Acts of Mark*.

11.3. Publication in Syria

Both John and Mark are associated with literary activities in Antioch, possibly also at a time corresponding to the dispersal of the Hellenistic Christians.

11.3.1. The Peshitta

The translation of the Syriac Peshitta version of the Old Testament is attributed to Mark by the East Syriac Lectionary entitled the *Garden of Delights* (*Gannat Bussame*), which was possibly written in the tenth century and which made use of many older sources, including Isho'dad and Theodore of Mopsuestia:

> Some people report that Mark himself translated the Old Testament from Hebrew into Syriac, and that he presented his translation to James, the brother of our Lord, and to the Apostles, who appended their approbation to it and gave it to the inhabitants of Syria. [3]

The mention of James and the apostles is consistent with a setting for Mark's Syrian activities during the initial expansion of Christianity into Syria following the martyrdom of Stephen (cf. Acts 8:1; 11:19), for those who were dispersed remained under the oversight of the Jerusalem church (cf. Acts 11:22), and the apostles were still said to have been resident in Jerusalem at that time (cf. Acts 8:14).

The same tradition was known to a ninth-century Muslim convert from Christianity named 'Ali ibn Rabban al-Tabari, who attributes quotations from the Old Testament Peshitta to "the books of the Syrians which Marcus has translated". [4] The attribution of the Peshitta to Mark is of unknown derivation. It was not universal: Bar Hebraeus knew three different theories of the Peshitta's origins, none of which attributed it to Mark. [5]

---

[3] Translation in Alphonso Mingana, *The Book of Religion and Empire* (Manchester: Manchester University Press, 1922), xx–xxi; cf. Michael Weitzman, *The Syriac Version of the Old Testament* (UCOP 56; Cambridge: Cambridge University Press, 2005), 248. The edited Syriac text with accompanying German translation is found in G. J. Reinink, ed. and trans., *Gannat Bussame, I, I. Die Adventssonntage* (CSCO 501–2; Leuven: Peeters, 1988); I was unable to locate this quotation in that edition, however.

[4] Mingana, *Religion and Empire*, 95, 98, 78; Cf. Weitzman, *The Syriac Version of the Old Testament*, 147, 249.

[5] Weitzman, *The Syriac Version*, 249.

11.3.2. The Writing of the Gospel in Antioch

Mark is also associated with the writing of a Gospel in Antioch; the medieval Islamic scholar Ibn Hazm of Cordoba (994–1064) claims that Mark wrote "his Gospel in Greek at Antioch"; he places this twenty-two years after the ascension, or in the early fifties, [6] though Ephrem, as discussed in Chapter 2, spoke of John/Mark and Lucius as having written their Gospels before "the discipleship of Paul", perhaps meaning that they wrote before the first missionary journey (c. 47–48 CE) during which Mark accompanied Barnabas and Paul.

The time at which Ephrem claimed that Mark wrote his Gospel could correspond with that of Mark's return to Antioch after his first missionary journey, as told in the *Acts of Mark*. Possibly a vestige of this is preserved in the *Acts of Barnabas* (6), where Paul is angry with John/Mark for delaying in Pamphylia with the "parchments" (μεμβράναι) rather than journeying directly to Antioch (*Act. Barn.* 6).

John is also said to have written a Gospel in Antioch by Ephrem in his commentary on the *Diatessaron*, who writes that "John wrote that [Gospel] in Greek, at Antioch". Evidence that John's writing was also placed in some sources at a time corresponding to the end of Mark's first missionary journey is provided by a twelfth-century Byzantine prologue, mentioned in the previous chapter, which claims that John wrote eleven years after the ascension, or about the time of John/Mark's return to Antioch, and that Luke wrote fifteen years after it, which would be around the time of the famine visit to Jerusalem (c. 45 CE; Acts 12:25; 13:1) and before Paul's first missionary journey; it adds that Luke's Gospel was addressed to Theophilus in Antioch. [7]

A few other Greek colophons relate that "John composed the Gospel named according to him after he returned to Ephesus from Paphos." [8] The city of Paphos was located on the southwestern coast of Cyprus and it is mentioned in the book of Acts as the city from which Paul, Barnabas and John/Mark sailed to Perga in Pamphylia in Asia Minor (Acts 13:13). The notice may reflect a narrative of John/Mark sailing from Cyprus to Pamphylia and then to Antioch, as in the *Acts of Mark*, and of his writing a Gospel in Antioch, only in this version, John is made to sail to Ephesus to write his Gospel rather than to Antioch via Pamphylia, in an apparent correction prompted by the dominant Johannine tradition of John's writing in Ephesus at the request of the Asian elders

---

[6] Muhammad Abu Laylah, *The Qur'an and the Gospels: A Comparative Study* (Cairo: El-Falah, 2005), 89, citing Ibn Hazm, *Al-Faisal*, vol. 2 (Cairo, Subayh, 1964), 20; Theodore Pulcini, *Exegesis as Polemical Discourse: Ibn Ḥazm on Jewish and Christian Scriptures* (Atlanta: Scholars Press, 1998), 101.

[7] Manuscript ε1135 = 1051. See: von Soden, *Die Schriften*, 298. The Byzantine colophons usually state that John wrote 30 or 32 years after the ascension (cf. Furlong, *Identity of John*, 118).

[8] See von Soden, *Die Schriften*, 312.

or bishops (cf. Clement of Alexandria, *apud* Eusebius, *Hist. eccl.* 6.14.5–7; *Canon Muratori*, ll. 9–16;[9] Victorinus, *Comm. Apoc.* 11.1; Jerome, *Comm. Matt.* pref.).

The *History of John*, which seems to have known the work of Ephrem (or vice versa),[10] perhaps also provides evidence for the conflation of an Antioch and Ephesus narrative of the writing of John's Gospel. It relates that when the apostles Peter and Paul "heard all that had happened in the whole country of the Ephesians", they came to Ephesus and persuaded John to write a Gospel:

> Peter and Paul entered Ephesus on a Monday, and for five days they were persuading him, while rejoicing, to compose a Gospel, but he was not willing, saying to them, "When the Spirit of holiness will it, I will write." And on the Sunday, at night, at the time when our Lord arose from the grave, the Apostles slumbered and slept. And at that glorious time of the Resurrection, the Spirit of holiness descended, and the whole place, in which they were dwelling, was in a flame; and those men who were awake, awakened their fellows, and they were amazed. And John took paper, and wrote his Gospel in one hour, and gave it to Paul and to Peter. And when the sun rose, they went down to the house of prayer, and read it before the whole city, and prayed, and partook of the body and blood of our Lord Jesus. And they came to the holy (man), and remained with him thirty days; and then they came to Jerusalem, to James, the brother of our Lord, and from there they came to Antioch.[11]

Bar Hebraeus provides a condensed version of this account, which he wrongly attributes to Eusebius, saying "And Eusebius says that Peter and Paul came to him to Ephesus and persuaded him to wrote (*Comm. Iohan.* prolog.).[12]

The narrative in the *History of John* seems to place the writing of John's Gospel at the time of the Syrian mission, when Peter and Paul were in Antioch (cf. Acts 11:25–27; Gal 2:11–13) and when James was overseeing the work in the city (cf. Acts 11:22; 12:17). It certainly is not consistent with the dominant Johannine tradition that John wrote in his old age at the request of the Asian elders. Indeed, here, Peter and Paul fill the role otherwise afforded to those Asian elders, presumably because in its source, they were present at Antioch when Mark wrote his Gospel.

The *History of John* concludes the account by relating that after John wrote his Gospel, Peter and Paul went to James in Jerusalem before journeying to Antioch. This echoes the account in the East Syriac *Garden of Delights*, which related that Mark translated the Old Testament into Syriac and brought it to James, who approved its use, possibly suggesting that the two narratives are variants of a common tradition.

---

[9] Numbered according to the corrected Latin text in Souter, *Text and Canon*, 208–11.

[10] Junod and Kaestli, *Acta Iohannis*, vol. 2, 748–49.

[11] The English translation is taken, with minor changes, from Wright, *Apocryphal Acts*, vol. 2, 58–59.

[12] Carr, *Bar-Hebraeus*, 136.

11.3.3. The Hebrew Gospel of Matthew

Both Mark and John are also associated with a Hebrew version of Matthew's Gospel. The *Acts of Barnabas* relates that during Barnabas and Mark's final Cypriot mission, Barnabas would heal the sick by placing upon them "a book in God's voice (Hebrew?), a writing of wonders and instructions", which he had been given by Matthew (*Act. Barn.* 15). In the *Acts of Barnabas* and the *Encomium of Barnabas*, Mark is later said to have deposited Barnabas' remains in a cave, together with the "lessons" (μαθήματα) which Barnabas had received from Matthew (*Act. Barn.* 24; *Encom. Barn.* 750–52).

There is also a tradition that John translated the Hebrew Gospel of Matthew into Greek, which is found in Eutychius, [13] Theophylact [14] and in a number of prologue readings found in Greek manuscripts from the tenth century and later. [15]

11.3.4. A Common Source of the Traditions

All these traditions of John and Mark variously composing or translating a writing are likely connected, arising from a variously-recycled narrative. Possibly it had related that John/Mark translated a Hebrew Gospel of Matthew into Greek at Antioch at the end of his first missionary journey, which was later brought to Jerusalem for approval. This may have been reinterpreted into the claim that he had translated the Peshitta, since the translation of the Gospel had come to be associated with John the Evangelist. This translation of a Gospel into Greek then came to be interpreted as his composing of a Gospel in Greek, and the tradition was then later passed down under the names of both John and Mark, in conformity to the pattern of the reduplication of traditions.

11.4. The Dormition Traditions

The traditions that John remained in Jerusalem until Mary's death, usually placed around ten to fifteen years after the ascension, or in the 40s, may correlate with John/Mark's presumably final departure from Jerusalem at the time

---

[13] *PG* 111:981.

[14] Greek text in von Soden, *Die Schriften*, 322.

[15] See Constantin von Tischendorf, Caspar René Gregory, and Ezra Abbot, eds., *Novum Testamentum Graece*, vol. 1 (Leipzig: Giesecke & Devrient, 1869–94), 211. Cf. von Soden, *Die Schriften*, 298.

of his journey to Antioch in the company of Barnabas and Paul (cf. Acts 12:25), which is usually dated around 46 CE but may have been earlier. [16]

The dormition traditions are possibly reflected, howbeit in a confused way, in Severus' *Homily*. As noted in Chapter 3, Severus has a unique account of Mark's baptism in which he and his mother were baptised by John at the request of Mary, Jesus' mother. Severus' version of Mark's baptism, which departs from the tradition that Mark was baptised by Peter, may reflect an attempt at reconciling traditions which associated John/Mark and his mother Mary with John and Mary, the mother of Jesus.

Later in Severus' account, Mark is said to have sailed to Jerusalem from Rome after being commissioned to preach in Egypt, in order to receive a last blessing from his mother Mary before her death. This would parallel the dormition tradition of John the Evangelist departing Jerusalem following Mary's death in the city. The account goes on to relate that as John/Mark was seeking a ship to Barca, the Virgin Mary appeared to him, instructing him to go to Egypt. [17] Mark is thus blessed by his mother Mary and commissioned by Mary the (adopted) mother of John. Probably the earlier form of the tradition associated John/Mark with the dormition, with Mary having been constructed into two different figures as a consequence of the loss of the identification of John/Mark with John the Evangelist.

The tradition that John remained with Mary until her death, related by Arethas and other sources, is possibly reflected in the version of the story of Mark's abandonment of Paula and Barnabas (Acts 13:4–13) found in the *Encomium of SS. Peter and Paul* (*Enc. Petri et Pauli* 102), Severus' *Homily* [18] and in the *Encomium of Barnabas* (411–12); while Acts states that Mark returned to Jerusalem (Acts 13:13), these sources add that he returned "to his mother".

11.5. The Desertion

The book of Acts records that after travelling to Antioch, Mark accompanied Paul and Barnabas through Cyprus before abandoning the mission at Perga, from whence he returned to Jerusalem (Acts 13:4–13). As discussed previously, a number of later versions of this story attribute Mark's abandonment of

---

[16] Riesner places it c. 45 (*Paul's Early Period*, 136); cf. Martin Hengel and Anna Maria Schwemer, *Paul between Damascus and Antioch: The Unknown Years* (Louisville, Ky.: Westminster John Knox, 1997), 243, who place it in 44/45.

[17] Bargès, *Homélie sur St Marc,* 39–42.

[18] Bargès, *Homélie sur St Marc*, 26–27.

the mission to cowardice, on account of seeing the afflictions that the apostles endured.

Mark's departure from Asia on account of cowardice is possibly reflected in the various claims that John exhibited fear and/or cowardice at entering his assigned labours. Thus, in the Syriac *History of John*, Jesus appears to John while he is journeying to Asia and exhorts him not to be afraid (6–7). In the *Prochorus Acts*, John began weeping when he discovered that his lot was to go to Asia, on account of the afflictions he would face in the sea, but he repents in the presence of Peter (5). Similarly, the Apocalypse *Andəmta* records that when John learned that his lot was to preach in the land of Greece, he did not wish to journey there, saying: "I will not go to a land where many idols are worshiped; I was always afraid." Peter then rebukes him for being "an example of cowardice" and accompanies him there himself before returning (presumably to Jerusalem). [19] The reference to the accompaniment of Peter perhaps represents conflation with the account of Mark and Peter preaching together in Bethany following the ascension, related by Mawhub (*Hist. Patr. Eccl. Alex.* 1.1), and with Prochorus' accompaniment of John to Patmos found in the *Prochorus Acts*.

11.6. The Further Travels of Mark

The second Cypriot mission of Barnabas and Mark does not seem to be reflected in the Johannine tradition, unless it is encompassed in the statement found in Syriac manuscript 16401 that John preached in "the islands next to Asia".

As noted in the discussion of the Cypriot narratives in Chapter 4, Mark seems to have been understood as journeying to Ephesus from Cyprus following Barnabas' martyrdom, sometime in the early reign of Nero (c. 54). Indeed, as discussed in Chapter 1, the imprisonment of Paul spoken of in Colossians (Col 4:10), at which time Mark was with Paul, is often thought to have taken place in Ephesus around the year 54. 2 Tim 4:11 speaks of Mark being summoned from Asia Minor to Rome by the apostle Paul, probably in the early or mid-60s. And as noted in Chapter 4, the *Life of Auxibius* claimed that after finding Paul (probably in Ephesus), Mark remained with the apostle until his death, presumably in Rome.

These movements correspond comfortably with the Johannine tradition. John is said in the *Prochorus Acts* (162) to have been fifty years old when he arrived in Ephesus, which would likely correspond to the decade of the 50s and

---

[19] Cowley, *Traditional Interpretation*, 176.

almost certainly no later than the early 60s; and the Syriac *History of John* claims that John settled in Ephesus during Nero's reign (54–68). [20]

Furthermore, John was also placed in Rome at about the time at which Mark was summoned to the city by Paul. Thus, Tertullian stated that John was immersed in boiling oil at Rome, which he speaks of in the same context as the martyrdoms of Peter and Paul, which are usually placed around 65–67 C.E; he added that John was then sent into exile. Furthermore, Jerome cited Tertullian as placing the immersion in oil during the reign of Nero. Thus, the John of tradition was in Ephesus and Rome at roughly the same time as John/Mark.

Clement of Alexandria relates that John returned to Ephesus from exile "after the death of the tyrant" (*Quis div.* 42), who was interpreted in the previous chapter of Nero. Clement goes on to relate that John travelled through Asia Minor, appointing bishops and ordering the churches (*Quis div.* 42). The *Acts of John* may suggest that John visited the seven churches of Asia in order (see Chapter 10). According to Irenaeus, John remained in Ephesus until his death in Trajan's reign (*apud* Eusebius, *Hist. eccl.* 3.23.4 = Irenaeus, *Haer.* 2.22.5); the *Acts of John* relates how he was buried near Ephesus (106–15).

The John/Mark traditions go more or less silent after he is brought to Rome during Nero's reign, at which point the Johannine tradition becomes clearly attested. This may be because that the Johannine narrative was mostly preserved under the name of John/Mark for the early years and John the Evangelist for the later ones. A possible exception to this dearth of traditions is perhaps to be found in the scattered notices concerning his death. Calmet seems to have known of a tradition of John/Mark's burial in Ephesus, for after relating the claims of the Greeks that John/Mark was called an apostle and had healed the sick in Ephesus with his shadow, he remarks that the tomb of John/Mark (whom he distinguishes from Mark the Evangelist) had been celebrated in Ephesus. [21] Unfortunately no further details are provided.

Also of interest is the notice given in the *Synopsis*, wrongly attributed to Dorotheus of Tyre (d. c. 361) and perhaps written between the sixth and eighth century, which provides a summary of the account of Mark's martyrdom in the *Martyrdom of Mark*, which it dates to the reign of Trajan. [22] A similar account in the *Chronicon Paschale* (seventh century) likewise places the martyrdom of "Mark, the evangelist and bishop of Alexandria" during Trajan's reign. [23] While this may

---

[20] Wright, *Apocryphal Acts*, vol. 2, 9.
[21] Calmet, *Dictionnaire historique,* vol. 2, 661.
[22] Translated by the author from the Greek text in von Soden, *Die Schriften*, 307.
[23] Greek text in Lightfoot, *Apostolic Fathers,* part 1, vol. 1, 65.

be an unrelated and coincidental mistake, [24] it might also reflect the tradition of John's death in the reign of Trajan, as Bacon has suggested. [25]

Lastly, the death of John/Mark is remembered by both the Greeks and Latins on 27 September, [26] which also happens to be the day after which the repose of John the Evangelist is remembered in the Eastern Church. [27] Furthermore, 27 September was observed in the Ethiopic tradition as the feast day of the sons of Zebedee, [28] and as the feast day of John's exile in 's-Hertogenbosch in the Netherlands. [29] These things again might again evince evidence that John/Mark and John the Evangelist were once confused or identified, before John/Mark came to be identified with Mark the Evangelist and John with John the son of Zebedee.

By contrast, the feast day of the Apostle John in the West is 27 December; the same date is given as that on which James and John received their crowns (of martyrdom) in Jerusalem, according to the Syriac martyrology, composed in Edessa in 411 from Greek sources. [30] The Armenian martyrology, from perhaps as early as the third century, remembers this John on 28 December, along with his brother James. [31] The feast day of Mark the Evangelist, commemorating his martyrdom in Alexandria, is remembered on 26 April in the Coptic Church (found already in the *Martyrdom of Mark* written sometime between the second and fourth century) and 25 April in the Roman Catholic, Eastern Orthodox and West Syriac Churches.

---

[24] Compare the confusion in the *Martyrdom of Mark* concerning the reign in which Mark was martyred, discussed in Chapter 1. Of course this confusion may actually have arisen on account of the conflation of three separate figures.

[25] Benjamin W. Bacon, *The Beginnings of Gospel Story: A Historical-Critical Inquiry into the Sources and Structure of the Gospel According to Mark, With Expository Notes Upon the Text, For English Readers* (New Haven, Conn.: Yale University Press, 1909), 120 n.1.

[26] Calmet, *Dictionnaire historique*, vol. 2, 661.

[27] Culpepper, *John*, 172; Gumerlock, "Chromatius of Aquileia," 62 n. 2; cf. Eisler, *Enigma*, 126.

[28] Eisler, *Enigma*, 61–2.

[29] Culpepper, *John*, 173.

[30] Marie-Émile Boismard, *Le martyre de Jean l'apôtre* (CRB 35; Paris, Gabalda, 1996), 21–22.

[31] See William D. Davies and Dale C. Allison Jr., *A Critical and Exegetical Commentary on the Gospel according to Saint Matthew*, vol. 3 (ICC; Edinburgh: T. & T. Clark, 1997), 91 n. 39; cf. Eisler, *Enigma*, 60.

11.7. Conclusion

While the confused state of medieval traditions in general would no doubt yield a number of correlations between any two figures,[32] a consistent pattern emerges in the case of John and Mark that seems to go beyond any chance configuration. While some of these correlations could be coincidental, the extent of the correlations for John and Mark is untypical for separate figures and is perhaps otherwise unattested. Certainly, such correlation does not exist between John/Mark and Mark the Evangelist, where the two figures have had to merged in ways that leave behind an obvious trail of conflation.

Thus, in each case, the narrative begins in Jerusalem and proceeds through Antioch, Seleucia, Cyprus and Antioch. Traditions concerning John the Evangelist are silent during the time of John/Marks mission with Paul and Barnabas and his later Cypriot mission with Barnabas, but both figures appear in Asia Minor in the 50s and in Rome in the 60. Both are attested as being buried in Ephesus, both are said to have died in Trajan's reign, and the death of both is remembered at the same time.

This unintended complementarity may suggest that the two were identified in ancient sources. Indeed, since there is often no obvious priority of tradition (e.g. the placement of both Mark and John in Ephesus and Rome during Nero's reign is independently and anciently attested for both), it may be that the two figures were identified on a historical (that is, actual) level, though an examination of this question would go beyond the scope of the present study. It can, however, be noted that John/Mark correlates well with the Beloved Disciple of the Fourth Gospel (Jerusalemite, learned, aristocratic, priestly connections), and as noted in the Introduction, a number of scholars have argued that John/Mark was the Beloved Disciple.

Two different processes seem to have converged to obscure this complementarity. First, John's early Antioch ministry and his departure from Jerusalem following Mary's death were likely been displaced by the narrative of his Asian residence in Tiberius' reign. Secondly, John/Mark's movements (particularly the later ones) have been somewhat obscured in the sources by the various attempts at conforming his narrative to those of Mark the Evangelist and the Alexandrian Mark, even in some cases despite the attestation of these journeys in canonical texts.

---

[32] E.g. both John and Luke are said to have died in Ephesus (ε 530 = miniscule 724, from c. 1520 CE, in von Soden, *Die Schriften*, 307); there is also the claim that the gospel of Luke was written "with St. Peter having entrusted it" (von Soden, *Die Schriften*, 303–4), which is an obvious mistake for "Paul".

Chapter 12

The Origins of the Shared Traditions

In this study, attention has been drawn to traditions shared by John/Mark and John the Evangelist. These have included the placement of John/Mark in narratives derived from the Fourth Gospel, sometimes in roles otherwise associated with the Beloved Disciple, including his presence at the wedding at Cana and his role as host of the Last Supper and as a witness of the crucifixion; the reduplication of Markan and Johannine traditions, such as the attribution to both of a father named Aristobulus and the description of both as a priest wearing the sacerdotal plate; and the attribution to both Mark and John of a narrative framework which begins in Jerusalem and ends in Ephesus, via Syria, Asia Minor and Rome. Notice was also made of the attribution to Mark of a Gospel containing a Logos theology and/or doctrine of the divinity of Christ

This chapter will attempt to identify the origins and the sources of the Johannine and Markan versions of these traditions and to delineate their transmission. The suggested sources will be Hegesippus' *Memoirs* for the non-Zebedean portrayals of John in western sources, a lost Gospel prologue, perhaps drawn from Hegesippus, for the depiction of Mark as a priest, Africanus' *Chronography* for the Coptic traditions of Mark and for the *Acts of Mark* and a lost Cypriot source of Barnabas' mission and martyrdom for the Cypriot works. It will also be suggested that there was a now lost, unidentified common source from which all these traditions drew, and which provided an account of John/Mark's early life and Syrian mission which was used by Hegesippus, Africanus, the *Acts of Mark* and the Syriac Johannine traditions.

These reconstructions are, of course, only speculative and tentative in nature. It will perhaps be impossible to more clearly identify the sources and the process of transmission by which the traditions were reduplicated.

12.1 The Source of the Johannine Reduplicated Traditions

It can be noted that, generally speaking, the reduplicated traditions are extant under the name of Mark in Coptic and Cypriot sources and in the *Acts of Mark*, and under the name of John in western, Latin sources. Greek and Syriac sources, however, exhibit variation. The association of these traditions with either Mark or John can be summarised as follows:

Table 12.1: Reduplicated Traditions

	Latin	*Acts of Mark*	Cypriot	Greek	Coptic	Syrian
Aristocrat	John [1]	Mark	X	Mark [2] / John [3]	Mark [4]	X
Aristobulus	John [5]	X	Mark [6]	Mark [7] / John [8]	Mark [9]	X
Cana	X	Mark*	X	X	Mark [10]	X
Carrying Water	X	Mark	Mark [11]	John [12]	Mark [13]	X
Passover	X	Mark	Mark [14]	John [15]	Mark [16]	X
Naked Youth	John [17]	X	X	Mark / James [18]	Mark / James [19]	John [20]
Virgin	John [21]	X	X	John [22]	Mark [23]	John [24]
Priest	Mark [25]	X	X	John [26]	X	X

* Implied.

---

[1] Jerome (*Epist.* 127.5).

[2] Procopius the Deacon (*Encom. in Marc.*).

[3] *Memorial of Saint John*.

[4] Severus (*Hom. St. Marc.*).

[5] Julian Peter, Heleca and possibly Braulio of Saragossa (590–651).

[6] Archbishop Kyprianos makes Mary, Mark's mother, the daughter of Aristobulus.

[7] The *Menaion* makes Aristobulus the brother of Barnabas.

[8] The *Synaxarion of Constantinople*.

[9] Mawhub (*Hist. Patr. Eccl. Alex.* 1.1); Ibn Kabar (*lamp. tenebr.*).

[10] Mawhub (*Hist. Patr. Eccl. Alex.* 1.1); Ibn Kabar (*lamp. tenebr.*).

[11] *Encomium of Barnabas*.

[12] Epiphanius the Monk (*Vit. Virg.* 20).

[13] Mawhub (*Hist. Patr. Eccl. Alex.* 1.1); Ibn Kabar (*lamp. tenebr.*).

[14] *Encomium of Barnabas*.

[15] Hippolytus of Thebes, *Chron.* 4.

[16] Mawhub (*Hist. Patr. Eccl. Alex.* 1.1); Ibn Kabar (*lamp. tenebr.*).

[17] Ambrose (*Enarrat. Ps. 36*, 53). Peter Chrysologus (*Sermo*, 78; cf. 150, 170); Gregory the Great (*Mor.* 14.57), Bede (*In Marci Evang. Exp.* 14).

[18] Both names are mentioned in an Arabic marginal note in a Coptic manuscript.

[19] James in Epiphanius (*Pan.* 78.13.3); James or Mark in a Greek catena.

[20] Isho'dad of Merv (*Comm. Marc.* 10).

[21] Tertullian (*De. mon.* 17); Jerome (*Jov.* 1.26).

[22] *Acts of John* 113; Methodius of Patara (*De res.* 1.59.6).

[23] Severus (*Hom. St. Marc.*).

[24] Ephrem (*Virg.* 15.4).

[25] *Monarch. Prolog.* Marc.; the *Early Commentary on Mark*; Bede (*In Marci Evang. Exp.* Epist. ad Accam); the two Hiberno-Latin manuscripts; the *Passion of Mark*.

[26] Polycrates (*apud* Eusebius, *Hist. eccl.* 5.24.2).

The Johannine form of the traditions are sometimes attested early. The identification of John as the young man who fled naked is already found in Ambrose of Milan (c. 340–397). This tradition could not have arisen in connection with the Zebedean John, who was one of the twelve apostles who are said to have fled before the crucifixion (Mark 14:27, 51; Matt 26:31–35, 56b). Perhaps it arose from the identification of the young man with the Beloved Disciple, who followed Jesus after his arrest (John 18:15), as in Bede (*In Marci Evang. Exp.* 14); and/or it may have been related to the tradition of Mark as the owner of the house in which the supper was held.

Jerome (c. 347–420) preserves a non-Zebedean depiction of John as an aristocratic Jerusalemite, which is discordant with any identification of this figure with John the son of Zebedee, even if Jerome harbours no suspicion that he was dealing with a conflated figure. His depiction is associated with the Beloved Disciple, but it may also be related to the depiction of John/Mark as belonging to Jerusalem's social elite.

Another non-Zebedean depiction of John is furnished at the end of the second century by Polycrates, who speaks of him as a priest wearing the priestly crown. There are no indications that the Apostle John was of priestly background or that he was a Levite. Mark, however, did have Levitical connections and may have been a Levite himself; there are also portrayals of Mark as a priest, first found in extant sources in the late fourth-century Monarchian Prologue to Mark.

Thus, Johannine forms of the reduplicated traditions are attested from the early centuries of the era, and any potential common source must therefore be even older. This, along with the predominantly western provenance of the reduplicated traditions in their Johannine form may point to Hegesippus as a probable source of the western traditions, for he published his *Memoirs* in Rome sometime between 150 and 180.[27] His *Memoirs*, furthermore, were known to Jerome. The Palestinian subject matter of the traditions is also consistent with Hegesippus, whose work is said to have related traditions concerning the relatives of the Lord (*apud* Eusebius, *Hist. eccl.* 3.20.1).

Hegesippus also recorded that James was ordained as the first bishop of Jerusalem and provided an account of his martyrdom (*apud* Eusebius, *Hist. eccl.* 2.23.3–18). Furthermore, he related traditions concerning Simeon, the second bishop of the Jerusalem church (4.22.4–6), the Jewish sects (4.22.7) and other unwritten Jewish traditions (4.22.8). As discussed in Chapter 7, Hippolytus of Thebes in his *Chronicle* speaks about the ordination of James in the context of relating dormition traditions, which were perhaps also derived from Hegesippus. It was also suggested that Hegesippus had been the source of the Zion traditions in Epiphanius and Eutychius.

---

[27] Ralph P. Martin, *James* (WBC 48; Dallas: Word, 1998), xlix; Painter, *Just James*, 113.

The nature of Hegesippus' work is indicated by Jerome, who speaks of him as "composing together all the histories of ecclesiastical events (*ecclesiasticorum actuum texens historias*) from the passion of the Lord until his own time" (*Vir.* 22). Jerome's *texens* ("weaving") here may suggest that Hegesippus wove various histories into a single narrative.

Possibly this "weaving" of narratives resulted in the conflation, found in the Greek *Menaion*, of John's father, Aristobulus, with a probably distinct Judean figure of the same name who was said to have been one of the Seventy, as well as with a missionary of the same name who is said to have been ordained as a bishop by Paul and sent to Britain, where he died. [28] Heleca, bishop of Saragossa (590–651), similarly writes that Aristobulus, whom he identifies with Zebedee, was one of the seventy-two disciples and that he was sent to "England" from Rome, where he was martyred in the second year of Nero. [29] These conflations are absent from Coptic sources, which maintain the Aristobulus tradition within a Markan context.

12.1.1. Mark the Priest

The tradition of Mark as a priest, found in the Monarchian Prologue, the Valois fragment and other sources is unique among the reduplicated traditions for two reasons: it is preserved in western sources under the name of Mark, rather than John, and (as already noted) there are no equivalents to be found among Coptic or Cypriot sources or in the *Acts of Mark*, which only relate that Mark was of Levitical heritage. It was argued in Chapter 8 that Hegesippus was the source for this depiction of Mark; this is problematic however, for the thesis that the western reduplicated traditions were also drawn from him, since these are preserved under the name of John.

Any answer is necessarily speculative. Possibly Hegesippus variously spoke of the same figure as both John and Mark. While he perhaps generally spoke of him under the name of John, the name of Mark might have been employed in the priestly context on account of its inclusion of the epithet of ὁ κολοβοδάκτυλος, which was perhaps intertwined with the pun on his name of *murcus*.

Possibly this depiction of John/Mark as a priest wearing the sacerdotal plate was later employed in a primitive Gospel prologue, which spoke of his teaching concerning the divine Logos, which would have then been later modified by the Anti-Marcionite Prologue to Mark and the Monarchian Prologue to Mark. Hippolytus' reference to Mark as ὁ κολοβοδάκτυλος was also mentioned in the context of his claim that Mark's Gospel answered Marcion's errors concerning

---

[28] See Ussher, *Works*, vol. 5, 20; cf. *Prologue from Ochrid* (March 16). The Aristobulus known as the bishop of Britain may have instead been a missionary to Britonia (modern Mondonedo), in Spain; see ODC 103.

[29] Ussher, *Works*, vol. 5, 21.

the Logos, perhaps because he too drew from a primitive Gospel prologue which both spoke of Mark as ὁ κολοβοδάκτυλος and which characterised his Gospel as one containing a Logos doctrine. Hippolytus apparently knew, however, that this Mark, ὁ κολοβοδάκτυλος, was the author of the Fourth Gospel, as he makes no attempt at correcting or qualifying his statement.

12.2. The Source of Non-Western Markan Traditions

As discussed in Chapter 5, the close relationship between the Coptic and Cypriot sources and the *Acts of Mark* suggests that they were dependent upon a common source of Markan traditions. Of all these, Coptic traditions have preserved the most obvious and pronounced allusions to the figure of the Beloved Disciple in their depiction of John/Mark as the host of the Last Supper and as witness of the crucifixion. It is difficult to conceive how such traditions could have been introduced after the identification of John/Mark with the Alexandrian one; they presumably survived because they were transmitted as part of an established John/Mark corpus of traditions which was assimilated to the Alexandrian Mark.

12.2.1. Hegesippus and the Reduplicated Markan Traditions

Probably the Markan reduplicated traditions of Coptic and Cypriot sources and the *Acts of Mark* shared a common source with Hegesippus, who seems to have transmitted some of the same traditions under the name of John. As already noted, Coptic sources and the *Acts of Mark*, though speaking of Mark's Levitical heritage, exhibit no awareness of the portrayal of John/Mark as a priest wearing the sacerdotal plate, which seems to have originated with Hegesippus. They also fail to exhibit any knowledge of the western conflation of Aristobulus the Roman missionary to Britain with John/Mark's father, which may have originated with Hegesippus.

Positive evidence for the independent use of common sources by Hegesippus and the Coptic tradition is provided by the extant accounts of the martyrdom of James the Just. In Hegesippus' account, James is said to have been preaching Jesus from a tower on the temple to the crowds who had assembled during Passover (*apud* Eusebius, *Hist. eccl.* 2.23.10–14), until the "scribes and Pharisees" threw him down from the temple and began to stone him (2.23.16). After this, a fuller is said to have taken a club and beaten James in the head, killing him, and he is afterwards buried near the temple. Hegesippus adds that there was a memorial on the spot which was still there in his day (2.23.18).

These different attempts at killing James likely represent a conflation of multiple martyrdom narratives involving throwing down from temple, stoning and/or beating. [30] Another account of James the Just's martyrdom, which Eusebius drew from Clement of Alexandria, relates that James was thrown down from the temple before being finished off with a club (*apud* Eusebius, *Hist. eccl.* 2.1.5); Clement makes no mention of James being stoned or buried near the temple, as found in Hegesippus' version.

Furthermore, these omitted details show up in other texts in association with the martyrdom of James the son of Alphaeus. Thus, Ps.-Hippolytus describes James the son of Alphaeus as having been stoned to death in Jerusalem, adding that he was buried near the temple (*De LXX Discip.*). There is no mention of this James being thrown down from the temple or beaten with a club, as in Clement's description of the martyrdom of James the Just. The probably fifth-century Latin *Incomplete Commentary on Matthew* also speaks only of the stoning of James the son of Alphaeus in Jerusalem. [31]

The Ethiopic work, the *Contendings of the Apostles*, which was probably a translation of a Coptic work written in the sixth century or later, [32] separately speaks of both the martyrdoms of James the son of Alphaeus and James the Just. As in other sources, the son of Alphaeus is said to have been stoned to death in Jerusalem and buried near the temple, [33] while the account of the martyrdom of James the Just in the *Contendings of the Apostles* reads similarly (with some minor differences) to that of Clement. Thus, James the Just is addressing the Jerusalem crowds and the priests and Pharisees take him to a pinnacle of the temple and throw him down; a fuller then finishes James off with his club. This James is said to have been buried, not near the temple, but in a synagogue, a detail not supplied by Clement. [34] This perhaps refers to the Church of Holy Zion in Jerusalem, which as noted in Chapter 7, was referred to as a synagogue by a source known to Epiphanius.

Interestingly, the account dates the martyrdom of James the son of Alphaeus during the reign of Claudius (41–54). Hegesippus' account, as given by Eusebius, places the martyrdom of James the Just shortly before the siege of Jerusalem (70 CE), but Epiphanius, whose account of James was likely indirectly dependent on Hegesippus (see Chapter 8), provides two dates for James' martyrdom, claiming that it took place both twenty-four years after the ascension and immediately before the siege of Jerusalem (*Pan.* 78.14.5). The first date, twenty-four years after the ascension, could correspond either to the end of Claudius' reign (agreeable to the account of James the son of Alphaeus in the

---

[30] Cf. Martin, *James*, lii; Painter, *Just James*, 119.

[31] Homily 41 on Matt 22, in James Kellerman, trans., Thomas C. Oden, ed., *Incomplete Commentary on Matthew (Opus Imperfectum)*, vol. 2 (Downers Grove, Ill.: IVP, 2010), 328.

[32] Budge, *Contendings*, viii.

[33] Budge, *Contendings*, 265–66.

[34] Budge, *Contendings*, 89.

Contendings) or to the beginning of Nero's. While the evidence is unfortunately not clear enough to affirm with certainty that Epiphanius' James died in Claudius' reign, the alternative dating he provides does not correspond with the period immediately before the siege of Jerusalem, providing evidence that Epiphanius' James was a conflated figure, as Hegesippus' was. [35]

Table 12.2.1: Traditions Associated with James the Son of Alphaeus and James the Just

	Thrown from temple	Killed with club	Stoned to death	Claudian dating	Just prior to 70 CE	Buried near temple
James of Alphaeus			X	X		X
James the Just	X	X			X	
James in Hegesippus	X	X	X	?	X	X

It thus seems that Hegesippus conflated an account of the martyrdom of James the son of Alphaeus with that of James the Just, both of whom were often confused in the sources. [36] Unlike Hegesippus, the *Contendings of the Apostles* maintains unconflated accounts of the martyrdoms of James the Just and James the son of Alphaeus, suggesting that the Coptic sources from which it was translated transmitted these traditions independently of Hegesippus, as Clement likely did also.

There are no compelling reasons for assuming that Hegesippus' sources were unknown outside of his own work. [37] And Budge, the editor of the *Contendings*, posited on separate grounds that the *Contendings* preserves traditions derived from Semitic documents (Hebrew or Syriac) that date to as early as the second century. [38] Such sources might have been independently known to Hegesippus who, according to Eusebius, made use of Hebrew (and possibly Aramaic) and Syriac documents (cf. Eusebius, *Hist. eccl.* 4.22.8). Possibly the John/Mark traditions were transmitted in the same common source or sources.

---

[35] This discussion of the possible conflation of the martyrdoms of James the Just and James the son of Alphaeus has been summarised from Furlong, *Identity of John*, 29–31.

[36] Broek, *Pseudo-Cyril*, 18; 28.

[37] The possibility that Hegesippus' sources may have survived independently of Hegesippus is accepted by Painter (*Just James*, 121122).

[38] Budge, *Contendings*, viii.

12.2.2. Proposed Source: Africanus

The *Acts of Mark*, *Encomium of Barnabas* and sources of Coptic Markan traditions may have been dependent upon the lost *Chronography* (c. 221) of the
learned Julius Africanus, who related traditions which had been handed down
in Palestine by the relatives of the Lord (the Desposyni) (*apud* Eusebius, *Hist.
eccl.* 1.7.14). He was possibly a native of Jerusalem [39] or was at least well-
travelled in Judea, possessing strong ties with the town of Emmaus. [40] He knew
at least some Hebrew, and may have been fluent; it is likely he also knew some
Syriac, since he served at one time at the court of King Abgar VIII in Edessa. [41]
The *Chronography*'s place of writing is unknown, though Alexandria has been
suggested, [42] and Colin Roberts in his famous study on Egyptian Christianity
lists Julius Africanus among the more widely-read authors in Egypt. [43] Indeed,
Africanus has been suggested as a source for some of Mawhub's material. [44]
Africanus was also likely not dependent upon Hegesippus for his material as
Eusebius related Palestinian traditions from Africanus and Hegesippus separately. [45] All of these factors render Africanus a credible candidate for the
source of the Markan traditions.

Presumably the common source or sources underlying the Johannine and
Markan traditions had spoken of John/Mark as the Beloved Disciple. Possibly
both the names of Mark and John were variously used in the accounts; in any
case, Hegesippus apparently chose to employ the name of John for his account,
whereas the originator of the Markan traditions elected to discuss him under
the name of Mark.

As was argued in Chapter 5, the claim that Mark was the one carrying the
jar of water probably arose by conflation with the tradition of Mark as one of

---

[39] Martin Wallraff, ed., *Iulius Africanus, Chronographiae: The Extant Fragments*, trans.
William Adler (GCS NF 15; Berlin: de Gruyter, 2007), xv–xvi.

[40] Wallraff, ed., *Iulius Africanus*, xiv–xv. According to the early fourteenth-century ecclesiastical historian, Nicephorus Callistus Xanthopulus of Constantinople, Africanus was
from Emmaus (see excerpt T2c in Wallraff, ed., *Iulius Africanus*, 6).

[41] Wallraff, ed., *Iulius Africanus*, xiv–xv.

[42] Alexandria is given as the place of writing by Richard W. Burgess with Witold Witakowski, *Studies in Eusebian and Post-Eusebian Chronography* (Hist. Einzel. 135; Stuttgart:
Steiner, 1999), 80.

[43] Colin H. Roberts, *Manuscript, Society and Belief in Early Christian Egypt* (London:
Oxford University Press, 1977), 63.

[44] Witold Witakowski, "Coptic and Ethiopic Historical Writing," in *The Oxford History
of Historical Writing*, ed. Sarah Foot and Chase F. Robinson, vol. 2 (Oxford: University
Press, 2012), 141. Mawhub himself claimed to have used Greek and Coptic sources (*Hist.
Patr. Eccl. Alex.* 1.1) which he found in monasteries and in the possession of individual
Christians (*Hist. Patr. Eccl. Alex.* pref. 1, 4).

[45] Riesner notes the possibility of Africanus' dependence on Hegesippus, though he thinks
the evidence is inconclusive either way (*Paul's Early Period*, 185).

those who poured out the wine at the wedding of Cana. Possibly Africanus himself was responsible for this conflation.

However, if the conflation occurred within the Markan sources, this would raise the question of how John also came to be identified as the one carrying the jar of water. The answer, it would appear, is that this does not represent a typical reduplicated tradition, for its Johannine form is not extant in western sources, appearing instead in the work of Epiphanius the Monk, of Constantinople; [46] it was this Epiphanius who was the source for Hippolytus of Thebes, who, as discussed in Chapter 7, provides an account which closely follows the Markan traditions of Mark's house as the place where the Passover was eaten, when the apostles took refuge, and where the Lord appeared to the disciples, with the exception that these traditions are related under the name of John instead of Mark. Epiphanius the Monk likely simply redacted an account which pertained to the house of Mark by replacing his name with John's, perhaps on account of the later association of the Zion site with John (which was no doubt occasioned, in turn, by the association of this site with Mary's dormition). It was probably therefore only in this way that the tradition of Mark as the one carrying the jar of water came to be attributed to John as well, in a transmission which was quite separate from the Johannine forms of the reduplicated traditions found in western sources.

12.3. The Cypriot Mission of Mark and Barnabas

The *Encomium of Barnabas*, the *Acts of Barnabas* and the *Life of Auxibius* all relate traditions of the ministry of Barnabas and Mark in Cyprus and Barnabas' martyrdom in Salamis, which were no doubt all derived from a common Cypriot source. Presumably this source took up the narrative from where the Acts left off, with Barnabas and John/Mark leaving Jerusalem for Cyprus. It would then have provided an account of their ministry there, culminating in Barnabas' martyrdom. It may have then spoke of Mark sailing to see Paul in Ephesus and remaining with him until his death in Rome.

The *Acts of Mark* does not relate this Cypriot mission, but it exhibits awareness of the Cypriot traditions of the ministry of Barnabas and Mark, for it has conflated them with the Egyptian narrative of the Alexandrian Mark. Among Coptic sources, both Severus and the *Synaxarion for Baramouda* were familiar with the Cypriot narrative.

---

[46] *PG* 120:209.

12.4. The Source of the Syrian Narrative

No clear text or writer presents itself as the source of the narratives of the Syrian mission known to the *Prochorus Acts*, Ephrem, Dionysius bar Salibi and the two Ethiopic apocalyptic commentaries. It seems unlikely that they derived their information from the same source as the Coptic and Cypriot texts and the *Acts of Mark*, given that these all preserve the traditions under the name of Mark, not John. They also do not exhibit any depiction of John as a priest wearing the sacerdotal plate, which seems to have been a feature of Hegesippus' work, suggesting that they might not have been dependent upon Hegesippus either. This seems to leave the possibility that these sources independently drew from the same common source or sources used by Hegesippus and Africanus. This would perhaps be expected, since it would appear that the common sources of these two writers were written in Syriac, the language of many of the documents preserving vestiges of the Johannine narrative. Such a common source or sources would have originated anterior to Hegesippus, and presumably therefore in the first half of the second century, if not earlier.

12.5. Conclusion

Any explanation for how the shared traditions of John and Mark were transmitted is necessarily conjectural. It was noted that there is no dominant direction of reduplication; the priority of some of the traditions is with John and some with Mark. It was also noted that any common source must have been ancient, for it predated the earliest writers whose works contain reduplicated traditions, such as Jerome and Ambrose, if not Hegesippus, Polycrates and Hippolytus of Rome.

It was further suggested that Hegesippus was likely the conduit of these traditions in the West and that Africanus was likely the source of the Coptic traditions, as well as of some of the Markan traditions contained in the *Acts of Mark* and the *Encomium of Barnabas*. The Johannine traditions of the dormition and the mission in Antioch were, it was suggested, possibly derived from the ancient Syriac sources which had been used by Hegesippus and Africanus.

While these suggestions are tentative, they can account for a wide range of chronologically, linguistically and geographically diverse data (i.e. their explanatory scope is strong). Indeed, alternative suggestions for accounting for the evidence have not as yet been forthcoming.

Conclusion to the Study

This study has sought to situate John/Mark within the context of both Markan and Johannine traditions. In particular, it has followed his transformation from a Johannine figure into a Markan one.

The first part of the study sought to demonstrate that John/Mark was likely originally considered a quite separate figure from Mark the Evangelist and the Alexandrian Mark. The first step in the merging of these three narratives appears to have been the identification of the latter two Marks, perhaps by Eusebius in the early third century. The Evangelist seems to have been identified with John/Mark by around the turn of the fourth century, likely resulting in some cases in the transformation of the Evangelist from one who had been a disciple of Peter and had never seen Jesus to a Mark who was an early Judean Christian who had been among Jesus' seventy(-two) disciples. The identification of these figures continued to produce further and often unsophisticated attempts at the conflation of the hitherto separate Markan narratives. This is particularly evident in Coptic sources, which often refused to displace their own traditions with the Papian narrative, and which struggled to reconcile Judean and Egyptian depictions of Mark's background.

The second part of this study sought to provide evidence that John/Mark had been considered a Johannine figure in some early Christian sources. Thus, it drew attention to vestiges of a portrayal of John/Mark as a figure who played pivotal roles in the Johannine narrative. Indeed, he may have been identified as the Beloved Disciple, for he is made the host of the Last Supper and a witness of the crucifixion; there was also attributed to him a Gospel containing a Logos doctrine and/or doctrine of the divinity.

Attention was also drawn to reduplicated traditions, or traditions shared by both John and Mark: both are said to have been virgins, both are identified as the young man who fled naked, both are said to have been a priest wearing the sacerdotal plate, and both are identified with the site of the Church of Holy Mount Zion in Jerusalem. Some of these traditions are incongruous with the Apostle John; thus, John is said to have been an educated Jerusalem aristocrat, and he is even said to have been the son of a certain Aristobulus, the brother of Barnabas.

Lastly, there were the apparent correlations of John/Mark with the Johannine narrative and John the Evangelist with the John/Mark narrative, with both figures placed at the same key locations at around the same time, beginning in Jerusalem, and encompassing Antioch, Cyprus, Asia Minor and Rome before concluding in Ephesus. Nevertheless, the Johannine form of these traditions seems to have been distorted as a result of the placement of John's Asian ministry in the reign of Tiberius.

Despite the later identification of John/Mark with Mark the Evangelist and the subsequent displacement of John/Mark narratives, a remarkable amount of material does still exist which, when considered together, suggests that John/Mark, the cousin of Barnabas, was once identified with John, the Beloved Disciple and Ephesian Evangelist.

Appendix

The *Acts of Mark*, Chapters 1 to 8

An English translation of the *Acts of Mark* is not yet available. A translation of the relevant section concerning John/Mark (chapters 1–8) has therefore been prepared for this study, from the Greek text in Halkin's edition. [1] The rest of the *Acts of Mark* relates traditions belonging to Mark the Evangelist and to the Alexandrian Mark.

Chapter 1: Prologue

The divinely-taught doctrines of the divinely-wise and much-celebrated apostles and their Spirit-moved teaching which saves the world, having been preached by God's guidance to the boundaries of the inhabited world, and the judgment having rolled out like the flashings of the beams of the sun, the majority of the inhabited world was rescued from gloomy and Satanic godlessness and soul-destroying madness of idolatry and brought into the light of the knowledge of God. Since, therefore the admirable and thoroughly honourable apostle and evangelist Mark is also from the divinely-chosen chorus of the great and inspired apostles, he is suitably worthy of great praises and is celebrated with songs by the pious. For which reason, our lowness and moderation have been urged by scripture to pass down his praiseworthy and God-pleasing course of life and his useful travels and his wonder-working miracles, to the glory of Christ our God and for the benefit of the readers. Therefore, by the assisting aid of the almighty and one-natured trinity of the one divine nature, and of his kingdom, and having also confidence in the acceptable petitions of the God-beholding evangelist for help, let us begin, setting forth a written exposition.

---

[1] Halkin, "Actes," 343–71. I have also consulted the unpublished translation by Dr Mark A. House ("Deeds and Miracles and Testimony of the Holy and All-praiseworthy Apostle and Evangelist Mark"), who kindly shared his work with me.

Chapter 2: Mark's Youth and Knowledge of the Scriptures

This glorious apostle Mark, the lamp of the never-setting light and the very great (or "greatest") herald of the evangelical teaching concerning the divinity, was descended from pious-minded ancestors who were adorned with worthy practices and were drawn from the Levitical tribe. From childhood until his prime of life and maturity, he used to order his life temperately and modestly, keeping himself on the one hand from inopportune and damaging work done in vain, and clinging to every soul-profiting and wholesome good work. Persevering in fasting and prayer and petitions, and rejoicing in good deeds, he was celebrated and wondered at by all. And consulting the prophetic books and devoting himself to their reading, and initiated with respect to the hidden and hard-to-understand exposition of the God-inspired predictions by divine illumination, he harmoniously explained the interpretations of those elevated divine discourses with very great beauty and virtue, making them evident to everyone. From this, therefore, and also from his virtuous way of life, the people would call him the "speaker of mysteries" and "religious herald", as those reaping great benefit from his teaching.

Chapter 3: His Generosity and Other Virtues

Having his home in Jerusalem, he was allotted much wealth from his ancestors; but he distributed this to the needy and the poor, for this admirable apostle was generous and full of much compassion, receiving foreigners and those without means in a kind and courteous way and supplying their needs. He was also distinguished by many other forms of virtue besides these excellent virtuous deeds, and very rightly; for it was necessary that he, having been predestined for the discipleship of the only begotten Son of God and worthily called to every good work of virtue, pass to the highest place; and so thus to receive the divine illumination of the all-holy and life-giving Spirit and to become the most clear-seeing lamp and most radiant herald of the divine discourse pertaining to the gospel.

Chapter 4: He is Baptised by Peter; His Mother Entertains Jesus

And this blessed apostle was first called John, but when he received the washing of regeneration from the most sacred and all-venerable Peter, the leader of the apostles, he received the name Mark and took the position of his adopted son. And Mary, the mother of the all-blessed Mark, pursued an honourable and God-pleasing life. And seeing the crowded multitude following Christ our God, who became man for the salvation of the human race and accomplished very great and incredible wonders, she goes to him with great speed and earnestly intreats and beseeches him to come into her house. The most benevolent Jesus of great mercy, the God-man, hearkened to her, and the Creator of all things came into her house, the one who is present everywhere and fills all things with his divine and all-controlling power. And he, who supplies holiness and illumination to everyone and provides many good works, enlightened and sanctified all of those there. For what could be loftier and more pleasant than this saving stay and hospitality? That she, the mother of the divinely-speaking apostle, called in truth blessed and most honoured, received into her home the only begotten Son and Word of God who brought forth everything seen and unseen from that which was not existing and who on account of his great goodness and unspeakable compassion became a man. For the crowds, seeing the great signs, marvels and innumerable wonders which Christ, the Son of Most High God, was performing over very many years in the limits of Jerusalem, were exceedingly struck, as the evangelical theology declares. For he raised and made the alive the dead by only a word, he made the blind to see, he healed those who were paralysed and who were demon possessed, he walked on the surface of the seas, rebuking the sea and the winds with authority, he made calm and smooth the swells of a violent wave. From five loaves he fed multitudes, and he healed those who were half wasted away and terribly leprous and those who were sick, and he granted healing to an innumerable crowd that was taken in grievous and distressing sicknesses. For he is the Son of God and God, the Christ who did these things, of the same nature as the Father and the Holy Spirit, the one sustaining the universe, who upholds all creation by his divine and mighty command. And these things proceeded in this way; let the account move to the following things.

Chapter 5: Mark Follows the Baptist and Jesus; Peter's Release

Therefore, the glorious apostle Mark first began following the holy and most loud-voiced John, the forerunner; but when the one and only Son of God was going from Jerusalem into Galilee, he followed him. But when the most sacred and all-venerable Peter, the leader of the apostles, was cast from a difficult to escape and entirely secured prison through the appearance of a holy angel, and was rescued from the hands of the utterly abominable and thrice-accursed Herod and from the unsubstantiated and falsely-contrived betrayal of the villainous and very difficult Judeans, having run a straight course out of the prison, came to the house of the thrice-happy Mark, and sent up a hymn of thanksgiving to God and told all the brothers about the miracle which had happened to him, of how Christ our God had freed him instantly and miraculously from the savage and bloodthirsty accusation of the guilty Judeans. All therefore rejoiced, lifting up the befitting thanksgiving to Christ, our God.

Chapter 6: The Passover at Mark's House; Preaching in Antioch

Therefore, after this, as has been said above, he called the celebrated Mark his adopted son. And this has reached to us from tradition and by succession that the one carrying the jar of water and the one having have heard from those who were sent: "Christ, who sent us, will keep the Passover at your place" – for his willing suffering had drawn near – was the divinely-sounding Mark. And after the voluntary and life-giving suffering of Christ our God, and his world-saving resurrection on the third day, and his ascension into the heavens, to his consubstantial Father and God, and the salvation and radiant manifestation of the life-giving and all-holy Spirit, who is sent forth from the Father and rests in the Son, and the divine illumination which came to the divinely-discoursing apostles, the divinely-voiced evangelist Mark, having received from the apostles in Jerusalem, wise in divine things, the saving teachings that were set forth in writing, arrived in the great Antioch, the most conspicuous of cities, with the most holy and admirable apostle Barnabas. And they began (to preach) the God-given and most saving proclamation, and they were very readily received by the Antiochians. And many who were abandoning the error and wickedness of idols though the teaching of these inspired apostles converted to the Christian way and have become sons of light.

But having set out from there, the divinely-minded Mark reached Seleucia. Then the one entrusted with the undertaking of the archon's authority in that region, who was profane and an idolater, happened upon some citizens; after hearing that the divine apostle Mark had taken up residence there, preaching freely the word of godliness, he was greatly disturbed and ordered for him to be detained. When the celebrated apostle was arrested and guarded in prison, he was looking into how to get rid of him by death. After a few days had passed, an angel of the Lord released him out of those very grievous chains and said to him: "Depart into the city of the Caesareans and preach the word the truth there!" When the angel had said these words to him and had left his sight, and after those indissoluble chains were loosed, Mark went out from the prison. And being very ready to complete God's commands, he arrives in Caesarea of Palestine. Spending much time there as a teacher of godliness, having instructed most of the godless and profane, brought them into the light of the divine knowledge and made them Christians.

Chapter 7: Mission in Cyprus; Conversion of Sergius

After that, having departed from Palestine and having boarded the ship he sailed away and reached the great island of the Cypriots. And while going around the island and announcing the proclamation of godliness to everyone, he accomplishes great wonders in the name of Christ the God, who is preached by him, healing incurable diseases and bringing most of the people from wickedness to godliness and to orthodox worship, and working godly thinking through the washing of regeneration.

When these God-pleasing works had been completed by him in Cyprus, having after a little while been instructed by the all-holy and life-engendering Spirit, he passed from those borders, and having reached Pamphylia, he spent time there. At that time also the most divine discourser of God and great teacher of the world, Paul the apostle, prevailed over the wizard and false prophet Bar-Jesus and put him completely to shame. And with righteousness and divine judgment he struck blind Elymas, the sorcerer and deceiver. And Sergius the proconsul became a partaker of the pious worship and he received the gift of holy baptism from the admirable and venerable apostle Paul, with all his house. For these impure and all-abominable Bar-Jesus and Elymas, having become deceivers, liars and leaders of the blind to destruction, and attempting also to corrupt the appointed things, priding themselves in the nothingness of falsehood, have become strangers to the truth, having led astray not a few of the unstable and simple to their own impiety and soul-destroying emptiness of mind. But likewise, just as the darkness is scattered by introduction of light, so also the God-taught and soul-saving teaching, having shined forth, and the marvel of their great wonders, has utterly destroyed the soul-destroying and unreal things done vainly, and has made those deceived by them both godly and orthodox through the washing of regeneration. And so it is with that; and the things remaining to the account are worthy to say.

Chapter 8: Mark at Antioch and Jerusalem

Then the most holy Mark wished to reach the western lands of the Gauls; this was not carried out, on account of a divine revelation; but having learned that the most holy Paul, the herald of truth, was spending time in great Antioch with the glorious Barnabas, who were openly preaching the divinely-given and saving teachings, he left for them. And having spent time with them there for not a short time and having announced the word of godliness to all, he was filled with gladness and joy, seeing the flock of Christ growing yet more daily. After these things, leaving them, he came to Jerusalem together with Simeon, called Niger. Coming into the temple, having gathered all the brothers, and having lifted up befitting supplication and laudatory hymn singing to the master of all things with them, to Christ the God for sufficient days, he rejoiced, being spiritually overjoyed.

Bibliography

Abu Laylah, Muhammad. *The Qur'an and the Gospels: A Comparative Study*. Cairo: El-Falah, 2005.

Achtemeier, Paul J. *1 Peter: A Commentary on First Peter*. Hermeneia; Minneapolis: Fortress, 1996.

Aland, Kurt, ed. *Synopsis Quatturo Evangeliorum: Locis Parallelis Evangeliorum Apocryphorum Et Patrum Adhibitis Edidit*. 15th ed. Stuttgart: Deutsche Bibelgesellschaft, 2001.

Allen, Rupert. "Mark 14, 51–52 and Coptic Hagiography." *Biblica* 89 (2008): 265–68.

Anon., ed. and trans. *The Holy Psalmody*. Lynnwood, Wash.: Saint Mary's Coptic Orthodox Church, 1997.

Anon., trans. *Morals on the Book of Job by S. Gregory the Great, the First Pope of That Name, Translated, with Notes and Indices*. 3 vols. Oxford: John Henry Parker, 1845.

Aquinas, Thomas. *In Evangelia S. Matthaei et S. Ioannis Commentaria*. 2 vols. Turin: Typographia Pontificia 1893–94.

Arndt, William, Frederick W. Danker, and Walter Bauer, eds. *A Greek-English Lexicon of the New Testament and Other Early Christian Literature*. 3rd ed. Chicago: University of Chicago Press, 2000.

Attridge, Harold W. "The Restless Quest for the Beloved Disciple." Pages 71–80 in *Early Christian Voices in Texts, Traditions, and Symbols: Essays in Honor of François Bovon*. Edited by David H. Warren, Ann Graham Brock and David W. Pao. Biblical Interpretation Series 66. Leiden: Brill, 2003.

Aune, David E. "The Odes of Solomon and Early Christian Prophecy." *New Testament Studies* 28 (1982): 435–60.

–. *Prophecy in Early Christianity and the Ancient Mediterranean World*. Grand Rapids: Eerdmans, 1983.

–. *Revelation 1–5*. Word Biblical Commentary 52A. Dallas: Word, 1998.

Baarda, Tjitze. "The Etymology of the Name of the Evangelist Mark in the *Legenda Aurea* of Jacobus a Voragine." *Nederlands archief voor kerkgeschiedenis* 72 (1992): 1–12.

Bacon, Benjamin W. *The Beginnings of Gospel Story: A Historical-Critical Inquiry into the Sources and Structure of the Gospel According to Mark, With Expository Notes Upon the Text, For English Readers*. New Haven, Conn.: Yale University Press, 1909.

–. *The Fourth Gospel in Research and Debate: A Series of Essays on Problems Concerning the Origin and Value of the Anonymous Writings Attributed to the Apostle John*. New York: Moffat, 1910.

Badham, Francis Pritchett. "The Martyrdom of John the Apostle." *American Journal of Theology* 8 (1904): 539–54.

Bagatti, Bellarmino. *The Church from the Gentiles in Palestine*. Translated by Eugene Hoade. Publications of the Studium Biblicum Franciscanum. Collectio minor 4. Jerusalem: Franciscan Printing Press, 1971.

Bardsley, Herbert J. *Reconstructions of Early Christian Documents*. London: SPCK, 1935.

Bargès, Jean J. L., trans. *Homélie sur St Marc, apôtre et évangéliste par Anba Sévère, évêque de Nestéraweh*. Paris: Leroux, 1877.

Barrett, Charles K. *A Critical and Exegetical Commentary on the Acts of the Apostles*. 2 vols. International Critical Commentary. Edinburgh: T. & T. Clark, 1994–1998.

Barth, Markus and Helmut Blanke. *Colossians: A New Translation with Introduction and Commentary*. Translated by Astrid B. Beck. Anchor Bible 34B. New York: Doubleday, 1994.

Bauckham, Richard. *The Testimony of the Beloved Disciple: Narrative, History, and Theology in the Gospel of John*. Grand Rapids: Baker, 2007.

–. *Jesus and the Eyewitnesses: The Gospels as Eyewitness Testimony*. 2nd ed. Grand Rapids: Eerdmans, 2017.

Beasley-Murray, George R. *John*. Word Biblical Commentary 36. 2nd ed. Dallas: Word, 2002.

Beck, Edmund, ed. *Des heiligen Ephraem des Syrers Hymnen de Virginitate*. Corpus Scriptorum Christianorum Orientalium 224. Leuven, 1962.

Bernard, John H. *A Critical and Exegetical Commentary on the Gospel According to St. John*. 2. vols. International Critical Commentary. New York: Scribner, 1929.

Bolland, Jean, ed. *Acta Sanctorum Martii*. Vol. 2. Paris: Victorem Palme, 1865.

Behr, John. *John the Theologian and his Paschal Gospel: A Prologue to Theology*. Oxford: University Press, 2019.

Bernhard, Andrew. "The Life and Martyrdom of John the Baptist: A Translation and Introduction." Pages 247–67 in *New Testament Apocrypha: More Noncanonical Scriptures*. Vol. 1. Edited by Tony Burke and Brent Landau. Grand Rapids: Eerdmans, 2016.

Bird, Michael F. "Mark: Interpreter of Peter and Disciple of Paul." Pages 30–61 in Paul and the Gospels: Christologies, Conflicts and Convergences. Edited by Michael F. Bird and Joel Willitts. London: T. & T. Clark, 2011.

Bishop, Eric F. F. "Simon and Lucius: Where did they come from? A Plea for Cyprus." *Expository Times* 51 (1939–40): 148–53.

Black, C. Clifton. *Mark: Images of an Apostolic Interpreter*. Minneapolis: Fortress, 2001.

Blomberg, Craig L. *The Historical Reliability of John's Gospel: Issues & Commentary*. Downers Grove, Ill.: IVP, 2001.

Boismard, Marie-Émile. *Le martyre de Jean l'apôtre*. Cahiers de la Revue biblique 35. Paris, Gabalda, 1996.

Boring, M. Eugene. *An Introduction to the New Testament: History, Literature, Theology*. Louisville, Ky.: Westminster John Knox, 2012.

Borleffs, Philip, ed. *Quinti Septimi Florentis Tertulliani Opera Pars IV*. Corpus Scriptorum Ecclesiasticorum Latinorum 76. Vienna: Tempsky, 1957.

Bourgel, Jonathan. "The Jewish-Christian's Move from Jerusalem as a Pragmatic Choice." Pages 107–37 in *Studies in Rabbinic Judaism and Early Christianity: Text and Context*. Edited by Dan Jaffé. Leiden: Brill, 2010.

Boxall, Ian. *Patmos in the Reception History of the Apocalypse*. Oxford: Oxford University Press, 2013.

Braun, François-Marie. *Jean le Théologien et son évangile dans l'Église ancienne*. 3 vols. Paris: Gabalda, 1959–1972.

Brent, Allen. *Hippolytus and the Roman Church in the Third Century: Communities in Tension Before the Emergence of a Monarch-Bishop*. Leiden: Brill, 1995.

–. "Tertullian on the Role of the Bishop." Pages 175–85 in *Tertullian and Paul*. Edited by Todd D. Still and David E. Wilhite. New York: Bloomsbury, 2013.

Brooks, James A. *Mark*. New American Commentary 23. Nashville: Broadman & Holman Publishers, 1991.

Brown, Raymond E. *The Gospel According to John (I–XII): Introduction, Translation, and Notes*. Anchor Bible 29. New Haven, Conn.: Yale University Press, 2008.

Bruce, Frederick F. "St John at Ephesus." *Bulletin of the John Rylands University Library* 60 (1978): 339–61.

–. *The Epistles to the Colossians, to Philemon, and to the Ephesians*. The New International Commentary on the New Testament. Grand Rapids: Eerdmans, 1984.

–. *The Book of the Acts*. The New International Commentary on the New Testament. Grand Rapids: Eerdmans, 1988.

–. *Paul: Apostle of the Heart Set Free*. Grand Rapids: Eerdmans, 2005.

Bruns, J. Edgar. "John Mark: A Riddle within the Johannine Enigma," *Scripture* 15 (1963): 88–92.

–. "The Confusion between John and John Mark in Antiquity." *Scripture* 17 (1965): 23–26.

Budge, Ernest Alfred Wallis, ed. and trans. *The Book of the Bee*. Oxford: Clarendon Press, 1886.

–. *The Contendings of the Apostles: Being the Histories and the Lives and Martyrdoms and Deaths of the Twelve Apostles and Evangelists*. Vol. 2: *The English Translation*. Oxford: Oxford University Press, 1901.

–. *The Chronography of Gregory Abû'l Faraj, the Son of Aaron, the Hebrew Physician Commonly Known as Bar Hebraeus*. London: Oxford University Press, 1932.

Burgess, Richard W., with Witold Witakowski. *Studies in Eusebian and Post-Eusebian Chronography*. Historia Einzelschriften 135. Stuttgart: Steiner, 1999.

Butler, Alban. *The Lives of the Fathers, Martyrs and Other Principal Saints*. Vol. 2. New York: P. J. Kenedy, 1903.

Cadbury, Henry J. "Lucius of Cyrene." Pages 489–99 in *The Acts of the Apostles*. Edited by F. J. Foakes Jackson and Kirsopp Lake. Vol. 5. Grand Rapids: Baker, 1979.

Cahill, Michael, trans. *The First Commentary on Mark: An Annotated Translation*. Oxford: Oxford University Press, 1998.

Callahan, Allen D. "The Acts of Saint Mark: And Introduction and Commentary." Ph.D. dissertation. Harvard University, 1992.

Calmet, Antoine. *Dictionnaire historique, critique, chronologique, géographique et littéral de la Bible*. 4 vols. 2nd ed. Geneva: Bousquet, 1730.

Capper, Brian J. "The Palestinian Cultural Context of Earliest Christian Community of Goods." Pages 346–47 in *The Book of Acts in its Palestinian Setting*. Edited by Richard Bauckham. The Book of Acts in its First Century Setting 4. Grand Rapids: Eerdmans, 1995.

–. " 'With the Oldest Monks ...' Light from Essene History on the Career of the Beloved Disciple?" *Journal of Theological Studies* 49 (1998): 26–36.

Carmignac, Jean "Les Affinités qumrâniennes de la onzième Ode de Salomon." *Revue de Qumran* 3 (1961): 71–102.

Carr, Eardley W., ed. and trans. *Gregory Abu'l Faraj Commonly Called Bar-Hebraeus: Commentary on the Gospels from the Horreum Mysteriorum*. London: SPCK, 1925.

Carson, Donald, and Douglas J. Moo, An Introduction to the New Testament. 2nd ed. Grand Rapids: Zondervan, 2005.

Cave, William. *A Complete History of the Lives, Acts, and Martyrdoms of the Holy Apostles*. Vol. 1. Philadelphia: Solomon Wyatt, 1810.

Chabot, Jean-Baptiste. *Chronique de Michel le Syrien, Patriarche Jacobite d'Antioch (1166–1199)*. Vol. 1. Paris, Leroux, 1899.

Chaise, Filbert de la. "A l'origine des récits apocryphes du 'Transitus Mariae.'" *Ephemerides Mariologicae* 29 (1979): 77–90.

Chapman, John. *Notes on the Early History of the Vulgate Gospels*. Oxford: Clarendon Press, 1908.

Charles, Robert H. *A Critical and Exegetical Commentary on the Revelation of St. John*. 2 vols. International Critical Commentary. New York: Scribner, 1920.

Charlesworth, James H., ed. *The Old Testament Pseudepigrapha*. 2 vols. New York: Doubleday, 1983–1985.

Charlesworth, James H. "A Study in Shared Symbolism and Usage: The Qumran Community and the Johannine Community." Pages 97–152 in *The Bible and the Dead Sea Scrolls*. Vol. 3, *The Scrolls and Christian Origins*. Edited by James H. Charlesworth. Waco, Tex.: Baylor University Press, 2006.

Charlesworth, James H., and R. Alan Culpepper. "The Odes of Solomon and the Gospel of John." *Catholic Biblical Quarterly* 35 (1973): 298–322.

Clayton, Mary. *The Apocryphal Gospels of Mary in Anglo-Saxon England*. Cambridge: Cambridge University Press, 1998.

Coakley, James Farwell. "A Catalogue of the Syriac Manuscripts in the John Rylands Library." *Bulletin of the John Rylands University* 75 (1993): 105–207.

Colson, Jean. *L'énigme du disciple que Jésus aimait*. Théologie Historique 10. Paris: Beauchesne, 1969.

Concannon, Cavan W. "The Acts of Timothy: A New Translation and Introduction." Pages 396–405 in *New Testament Apocrypha: More Noncanonical Scriptures*. Vol. 1. Edited by Tony Burke and Brent Landau. Grand Rapids: Eerdmans, 2016.

Conybeare, Fred C. "Ein Zeugnis Ephräms über das Fehlen von c. 1 und 2 im Texte des Lucas." *Zeitschrift für die neutestamentliche Wissenschaft und die Kunde des Urchristentums* 3 (1902): 192–97.

Conzelmann, Hans. *Die Apostelgeschichte*. Handbuch zum Neuen Testament 7. Tübingen: J.C.B. Mohr (Paul Siebeck), 1963.

Cosby, Michael R. *Creation of History: The Transformation of Barnabas from Peacemaker to Warrior Saint*. Eugene, Oreg.: Cascade, 2017.

Cowley, Roger W. *The Traditional Interpretation of the Apocalypse of St John in the Ethiopian Orthodox Church*. Cambridge: Cambridge University Press, 1983.

Cramer, John Anthony, ed. *Catenae Graecorum Patrum in Novum Testamentum*. Oxford, 1844.

Cross, F. L., and Elizabeth A. Livingstone, eds. *The Oxford Dictionary of the Christian Church*. Oxford: Oxford University Press, 2005.

Crossley, James G. *The Date of Mark's Gospel: Insight from the Law in Earliest Christianity*. London: T. & T. Clark, 2004.

Crouch, Dora P. *Geology and Settlement: Greco-Roman Patterns*. Oxford: Oxford University Press, 2003.

Cullmann, Oscar. *The Johannine Circle*. Translated by John Bowden. London: SCM, 1976.

Culpepper, R. Alan. *John, the Son of Zebedee: The Life of a Legend*. Edinburgh: T. & T. Clark, 2000.

Cureton, William, ed. *Ignatius of Antioch, Corpus Ignatianum: A Complete Collection of the Ignatian Epistles, Genuine, Interpolated, and Spurious*. Berlin: Asher, 1849.

Daniélou, Jean. *Primitive Christian Symbols*. Translated by Donald Attwater. Baltimore: Helicon Press, 1964.

Davis, Stephen J. *The Early Coptic Papacy*. Vol.1. Cairo: The American University in Cairo Press, 2005.

Davies, William D., and Dale C. Allison Jr. *A Critical and Exegetical Commentary on the Gospel according to Saint Matthew*. 3 vols. International Critical Commentary. Edinburgh: T. & T. Clark, 1988–1997.

Deissmann, G. Adolf. *Bible Studies: Contributions Chiefly from Papyri and Inscriptions to the History of the Language, the Literature and the Religion of Hellenistic Judaism and Primitive Christianity*. Translated by Alexander Grieve. Edinburgh: T. & T. Clark, 1901.

–. *Light from the Ancient East the New Testament Illustrated by Recently Discovered Texts of the Graeco-Roman World*. Translated by Lionel Richard Mortimer Strachan. London: Hodder & Stoughton, 1910.

Delff, Heinrich. *Das vierte Evangelium: Ein authentischer Bericht über Jesus von Nazaret*. Husum: Delff, 1890.

Den Heijer, Johannes. "Réflexions sur la composition de *l'Histoire des Patriarches d'Alexandrie*: les auteurs des sources coptes." Pages 107–13 in *Coptic Studies, Acts of the Third International Congress of Coptic Studies*. Edited by Wlodzimierz Godlewski. Warsaw: PWN-Éditions scientifiques de Pologne, 1990.

Deppe, Dean B. *The Theological Intentions of Mark's Literary Devices: Markan Intercalations, Frames, Allusionary Repetitions, Narrative Surprises, and Three Types of Mirroring*. Eugene, Oreg.: Wipf and Stock, 2015.

Diekamp, Franz. *Hippolytos von Theben: Texte und Untersuchungen*. Münster: Aschendorff, 1898.

Dunn, James D. G. *The Epistles to the Colossians and to Philemon: A Commentary on the Greek Text*. The New International Commentary on the New Testament. Grand Rapids: Eerdmans, 1996.

Echle, Harry A. "The Baptism of the Apostles: A Fragment of Clement of Alexandria's Lost Work Ὑποτυπώσεις in the Pratum Spirituale of John Moschus." *Traditio* 3 (1945): 366–68.

Eckle, Wolfgang. *Den der Herr liebhatte: Rätsel um den Evangelisten Johannes. Zum historischen Verständnis seiner autobiographischen Andeutungen*. Hamburg: Kovac, 1991.

Eisler, Robert. *The Messiah Jesus and John the Baptist*. Translated by Alexander Haggerty Krappe. London: Methuen, 1931.

–. *The Enigma of the Fourth Gospel*. London: Methuen, 1938.

Elliott, John H. *1 Peter: A New Translation with Introduction and Commentary*. Anchor Bible 37B. New York: Doubleday, 2000.

Elliott, Keith, ed. and trans. *The Apocryphal New Testament: A Collection of Apocryphal Christian Literature in an English Translation Based on M. R. James*. Oxford: Clarendon Press, 1993.

Ellis, E. Earle. *The Making of the New Testament Documents*. Leiden: Brill, 2002.

Ellis, Frederick S., trans., and William Caxton, ed. *Jacobus de Voragine, The Golden Legend, or, Lives of the Saints*. 7 vols. London: Dent, 1900.

Emerton, John A. "Some Problems of Text and Language in the Odes of Solomon." *Journal of Theological Studies* 18 (1967): 372–406.

Erbes, Carl. "Der Apostel Johannes und der Jünger, welcher an der Brust des Herrn lag." *Zeitschrift für Kirchengeschichte* 33 (1912): 159–239.

Esbroeck, Michel van. "Deux listes d'apôtres conservées en syriaque." Pages 15–24 in *Third Symposium Syriacum 1980*. Edited by René Lavenant. Orientalia Christiana Analecta, 221. Rome: Pont. Institutum Studiorum Orientalium, 1983.

Evans, Craig A. *Word and Glory: On the Exegetical and Theological Background of John's Prologue*. Journal for the Study of the New Testament, Supplement Series 89. Sheffield: Sheffield Academic Press, 1993.

Evans, Ernest, ed. and trans. *Tertullian, Adversus Marcionem*. 2 vols. Oxford: The Clarendon Press, 1972.

Evetts, Basil, ed. and trans. "Severus of Al'Ashmunein (Hermopolis), History of the Patriarchs of the Coptic church of Alexandria, I, Mark to Theonas." Pages 99–214 in *Patrologia Orientalis* 1. Paris: Firmin-Didot, 1904.

Finegan, Jack. *The Archeology of the New Testament: The Mediterranean World of the Early Christian Apostles*. Boulder, Colo.: Westview Press, 1981.

–. *The Archeology of the New Testament: The Life of Jesus and the Beginning of the Early Church*. Rev. ed. Princeton: Princeton University Press, 1992.

Fitzmyer, Joseph A. *The Acts of the Apostles: A New Translation with Introduction and Commentary*. AB 31. New Haven, Conn.: Yale University Press, 1998.

–. *The Letter to Philemon: A New Translation with Introduction and Commentary*. AB 34C. New Haven, Conn.: Yale University Press, 2000.

Foat, Michael E., trans. "Encomium on SS. Peter and Paul Attributed to Severian of Gabala." Pages 65–101 in *Encomiastica from the Pierpont Morgan Library: Five Coptic Homilies Attributed to Anastasius of Euchaita, Epiphanius of Salamis, Isaac of Antinoe Severian of Gabala, and Theopempus of Antioch*. Corpus Scriptorum Christianorum Orientalium 545; Leuven: Peeters 1993.

France, Richard T. *The Gospel of Mark: A Commentary on the Greek Text*. New International Greek Testament Commentary. Grand Rapids: Eerdmans, 2002.

Franzmann, Majella. *The Odes of Solomon: An Analysis of the Poetical Structure and Form*. Novum Testamentum et Orbis Antiquus 20. Göttingen: Vandenhoeck & Ruprecht, 1991.

Furlong, Dean. "John the Evangelist: Revision and Reinterpretation in Early Christian Sources." Ph.D. dissertation. Vrije Universiteit Amsterdam, 2017.

–. *The Identity of John the Evangelist: Revision and Reinterpretation in Early Christian Sources*. Lanham, Md.: Lexington, 2020.

Gathercole, Simon. *The Composition of the Gospel of Thomas: Original Language and Influences*. Cambridge: Cambridge University Press, 2012.

Gibson, Margaret, ed. and trans. The Commentaries of Isho'dad of Merv: Bishop of Ḥadatha (c. 850 A.D.). Horae Semiticae 5. Vol. 1. Cambridge: Cambridge University Press, 1911.

Gildermeister, Johann, ed. *Theodosius de situ Terrae Sanctae im ächten Text und der Brevarius de Hierosolyma vervollstäandigt*. Bonn: Adolph Marcus, 1882.

Greenhalgh, Michael. *Marble Past, Monumental Present: Building With Antiquities in the Mediaeval Mediterranean*. Leiden: Brill, 2009.

Guelich, Robert A. *Mark 1–8:26*. Word Biblical Commentary 34A. Dallas: Word, 1998.

Gumerlock, Francis X. *Revelation and the First Century: Preterist Interpretations of the Apocalypse in Early Christianity*. Powder Springs, Ga.: American Vision, 2012.

–. "Chromatius of Aquileia on John 21:22 and Rev. 10:11." Pages 52–63 in *The Book of Revelation and Its Interpreters: Short Studies and an Annotated Bibliography*. Edited by Ian Boxall and Richard M. Tresley. London: Rowman, 2016.

Gunther, John J. "The Association of Mark and Barnabas with Egyptian Christianity (Part I)." *Evangelical Quarterly* 54 (1982): 219–33.

Haase, Felix, ed. *Apostel und Evangelisten in den orientalischen Überlieferungen*. Neutestamentliche Abhandlungen 9. Münster: Aschendorff, 1922.

Hackett, John. *A History of the Orthodox Church of Cyprus*. London: Methuen, 1901.

Halkin, François, ed. "Actes inédits de saint Marc." *Analecta Bollandiana* 87 (1969): 343–71.

Hamilton, Walter, trans. *Ammianus Marcellinus: The Later Roman Empire (A.D. 354–378)*. London: Penguin, 1986.

Hanna, William A., trans. *Ibn Kabar, The Lamp that Lit the Darkness*. St Louis: 2000.

Harlow, Daniel C. *The Greek Apocalypse of Baruch (3 Baruch) in Hellenistic Judaism and Early Christianity*. Studia in Veteris Testamenti pseudepigraphica 7. Leiden: Brill, 1996.

Harris, J. Rendel, and Alfonse Mingana, eds. *The Odes and Psalms of Solomon*. 2 vols. Manchester: Manchester University Press, 1920.

Harrison, Percy. *The Problem of the Pastoral Epistles*. London: Oxford University Press, 1921.

Heikel, Ivar A. *Eusebius Werke*. Vol. 7: *Die Demonstratio Evangelica*. Die Griechischen Christlichen Schriftsteller der ersten drei Jahrhunderte. Leipzig: Hinrichs, 1913.

Helm, August. *Die Chronik des Hieronymus*. Berlin: Akademie-Verlag, 1956.

Hengel, Martin. "Jakobus der Herrenbruder – der erste 'Papst'?" Pages 71–104 in *Glaube und Eschatologie: Festschrift für Werner Georg Kümmel zum 80. Geburtstag*. Edited by Erich Grässer and Otto Merk. Tübingen: J.C.B. Mohr (Paul Siebeck), 1985.

–. *The Johannine Question*. Translated by John Bowden. London: SCM Press, 1989.

–. *Studies in the Gospel of Mark*. Eugene, Oreg.: Wipf and Stock, 2003.

–. *Die vier Evangelien und das eine Evangelium von Jesus Christus: Studien zu ihrer Sammlung und Entstehung*. Wissenschaftliche Untersuchungen zum Neuen Testament 224. Tübingen: Mohr Siebeck, 2008.

–. *Saint Peter: The Underestimated Apostle*. Translated by Thomas H. Trapp. Grand Rapids: Eerdmans, 2010.

Hengel, Marin, and Anna Maria Schwemer. *Paul between Damascus and Antioch: The Unknown Years*. Louisville, Ky.: Westminster John Knox, 1997.

Henry, Matthew. *An Exposition of the Old and New Testament*. Vol. 5. London: Bagster, 1811.

Hilberg, Isidor, ed. *Sancti Eusebii Hieronymi Epistulae*. Corpus Scriptorum Ecclesiasticorum Latinorum 56. Vienna: 1918.

Holl, Karl, ed. *Epiphanius (Uncoratus und Panarion) III: Panarion haer. 65–80*. Die Griechischen Christlichen Schriftsteller der ersten drei Jahrhunderte 37. Leipzig: Hinrichs, 1933.

Jackson, H. Latimer. *The Problem of the Fourth Gospel*. Cambridge: Cambridge University Press, 1918.

James, Montague Rhodes, ed. and trans. *The Apocryphal New Testament: Being the Apocryphal Gospels, Acts, Epistles, and Apocalypses*. Oxford: Clarendon Press, 1924.

Johnson, Lewis. "Who was the Beloved Disciple?" *Expository Times* 77 (1966): 157–58.

Johnson, Luke Timothy. *The First and Second Letters to Timothy: A New Translation with Introduction and Commentary*. Anchor Bible 35A. New Haven, Conn.: Yale University Press, 2008.

Junod, Eric. "La virginité de l'apôtre Jean: recherché sur les origines scripturaires et patristique de cette tradition." Pages 113–36 in *Cahiers de Biblia Patristica* 1. Strasbourg: Centre d'Analyse et de Documentation Patristiques, 1987.

Junod, Eric, and Jean-Daniel Kaestli, eds. *Acta Iohannis*. 2 vols. Corpus Christianorum, Series Apocryphorum. Turnhout: Brepols, 1983.

Käsemann, Ernst. "Aufbau und Anliegen des johanneischen Prologs." Pages 75–99 in *Liberias Christiana Friedrich Delekat zum fünfundsechzigsten Geburtstag*. Edited by

Walter Matthias and Ernst Wolf. Beiträge zur evangelischen Theologie 26. Munich: Kaiser, 1957.

Keener, Craig S. *The IVP Bible Background Commentary: New Testament*. 2nd ed. Downers Grove, Ill.: IVP, 2014.

Kelhoffer, James A. *Miracle and Mission: The Authentication of Missionaries and Their Message in the Longer Ending of Mark*. Tübingen: Mohr Siebeck, 2000.

Kellerman, James, trans., and Thomas C. Oden, ed. *Incomplete Commentary on Matthew (Opus Imperfectum)*. 2 vols. Downers Grove, Ill.: IVP, 2010.

Klostermann, Erich, and Ernest Benz, eds. *Origenes Werke*. Vol. 10–11. Die griechischen christlichen Schriftsteller der ersten drei Jahrhunderte 38. Leipzig: Hinrichs, 1933–35.

Knight, George W. *The Pastoral Epistles: A Commentary on the Greek Text*. New International Greek Testament Commentary. Grand Rapids: Eerdmans, 1992.

Knox, John. *Marcion and the New Testament: An Essay in the Early History of the Canon*. Chicago: University of Chicago Press, 1942.

Kok, Michael J. "The Gospel on the Margins: The Ideological Function of the Patristic Tradition on the Evangelist Mark." Ph.D. dissertation. University of Sheffield, 2013.

Köstenberger, Andreas J. *A Theology of John's Gospel and Letters: The Word, the Christ, the Son of God*. Biblical Theology of the New Testament. Grand Rapids: Zondervan, 2009.

Kraeling, Carl H. *The Excavations of Dura-Europos: Final Report*, VIII, I. New Haven, Conn.: 1956.

Krueger, Derek. *Writing and Holiness: The Practice of Authorship in the Early Christian East*. Philadelphia: University of Pennsylvania Press, 2004.

Kümmel, Werner Georg. *Introduction to the New Testament*. Rev. ed. Translated by Howard Clark Lee. Nashville: Abingdon Press, 1973.

Kuruvilla, Abraham. "The Naked Runaway and the Enrobed Reporter of Mark 14 and 16: What Is the Author Doing with What He Is Saying?" *Journal of the Evangelical Theological Society* 54 (2011): 527–45.

Kysar, Robert. *The Fourth Evangelist and his Gospel: An Examination of Contemporary Scholarship*. Minneapolis: Augsburg, 1975.

Lalleman, Pieter J. *The Acts of John: A Two-stage Initiation into Johannine Gnosticism*. Leuven: Peeters, 1998.

Lake, Kirsopp, ed. and trans. Eusebius: *The Ecclesiastical History*, 2 vols. Loeb Classical Library. London: Heinemann; 1926.

Lambers-Petry, Doris. "How to Become a Christian Martyr: Reflections on the Death of James as Described by Josephus and in Early Christian Literature." Pages 101–24 in *Internationales Josephus-Kolloquium Paris 2001*. Edited by Folker Siegert and Jürgen U. Kalms. Münsteraner judaistische Studien 12. Münster, 2002.

Lampe, Geoffrey W. H. "A.D. 70 in Christian Reflection." Pages 153–71 in *Jesus and the Politics of his Day*. Edited by E. Bammel and C. F. D. Moule. Cambridge: Cambridge University Press, 1984.

Lampe, Peter. *Christians at Rome in the First Two Centuries: From Paul to Valentinus*. London: Continuum, 2003.

Lattke, Michael. *The Odes of Solomon: A Commentary*. Translated by Marianne Ehrhardt Hermeneia; Minneapolis: Fortress, 2009.

Lawlor, Hugh Jackson. *Eusebiana: Essays on the Ecclesiastical History of Eusebius Pamphili, c. 264–349*. Oxford: Clarendon Press, 1912.

Leloir, Louis, ed. *Saint Éphrem: Commentaire de l'Évangile concordant, texte syriaque (Manuscrit Chester Beatty 709)*. Chester Beatty Monographs 8. Dublin: Hodges Figgis, 1963.

Levine, Lee I. *Jerusalem: Portrait of the City in the Second Temple Period (538 B.C.E.–70 C.E.)*. Philadelphia: The Jewish Publication Society, 2002.

Lewis, Agnes Smith, ed. and trans. *The Mythological Acts of the Apostles*. Horae Semiticae 4. London: Clay, 1904.

Liddell, Henry George, Robert Scott, Henry Stuart Jones and Roderick McKenzie, eds. *A Greek-English Lexicon*. Oxford: Clarendon Press, 1996.

Lieu, Judith M. *Marcion and the Making of a Heretic: God and Scripture in the Second Century*. Cambridge: Cambridge University Press, 2015.

Lightfoot, Joseph B. *The Apostolic Fathers: Clement, Ignatius, and Polycarp*. 5 vols. London: Macmillan, 1889–90.

–. *The Acts of the Apostles: A Newly Discovered Commentary*. Edited by Ben Witherington III, Todd D. Still and Jeanette M. Hagen. The Lightfoot Legacy Set vol. 1. Downers Grove, Ill.: IVP, 2014.

Lipsius, Richard. A., and Max Bonnet, eds. *Acta Apostolorum Apocrypha*. Vol. 1/2, *Passio Andreae. Acta Andreae et Matthiae. Acta Petri et Andreae. Passio Bartholomaei. Acta Ioannis. Martyrium Matthaei*. Leipzig: 1898.

–. *Acta Apostolorum Apocrypha*. Vol. 2/2, *Acta Philippi et Acta Thomae, accedunt Acta Barnabae*. Leipzig: 1903.

Litwa, David M., ed. and trans. *Refutation of All Heresies: Text, Translation, and Notes*. Writings from the Greco-Roman World 40. Atlanta: SBL, 2015.

Lührmann, Dieter. *Das Markusevangelium*. Handbuch zum Neuen Testament 3. Tübingen: J.C.B. Mohr (Paul Siebeck), 1987.

MacCarthy, Carmel, trans. *Saint Ephrem's Commentary on Tatian's Diatessaron: An English translation of Chester Beatty Syriac MS 709*. Oxford: Oxford University Press, 1993.

MacDonald, Dennis R. "Legends of the Apostles." Pages 166–80 in *Eusebius, Christianity, and Judaism*. Edited by Harold Attridge and Gohei Hata. Detroit: Wayne State University Press, 1992.

MacDonald, Margaret Y. *Colossians and Ephesians*. Sacra Pagina 17. Collegeville, Minn.: The Liturgical Press, 2000.

Manson, Thomas W. *Studies in the Gospels and Epistles*. Philadelphia: Westminster, 1962.

Marcus, Joel. *Mark 1–8: A New Translation with Introduction and Commentary*. Anchor Bible 27. New Haven, Conn.: Yale University Press, 2008.

Marsh, John. *The Gospel of St. John*. Philadelphia: Westminster, 1978.

Martin, Ralph P. *2 Corinthians*. Word Biblical Commentary 40. Dallas: Word, 1986.

–. *James*. Word Biblical Commentary 48. Dallas: Word, 1998.

McDonald, Lee Martin. "The *Odes of Solomon* in Ancient Christianity: Reflections on Scripture and Canon." Pages 108–36 in *Sacra Scriptura: How "Non-Canonical" Texts Functioned in Early Judaism and Early Christianity*. Edited by James H. Charlesworth and Lee Martin McDonald. London: Bloomsbury, 2012.

McNally, Robert E. "Two Hiberno-Latin Texts on the Gospels." *Traditio* 15 (1959): 387–401.

–. "*Christus* in the Pseudo-Isidorean 'Liber de ortu et obitu patriarchum'" *Traditio* 21 (1965): 167–83.

Metzger, Bruce, and Bart Ehrman. *The Text of the New Testament: Its Transmission, Corruption, and Restoration*. 4th ed. Oxford: Oxford University Press, 2005.

Ramsay, William. *Luke the Physician*. London: Hodder & Stoughton, 1908.

Michaels, J. Ramsey. *1 Peter*. Word Biblical Commentary 49. Dallas: Word, 1998.

–. *The Gospel of John*. The New International Commentary on the New Testament. Grand Rapids: Eerdmans, 2010.

Mingana, Alphonse. *The Book of Religion and Empire*. Manchester: Manchester University Press, 1922.

–. "The Authorship of the Fourth Gospel." *Bulletin of the John Rylands University Library* 14 (1930): 333–39.

Mitford, Terence B. "Further Contributions to the Epigraphy of Cyprus." *American Journal of Archaeology* 65 (1961): 93–151.

Montgomery, James A. "The recently discovered Odes of Solomon." *Biblical World* 36 (1910): 93–100.

Morris, Leon. *Studies in the Fourth Gospel*. Grand Rapids: Eerdmans, 1969.

–. *The Gospel According to John*. The New International Commentary on the New Testament. Grand Rapids: Eerdmans, 1995.

Mounce, William D. *Pastoral Epistles*. Word Biblical Commentary 46. Dallas: Word, 2000.

Müller, Jac J. *The Epistles of Paul to the Philippians and to Philemon*. The New International Commentary on the New Testament. Grand Rapids: Eerdmans, 1955.

Murphy-O'Connor, Jerome. "The Cenacle – Setting for Acts 2:44–45." Pages 303–21 in *The Book of Acts in its Palestinian Setting*. Edited by Richard Bauckham. The Book of Acts in its First Century Setting 4. Grand Rapids: Eerdmans, 1995.

Nagel, Titus. *Die Rezeption des Johannesevangeliums im 2. Jahrhundert: Studien zur vorirenäischen Aneignung und Auslegung des vierten Evangeliums in christlicher und christlich-gnostischer Literatur*. Leipzig: Evangelische Verlagsanstalt, 2000.

Nau, François, "Histoire de saint Jean Baptiste attribuée à saint Marc l'Évangéliste." Pages 521–41 in *Patrologia Orientalis* 4. Paris: Firmin-Didot, 1908.

Nelson, Robert S. *The Iconography of Preface and Miniature in the Byzantine Gospel Book*. New York: New York University Press, 1980.

Neusner, Jacob, trans. *The Mishnah: A New Translation*. New Haven, Conn.: Yale University Press, 1988.

Neville, Leonora. *Heroes and Romans in Twelfth-Century Byzantium: The* Material for History *of Nikephorus Bryennios*. Cambridge: Cambridge University Press, 2012.

North, J. L. "*ΜΑΡΚΟΣ Ο ΚΟΛΟΒΟΔΑΚΤΥΛΟΣ*: Hippolytus, *Elenchus*, VII. 30." *Journal of Theological Studies* 28 (1977): 498–507.

Oberhummer, Eugene. "Keryneia 2." Columns 344–47 in *Paulys Realencyclopädie der classischen Altertumswissenschaft* 11, 1921.

Oden, Thomas C. *African Memory of Mark: Reassessing Early Church Tradition*. Downers Grove, Ill.: IVP, 2011.

Öhler, Markus. *Barnabas*. Wissenschaftliche Untersuchungen zum Neuen Testament 156. Tübingen: Mohr Siebeck, 2003.

Orchard, Bernard and Harold Riley. *The Order of the Synoptics: Why Three Synoptic Gospels?* Macon, Ga.: Mercer University Press, 1987.

Orlandi, Tito, ed. *Studi Copti. 1. Un encomio di Marco Evangelista. 2. Le fonti copte della Storia dei Patriarchi di Alessandria. 3. La leggenda di S. Mercurio*. Testi e documenti per lo studio dell'antichità 22. Milan: Cisalpino, 1968.

Painter, John. *Mark's Gospel: Worlds in Conflict*. London: Routledge, 1997.

–. *Just James: The Brother of Jesus in History and Tradition*. Edinburgh: Fortress, 1999.

Parker, Pierson. "John and John Mark." *Journal of Biblical Literature* 79 (1960): 97–110.

–. "John the Son of Zebedee and the Fourth Gospel." *Journal of Biblical Literature* 81 (1962): 35–43.

–. "The Posteriority of Mark." Pages 67–142 in William R. Farner, ed., *New Synoptic Studies: The Cambridge Gospel Conference and Beyond*. Macon, Ga.: Mercer University Press, 1983.

Pearson, Birger A. "Earliest Christianity in Egypt: Some Observations." Pages 132–59 in *The Roots of Egyptian Christianity*. Edited by Birger A. Pearson and James A. Goehring. Philadelphia: Fortress, 1986.

Pixner, Bargil. *Paths of the Messiah and Sites of the Early Christian Church from Galilee to Jerusalem*. San Francisco: Ignatius Press, 2010.

Plummer, Alfred. *The Gospel according to St Mark*. Cambridge: Cambridge University Press, 1914.

Pohlsander, Hans A., ed. *Sources for the History of Cyprus, 7: Greek Texts of the Fourth to Thirteenth Centuries*. Greece and Cyprus Research Center, 1999.

Pollard, Thomas Evan. *Johannine Christology and the Early Church*. Cambridge: Cambridge University Press, 1970.

Possinus, Petrus (Pierre Poussines), ed. *Catena Graecorum Patrum in Evangelium Secundum Marcum*. Rome, 1673.

Pratscher, Wilhelm. *Der Herrenbruder Jakobus und die Jakobustraditionen*. Forschungen zur Religion und Literatur des Alten und Neuen Testaments 139. Göttingen: Vandenhoeck & Ruprecht, 1987.

Pretty, Robert A., trans. *Adamantius: Dialogue on the True Faith in God*. Leuven: Peeters, 1997.

Prigent, Pierre. *Commentary on the Apocalypse of St. John*. Translated by Wendy Pradels. Tübingen: Mohr Siebeck, 2004.

Pringle, Denys. *The Churches of the Crusader Kingdom of Jerusalem: A Corpus*. Vol. 3, *The City of Jerusalem*. Cambridge: Cambridge University Press, 2010.

Pulcini, Theodore. *Exegesis as Polemical Discourse: Ibn Ḥazm on Jewish and Christian Scriptures*. Atlanta: Scholars Press, 1998.

Radice, Betty, ed. *Pliny. Letters and Panegyricus*, 2 vols. Loeb Classical Library. Cambridge, Mass.: Harvard University Press, 1969.

Ramelli, Ilaria. "John the Evangelist's Work: An Overlooked Redaktionsgeschichtliche Theory from the Patristic Age." Pages 30–52 in *The Origins of John's Gospel*. Edited by Stanley E. Porter and Hughson T. Ong. Leiden: Brill, 2016.

Ratzinger, Joseph. *Jesus of Nazareth: The Infancy Narratives*. Translated by Philip J. Whitmore. New York: Doubleday, 2007.

Regul, Jürgen. Die antimarcionitischen Evangelienprologe. *Vetus Latina: Die Reste der altlateinischen Bibel* 6. Freiburg: Verlag Herder, 1969.

Riesner, Rainer. *Paul's Early Period: Chronology, Mission Strategy, Theology*. Translated by Doug Stott. Grand Rapids: Eerdmans, 1998.

–. "Once More: Luke-Acts and the Pastoral Epistles." Pages 239–58 in *History and Exegesis: New Testament Essays in Honor of Dr. E. Earle Ellis for his 80th Birthday*. Edited by Sang-Won (Aaron) Son. London: T. & T. Clark, 2006.

Roberts, Colin H. *Manuscript, Society and Belief in Early Christian Egypt*. London: Oxford University Press, 1977.

Robinson, John A. T. *Redating the New Testament*. London: SCM, 1976.

–. *The Priority of John*. London: SCM, 1985.

Roetzel, Calvin J. *Paul: The Man and the Myth*. Minneapolis: Fortress Press, 1999.

Ropes, James H. *A Critical and Exegetical Commentary on the Epistle of St. James*. International Critical Commentary. New York: Scribner, 1916.

Routh, Martin Joseph. *Reliquiae Sacrae, sive, Auctorum fere iam Perditorum Secundi Tertiique Saeculi post Christum Natum quae Supersunt*. Vol. 1. Oxford: Cooke, 1814.

Salmon, George. *A Historical Introduction to the Study of the Books of the New Testament*. London: John Murray, 1899.

Schäferdiek, Knut. "Herkunft und Interesse der alten Johannesakten." *Zeitschrift für die neutestamentliche Wissenschaft und die Kunde der älteren Kirche* 74 (1983): 247–67.

Shenouda III, Pope. *The Beholder of God: Mark the Evangelist, Saint and Martyr.* Translated by Samir F. Mikhail and Maged S. Mikhail from the 4th ed. Santa Monica: 1995.

Sheridan, Mark. "The Encomium in Coptic Sermons of the Late Sixth Century." Pages 443–64 in Christianity in Egypt: Literary Production and Intellectual Trends. Studies in Honor of Tito Orlandi. Edited by Paola Buzi and Alberto Camplani. Rome: Institutum Patristicum Augustinianum, 2011.

Schenkl, G., ed. *Ambrose: Expositio Evangelii secundum Lucam.* Corpus Scriptorum Ecclesiasticorum Latinorum 32/4. Vienna: Akademie der Wissenschaften, 1902.

Schermann, Theodor, ed. *Prophetarum Vitae Fabulosae Indices Apostolorum Discipulorumque Domini.* Leipzig: Teubner 1907.

Schneemelcher, Wilhelm, ed. *New Testament Apocrypha.* Vol. 2. Cambridge: James Clarke, 1992.

Sedlácek, Jaromier, ed. *Dionysius bar Salibi. Commentarii in Evangelia.* Corpus Scriptorum Christianorum Orientalium, Scriptores Syri 2/98. Rome: de Luigi, 1906.

Shoemaker, Stephen J. *The Ancient Traditions of the Virgin Mary's Dormition and Assumption.* Oxford: Oxford University Press, 2006.

–. *Mary in Early Christian Faith and Devotion* (New Haven, Conn.: Yale University Press, 2016)

Simcox, William. H. *The Revelation of S. John the Divine.* Cambridge Greek Testament for Schools and Colleges. Cambridge: Cambridge University Press, 1909.

Skarsaune, Oskar. "Fragments of Jewish Christian Literature Quoted in Some Greek and Latin Fathers." Pages 325–78 in *Jewish Believers in the Jesus: The Early Centuries.* Edited by Oskar Skarsaune and Reidar Hvalvik. Peabody, Mass.: Hendrickson, 2007.

Smalley, Stephen. *John, Evangelist and Interpreter.* 2nd ed. London: Paternoster, 1997.

Smith, Preserved. "The Disciples of John and the Odes of Solomon." *The Monist* 25 (1915): 161–99.

Snyder, Glenn E. "The Acts of Barnabas: A New Translation and Introduction." Pages 317–36 in *New Testament Apocrypha: More Noncanonical Scriptures.* Vol. 1. Edited by Tony Burke and Brent Landau. Grand Rapids: Eerdmans, 2016.

Snyder, Julia A. *Language and Identity in Ancient Narratives: The Relationship between Speech Patterns and Social Context in the Acts of the Apostles, Acts of John, and Acts of Philip.* Wissenschaftliche Untersuchungen zum Neuen Testament 370. Tübingen: Mohr Siebeck, 2014.

Soliman, Sameh Farouk. "Two Epithets of Mark the Evangelist: Coptic ⲑⲉⲱⲣⲓⲙⲟⲥ and Byzantine Greek θεόπτης." *Greek, Roman, and Byzantine Studies* 54 (2014): 494–506.

Sordi, Marta. *The Christians and the Roman Empire.* Translated by Annabel Bedini. London: Routledge, 1994.

Souter, Alexander. "A Suggested Relationship between Titus and Luke." *Expository Times* 18 (1907): 285; 335–36.

–. *The Text and Canon of the New Testament.* New York: Scribner, 1913.

Stade, Christopher, trans. *The Explanation by the Blessed Theophylact of the Holy Gospel According to St. Mark.* House Springs, Mo.: Chrysostom Press, 1993.

Stegemann, Ekkehard W., and Wolfgang Stegemann. *The Jesus Movement: A Social History of its First Century.* Translated by O. C. Dean. Edinburgh: T. & T. Clark, 1999.

Stevenson, Kenneth. "Animal Rites: The Four Living Creatures in Patristic Exegesis and Liturgy," *Studia patristica* 34 (2001): 470–92.

Stökl Ben Ezra, Daniel. *The Impact of Yom Kippur on Early Christianity*. Wissenschaftliche Untersuchungen zum Neuen Testament 163. Tübingen: Mohr Siebeck, 2003.

al-Suryani, Ṣamu'il, and Nabih K. Dawud, eds., *Ta'rikh al-aba' al-baṭarika li-l-anba Yusab usquf Fuwwa*. Cairo: 1987.

Swete, Henry Barclay. *The Gospel according to St. Mark. The Greek Text with Introduction, Notes and Indices*. London: Macmillan, 1898.

Taniguchi, Yuko, François Bovon and Athanasios Antonopoulos. "The Memorial of Saint John the Theologian (BHG 919fb)." Pages 333–52 in *The Apocryphal Acts of the Apostles*. Edited by François Bovon, Ann G. Brock, and C. R. Matthews. Cambridge, Mass.: Harvard University Press, 1999.

Taylor, Joan. *Christians and the Holy Places: The Myth of Jewish-Christian Origins*. Oxford: Oxford University Press, 1993.

Taylor, R. O. P. "The Ministry of Mark," *Expository Times* 54 (1942–43): 136–38.

Telfer, William. "Was Hegesippus a Jew?" *Harvard Theological Review* 53 (1960): 143–53.

Thornecroft, J. K. "The Redactor and the 'Beloved' in John," *Expository Times* 98 (1986–87): 135–39.

Thornton, Claus-Jürgen. *Der Zeuge des Zeugen: Lukas als Historiker der Paulusreisen*. Wissenschaftliche Untersuchungen zum Neuen Testament 56. Tübingen: J.C.B. Mohr (Paul Siebeck), 1991.

Trebilco, Paul. *The Early Christians in Ephesus from Paul to Ignatius*. Grand Rapids: Eerdmans, 2007.

Trench, Richard. *The Hulsean Lectures for 1845 and 1846*. London: Macmillan, 1880.

Unger, Dominic J., trans. *St. Irenaeus of Lyons Against the Heresies, Book 1*. Ancient Christian Writers 55. New York: Newman Press, 1992.

Usener, Hermann, ed. *Acta S. Timothei*. Bonn: Caroli Georgi Universitas, 1877.

Ussher, James. *The Whole Works of the Most Rev. James Ussher, D.D.* 17 vols. Edited by Charles Richard Elrington. Dublin: Hodges, 1864.

Valesius, Henricus (Henri de Valois), ed. *Eusebius: The History of the Church from our Lord's Incarnation to the Twelfth Year of the Emperour Mauricius Tiberius, or the Year of Christ 594*. Cambridge, 1683.

Van den Broek, Roelof, ed. *Pseudo-Cyril of Jerusalem On the Life and the Passion of Christ: A Coptic Apocryphon*. Supplements to Vigiliae Christianae 118. Leiden, Brill, 2012.

Van Deun, Peter, and Jaques Noret, eds. *Hagiographica Cypria*. Corpus Christianorum, Series Graeca 26. Turnhout: Brepols, 1993.

Van Tilborg, Sjef. *Reading John in Ephesus*. Leiden: Brill, 1996.

Volfing, Annette. *John the Evangelist and Medieval German Writing: Imitating the Inimitable*. New York: Oxford University Press, 2001.

Vollers, Karl, and Ernst Von Dobschutz. "Ein spanisch-arabisches Evangelien-fragment." *Zeitschrift der deutschen morgenländischen Gesellschaft* 56 (1902): 633–48.

Von Soden, Hermann Freiherr. *Die Schriften des Neuen Testaments in ihrer ältesten erreichbaren Textgestalt*. Vol. 1. Berlin: Duncker, 1902.

Völter, Daniel. *Mater Dolorosa und der Lieblingsjünger des Johannesevangeliums*. Strasburg: Heitz, 1907.

–. *Die Offenbarung Johannis*. 2nd ed. Strassburg: Heitz, 1911.

Von Tischendorf, Constantin, Caspar René Gregory and Ezra Abbot, eds. *Novum Testamentum Graece*. Vol. 1. Leipzig: Giesecke & Devrient, 1869.

Vööbus, Arthur. "Neues Licht zur Frage der Originalsprache der Oden Salomos." *Le Muséon* 75 (1962): 275–90.

Wallraff, Martin, ed. *Iulius Africanus, Chronographiae: The Extant Fragments*. Translated by William Adler. Die griechischen christlichen Schriftsteller der ersten Jahrhunderte, Neue Folge 15. Berlin: de Gruyter, 2007.

Watson, Francis. *Gospel Writing: A Canonical Perspective*. Grand Rapids: Eerdmans, 2013.

Weidmann, Frederick W. *Polycarp and John: The Harris Fragments and Their Challenge to the Literary Traditions*. Notre Dame, Ind.: University of Notre Dame Press, 1999.

Weinrich, William C., ed. *Revelation*. Ancient Christian Commentary on Scripture: New Testament 12. Downers Grove, Ill.: IVP, 2005.

Weiss, Johannes. *Das älteste Evangelium: Ein Beitrag zum Verständnis des Markus-Evangeliums und der ältesten evangelischen Überlieferung*. Göttingen: Vandenhoeck & Ruprecht, 1903.

–. *Earliest Christianity: A History of the Period A.D. 30–150*. Translated by Frederick Grant. 2 vols. New York: Harper, 1959.

Weitzman, Michael. *The Syriac Version of the Old Testament*. University of Cambridge Oriental Publications 56. Cambridge University Press, 2005.

Whiteley, Denys E. H. "Was John Written by a Sadducee?" *Aufstieg und Niedergang der Römischen Welt* 2.25.3 (1985): 2481–505.

Wilkinson, John, trans. *Egeria's Travels*. London: SPCK, 1971.

–. *Jerusalem Pilgrims before the Crusades*. Warminster, UK: Aris and Phillips, 1977.

Williams, Margaret H. "Palestinian Jewish Personal Names in Acts." Pages 79–113 in *The Book of Acts in its Palestinian Setting*. Edited by Richard Bauckham. The Book of Acts in its First Century Setting 4. Grand Rapids: Eerdmans, 1995.

Wellhausen, Julius. *Das Evangelium Johannis*. Berlin: Reimer, 1908.

Wilson, James M. *The Western Text of the Acts of the Apostles, translated from Codex Bezae*. London: SPCK, 1923.

Winn, Adam. *The Purpose of Mark's Gospel: An Early Christian Response to Roman Imperial Propaganda*. Wissenschaftliche Untersuchungen zum Neuen Testament 245. Tübingen: Mohr Siebeck, 2008.

Witakowski, Witold. "Coptic and Ethiopic Historical Writing." Pages 138–54 in *The Oxford History of Historical Writing*. Edited by Sarah Foot and Chase F. Robinson. Vol. 2. Oxford: University Press, 2012.

Witherington III, Ben. *The Acts of the Apostles: A Socio-Rhetorical Commentary*. Grand Rapids: Eerdmans, 1998.

–. "What's in a Name? Rethinking the Historical Figure of the Beloved Disciple in the Fourth Gospel." Pages 203–12 in *John, Jesus, and History*. Vol. 2, *Aspects of Historicity in the Fourth Gospel*. Edited by Paul N. Anderson, Felix Just and Tom Thatcher. Atlanta: SBL, 2009.

Wright, William. *Apocryphal Acts of the Apostles: Edited from Syriac Manuscripts in the British Museum and Other Libraries*. 2 vols. London: Williams and Norgate, 1871.

Wright, William. "Syriac Remains of S. Ignatius." Pages 73–124 in *The Apostolic Fathers, Part II: S. Ignatius, S. Polycarp: Revised Texts*. 3 vols. 2nd ed. London: Macmillan, 1889.

Youssef, Youhanna Nessim. "The homily of Severus of Naştrāwa on saint Mark." *Bulletin de la Société d'archéologie copte* 49 (2010): 143–62.

Zahn, Theodor, ed. *Acta Joannis unter Benutzung von C. v. Tischendorf's Nachlass*. Erlangen: Verlag von Andreas Deichert, 1880.

–. *Forschungen zur Geschichte des neutestamentlichen Kanons und der altkirchlichen Literatur*. Vol. 6, *Apostel und Apostelschüler in der Provinz Asien*. Leipzig: Deichert, 1900.

–. *Introduction to the New Testament*. Translated by John Moore Trout et al. 3 vols. Edinburgh: T. & T. Clark, 1909.

Zuckschwerdt, Ernst. "Das Naziraat des Herrenbruders Jakobus nach Hegesippus." *Zeitschrift für die neutestamentliche Wissenschaft und die Kunde der älteren Kirche* 68 (1977): 276–87.

Index of Sources

I. Old Testament

Exodus
19:6   140
28:36   125
28:36 (LXX)   39, 125, 133
28:36 (Peshitta)   137
30:23 (LXX)   16

Leviticus
21:18   37

Numbers
35:5 (LXX)   16

Deuteronomy
21:6 (LXX)   16

1 Samuel
1:10 (LXX)   139

2 Kings
4:12   37
11:12 (LXX)   139

Ezra
5:17 (LXX)

Nehemiah
5:16 (LXX)   16

Psalms
20:4 (LXX)   139
85:16 (LXX)   139
86:16   139
116:16   139
Proverbs
8:23   138
8:22   138

Isaiah
1:8   115
3:10   130
51:1   130

Jeremiah
31:31   96
33:17–18   141

Ezekiel
1:10   92

Daniel
11:4 (LXX)   16
12:8 (LXX)   16

Zechariah
6:11 (LXX)   139

II. Old Testament Apocrypha and Pseudepigrapha

Tobit		*2 Maccabees*	
8:6	16	10:3	16
Judith		*3 Maccabees*	
15:13	140	4:8	140
		4:19	16
Wisdom			
9:6	139	*4 Maccabees*	
		9:6	140

III. New Testament

Matthew		6:17	73
18:1–4	111	10:1	23, 24
19:1	111	22:8–12	109
26:6–16	83	22:10	52, 71, 82, 109
26:18	71, 82, 90	22:20–26	111
26:31–35,	189	22:26	111
26:56b	189		
		John	
Mark		1:1	99
3:17	112	1:1–3	93, 96
9:33–37	111	1:2	138
10:1	111	1:4–5	93
10:10	16	1:14	96, 138
14:13	52, 71, 82, 109	1:1–18	92
14:14	71, 72, 82	1:18	92, 96, 99
14:27	189	1:28	52, 89
14:50–51	109	1:35–42	88
14:51	105, 109	1:35–40	70
14:52	126, 130	1:35–37	102
14:54	109	1:35	76
16:9–20	*93*	1:38–39	89
		1:43	70, 76, 88, 102
Luke		2:1–10	52, 88, 102
1:2	24	2:1–2	70, 76, 88
1:32	139	2:11	96
1:35	139	3:8	138
1:38	139	3:13	96
1:48	139	4:54	96
2:35	158	5:1–8	80, 89, 102
5:17	73	6:53	33

John (cont.)

6:62	96
7:2	138
7:37	138
10:40	52, 89
11:1	52, 90
11:18	52, 90
12:1	52, 90
13:30	84
13:23	90, 102, 124
13:34	96
14:21	138
15:10	96
15:16	138
18:2–3	84
18:15	108, 110
19:25–27	90, 102, 108, 139
20:19–26	119
20:19	52, 91, 92, 117
20:24–29	102
21:18	138
21:20–24	124
21:24	92

Acts

1:12–13	117
2:1–13	119
4:13	108
4:36	72, 106
6:5	156
6:7	37
8:1	25, 72, 177
8:14	177
11:19	72, 175, 177
11:20	25
11:22	155, 177, 179
11:25–27 27,	155, 179
11:28	25, 26
12:1–12	70
12:4–10	29
12:12–16	25
12:12	3, 8, 9, 13, 28, 34
12:13	9, 28
12:17	9, 155, 179
12:25	3, 8, 9, 25, 27, 42, 178, 181
13:1–5	9, 15
13:1	25, 26, 57, 72, 178

13:4–14:25	76
13:4–13	181
13:5	3, 9
13:6–12	58, 77
13:13	3, 9, 12, 42, 56, 76, 178, 181
14:1–4	77
15:36–41	42, 56, 76
15:37–41	10
15:37–39	10
15:37	3, 8, 10
15:39	3, 8, 10, 42, 55, 57, 62
20:19	52
21:20	159
24:31–35	11
25:20	16

1 Corinthians

9:25	140, 140

2 Corinthians

8:18	26
12:18	26

Galatians

2:11–13	155, 179

Philippians

2:6–11	138

Colossians

4:10–17	10
4:10–14	26
4:10	8, 10, 15, 24, 27, 42, 63, 100
4:11	24, 27
4:14	24, 27

2 Timothy

1:15–16	11
1:15	43
4:9	11
4:10–17	10
4:10	10, 43
4:11	8, 11, 12, 27, 36, 43, 63, 65
4:13	11, 56, 67
4:14	43

Philemon
23–24   10
24   8, 10, 27

1 Peter
5:13   8, 12, 18, 27, 28,
               32, 66, 70

1 John
4:10   138
4:12   96

4:19   138

Revelation
2:10   139
3:5   139
3:11   139
4:7   92
10:11   119
13:1   139
14:14   139

IV. Other Jewish Literature

Josephus
Antiquities
3.172   125
17.165–6   134

Mishnah and Talmud
m. Kippurim 8:1 A   128
Yoma 1.1   134
*bTaa*n 24b   129
bYoma 53b   129

Philo
On the Change of Names
               133

On the Migration of Abraham
               125

On Moses   125

Targum Onkelos
Exod 29:6   137

Targum Pseudo-Jonathan
Exod 19:6   140

V. Greek and Roman Literature

Manetho
Fragment 6   113

Ammianus Marcellinus
History 15.3   101

Pliny the Elder
Natural History
5.130   73

Pliny the Younger
Epistles
10.96   143–44

Suetonius
Lives of the Caesars
Augustus 24.1   101
Domitian 12.1–2 150

Tacitus
Histories
5.5   140

VI. Christian Literature

Acts of Barnabas

1–2	55–56
3	56
5	56
6	56, 178
7	73
8	57
9–11	57
10	59
11	57
12–14	57
14	57
15	57, 180
16	58
17	58
18	58
19	58
20	58
21	58
22	58
23	59, 65
24	59, 180
25	59

Acts of John

18	151, 152
19–25	151
30–36	151
37–45	151
48–54	151
55	151
58	151
59–60	151
63–86	152
88	153
106–115	152

Acts of John by Prochorus

3–4	156
5–6	156
7–8	156

8–14	156–57
44–46	157
50–51	157
81	157
151–52	157
154–56	157
162–65	157

Acts of Mark

1	97, 113
2	69, 98, 114
3	70, 97
4	70
5	70, 76
6	71, 175, 176
7	71, 176
8	71–72, 88, 176
9	74, 78, 176
10	74
11	74
12	74
15	74
19	74
21	74
22	74
27	74
28	74
33	74
34	74

Acts of Peter

5	19, 29, 73, 153
9	29

Acts of Thomas

1	153

Acts of Timothy

7	171

Africanus
Chronography   194

Alexander the Monk
Encomium of Barnabas
6–15   59
29–37   59
136–39   59
161   59
177–91   59
192–200   60
200–208   60
209–19   60
219–37   60
398–412   61
405–12   61
420–28   61
438–65   61
536–44   61
544–49   61
550–57   65
553–57   61
557–69   65
557–64   61
559–60   65
564–67   62
567–69   62
750–52   180

Ambrose
Commentary on Luke
Preface 8   92–93
2.61   158

Exposition of the Psalms
36   110
53   110

On the Offices of Ministers
2.20.101   111

Anti-Marcionite Prologues
To Mark   16

Apollonius
Against the Phrygian Heresy
                153

Apostolic Constitutions
                27

Thomas Aquinas
Commentary on Matthew
                99

Bar Hadbashaba
Commentary on Mark
10   110

Bar Hebraeus
Commentary on Mark
Prologue   30

Commentary on Matthew
10   110, 167

Bede
Explanation of the Gospel of Mark
Letter to Accam   37
14   110

Book of the Bee
44   159
48   30
49   30, 31
50   30

Book of Mary's Repose
1–2   118
51   118, 158
66   118, 158
70   118, 158

Chromatius
Commentary on Matthew
Prologue 6   99

Chronicon Pascale 183

John Chrysostom
Commentary on the Gospel of Mark
Prologue   35

Discourses
36   114

Homilies on Acts
26   13

Homilies on John
18:3   88

Clement of Alexandria
Hypotyposes   17–18

Who is the Rich Man?
                42, 149, 173

Ps.-Cyril
On the Life and the Passion of Christ
                91–92

Dialogue of Adamantius
5   23–24

Dionysius of Alexandria
On the Promises   12

Dionysius bar Salibi
Commentary on the Gospels
34   29
37   30
40   30

Ephrem
Commentary on Acts 27

Commentary on Tatian's Diatessaron
                26

Hymns on Virginity
15.4   112

Epiphanius of Salamis
Panarion
20.4.4   32–33

29.3.8–9   141
29.4.4   129
29.7.8   116
29.9   116
30.3   116
30.6   116
30.13   116
30.14   116
42.4.1–2   100
51.6.10–11   33
51.11.6   3
51.27.2   117
58.4.6   113
78.10.5–8   131
78.10.9–10   131
78.10.10   112
78.11.1   163
78.11.2–5   159
78.13.1   131
78.11.2   163
78.13.2–4a   130
78.13.2–5   126
78.13.3   109, 188
78.14.1–2   126
78.14.1   126
78.14.5   163

Weights and Measures
15   116

Epiphanius the Monk
Life of the Virgin   109

Encomium of SS. Peter and Paul
102   43
Epigram on Mark's Gospel
                97–98

Eusebius
Chronicle   21, 164

Ecclesiastical History
1.1.8   98
1.2.24   113

Ecclesiastical History
(cont.)
2.14.6   18, 79
2.15.2   32
2.16.1   19, 31
2.16.2   32
2.24.1   19, 31, 32
3.4.6   25
3.5.3   116
3.11.1–12.1   120
3.22.1   119
3.26.6   165
3.24.3   95
3.24.13   94, 98
3.25.6   151
3.39.6   165
4.22.3   141
4.22.8   116, 128, 140, 193
5.28.6   143, 144

Euthymius Zigabenus
First Commentary on Mark
                    37

Eutychius
Annals   115–16

Gregory the Great
Morals on the Book of Job
14.57   110

Harris Fragments
Fragment on Polycarp
                    112

Hegesippus
Memoirs   116, 124, 127, 129,
                    130, 132, 133, 141,
                    189, 191–92

Hippolytus
Antichrist
36   148

Apostolic Tradition
3.2–5   142

Odes on All the Scriptures
                    142

Refutation of All Heresies
Preface 6   142
7.30.1   18, 100
7.30.5–6   100

Hippolytus of Thebes
Chronicle
3   119
4   119
5   119, 120

Ps.-Hippolytus
On the Seventy Disciples
9   192
14   78
56   78
65   78

History of John   154–55

Irenaeus
Against Heresies
1.23.1   25
1.26.3   149
2.22.5   131
2.22.5   147, 183
3.1.1   15
3.10.1   25
3.11.1   149
3.11.3   102
3.11.8   93
5.30.1   149
5.33.4   15

Jerome
Against Jovinianus
1.26   111, 112, 148

Book of Hebrew Names
1.1   38

Book of Questions on Genesis
Gen 46:27   26

*Books on Church History and Contro-
versy*
45   125

Commentary on Galatians
6.10   131

Commentary on Matthew
Preface   94, 179
20.23   148

Commentary on Philemon
24   36

Epistles
127.5   108

Lives of Illustrious Men
1   176
7   25
8   21, 32, 33, 36
22   148, 190

Ibn Kabar
Lamp of Darkness   53

Isho'dad of Merv
Commentary on Mark
Prologue   28

Juvencus
Evangelical Histories
                          93

Lactantius
Divine Institutes
4.12   136

Epistles
39.2   136

Life of Auxibius
1–6   62
7   62, 64
7–8   64
8   62, 66
12   63, 66

Martyrdom of Mark
1   19, 153
3   19
4   19
5   19
6   19
7   19–20
9   20
11–15   20
18–20   20

Mawhub ibn Mansur ibn Mufarrij
*History of the Patriarchs of the Coptic
Church of Alexandria*
Preface   194
1.1   21, 50–52, 81, 89,
                          106, 109, 182, 188
1.3   21

Ps.-Melito
Departure of Mary
1   162, 163
2   162

Memorial of Saint John
                          96–97, 108

Methodius of Olympus
On the Resurrection
1.59.6   112

Michael of Antioch
Chronicle   29

Monarchian Prologue to Mark
                          35, 94–96

*The Names of the Twelve Apostles and
Their Parents*
                        82–83

Nicephorus
Ecclesiastical History
2   160
2.3   119

Odes of Solomon
3.3   138
6.1–2   138
9.11   139
11.16   138
12.12   138
16.18–19   138
19   136
20.1   136
20.7   136, 140
22.5   139
27.1–3   138
29.7–9   139
29.11   139
30.1–2   138
36.1–2   138
41.1–3   138
41.9   138
41.10–11   138
41.14   138

Origen
Commentary on Genesis
                        152

Commentary on John
10.3   94

Commentary on Matthew
                        18

Papias
Explanation of the Dominical Logia
                        14, 17–18, 24

Passion of Mark   39, 124

Peter, bishop of Alexandria
Acts of Peter   90–91, 92

Peter Chrysologus
Sermons
78   110
150   110
170   110

Peter Damian
Concerning the Perfection of the Monks
                        112

Polycrates
Letter to Victor   107, 123–24

Proclus of Constantinople
Homilies
4.5   113

Encomium of St Mark
                        33, 96, 108

Sedulius Scottus
Commentary on the Gospel of Mark
                        94

Severus of Nastrawa
Homily on Mark   44, 91

Synaxarion for Baramouda
                        54

Teaching of the Apostles
21   83

Tertullian
Against Marcion
4.5   17

Apology
5.4   141

Prescription Against Heretics
36   148

Theodore of Mopsuestia
Commentary on John
Prologue   94

Theodosius
On the Topography of the Holy Land
                        118

Theophylact
Explanation of the Gospel of Mark
Prologue   34, 93

Exposition of Acts   34

Victor of Antioch
Prologue to the Gospel of Mark
                        27

Victorinus
Commentary on Matthew
Prologue 5   93

Commentary on Revelation
                        93

Index of Modern Authors

Badham, Francis Pritchard 105
Bargès, Jean Joseph Léandre 44, 49
Bauckham, Richard 126–27, 134, 142
Bernard, John H. 134
Black, C. Clifton 9, 100, 105
Braun, François-Marie 134
Bruns, J. Edgar 87–89, 105, 107
Bruce, Frederick F. 134, 165
Colson, Jean 127, 134
Cullman, Oscar 3
Culpepper, R. Alan 3
Czachesz, István 63
Deissman, Gustav A. 144
Delff, Heinrich 134
Eisler, Robert 128, 134
Halkin, François 76
Harris, Rendel 133, 135–37
Guelich, Robert A. 7
Keener, Craig S.   8
Lambers-Petry, Doris 128
Lawlor, Hugh Jackson 127
Mingana, Alphonse 133, 135–37
Montgomery, James 137

Murphy-O'Connor, Jerome 115,116
Noret, Jaques 6
Orchard, Bernard 9
Orlandi, Tito 4
Pollard, Thomas Evan 18
Pratscher, Wilhelm 12
Riley, Harold 9
Robinson, John A. T.
Ropes, James H. 12
Shoemaker, Stephen 118, 163, 164
Smalley, Stephen 3
Smith, Morton 31
Soliman, Sameh Farouk 113
Stökl Ben Ezra, Daniel 128, 129
Taylor, Joan 116
Telfer, William 128
Watson, Francis 93
Weiss, Johannes 8
Winn, Adam 15
Van Deun, Peter 78
Van Tilborg, Sjef 144
Von Soden, Hermann Freiherr 35
Zahn, Theodor 93, 105

Index of Subjects

Acts of Mark 69, 75–80, 98, 107–109, 144, 175–76, 188, 191
Acts of John 151–53,
Acts of John by Prochorus 97, 107, 156–57
Acts of John in Rome 157
Africanus 187, 194
Agathon 45, 49
Alexander the Monk 59
Ambrose of Milan 92
Ananias, the cobbler 20, 44, 48
Anna 91, 120 *see also* Hannah
Antioch 9, 25, 29, 56, 71, 155, 167, 168–172, 175–79
Apocalypse Andəmta 170–71, 182
Apollonia 33, 78
Apollonius 153
Apostles, allotment tradition 19, 152–53, 156, 161
Arethas of Caesarea 160
Aristobulus 51, 53, 105–7, 188, 190
Auxibius 62
Azotus 51

Barnabas 9–10, 15, 42, 51, 55, 59, 106
– martyrdom of 62, 65
Babylon 28
Bar Jesus 58, 67, 203
Bar Hebraeus 30, 177, 179
Bede 37
Beloved Disciple 46, 87–88, 90–91, 108, 110, 138, 158, 187, 189, 191
Bernard the Monk 118
Bethany 52, 89–90
Bethesda, pool of 89
Book of John Concerning the Falling Asleep of Mary 161–62
Boukalou 20, 74
Braulio of Saragossa 107
Byblos 33, 78

Caesarea 11, 72, 77, 176
Cana, wedding at 52, 70, 83, 88–89, 188
Cenacle 114, 120 *see also* Zion Church
Chrysostom 13
Claudius 18, 21, 170, 176
Cleopas 120
Colophons 35
Cyrene (Cyprus) 57
Cyrene (North Africa) 19, 25, 50, 72, 106 *see also* Girne
Cypriot missions of Mark 58, 60–62, 64, 67, 75, 81–82, 182

Day of Atonement 39, 128–29
Dialogue of Adamantius 23–24
Dionysius of Alexandria 12
Dionysius bar Salibi 26, 29–30, 167–68
Domitian 141, 148–49, 157, 160
Drusiana 152, 154

Egeria 115, 117
Encomium of Barnabas 59–62, 65, 66, 70, 75, 78, 79, 80, 89, 109, 118, 180
Encomium on Mark the Evangelist 41–42, 61, 96
Encomium of SS. Peter and Paul 43–44, 81
Epaphras 10, 63
Ephesian imprisonment hypothesis 11
Ephesus 61, 66, 78, 144, 147–48, 151, 155–57, 163–68, 173, 179, 182–83
Ephrem the Syrian 26–27, 112, 178
Epiphanius of Salamis 32–33, 112, 115–16, 125–32, 140–43, 158, 163–64
Euphemus 57
Eusebius 50, 94, 115, 128–31
Evodius 29, 119–20

First Commentary on Mark 37

Gauls 71, 75, 101
Geez Commentary 168–172, 175
Girne (Cyprus) 73
Gospel of the Lord (Marcionite) 24

Hadrian 115
Hannah 45–46, 49, 91, 106 *see also*
    Anna
Hegesippus 100, 115–16, 124, 127–29,
    133, 140–43, 159, 187, 189–94, 196
Heleca, bishop of Saragossa 107
Henri de Valois 39, 124
Heracleides 58, 63, 64
Hiberno-Latin Manuscripts 37–38
Hilarius 111
History of John 154–55

Ibn Hazm 178
Ibn Kabar 53, 82–83, 109
Iconium 55, 77–78
Irenaeus 15–16, 93, 147–49, 159, 183
Isho'dad of Merv 28–29, 102

Jacob of Edessa 26
Jacobus de Voragine 38–39
James the Just 9, 109, 113, 120, 125–32,
    142–43, 155–56, 177, 179, 191–93
James, son of Alphaeus 142–43, 192–93
Jerusalem 45, 72, 81, 106, 114–16, 118,
    153, 156, 159–62, 182–82, 192–93
– Council of 55, 82
John, the Apostle 107
John the Baptist 70, 87–88
John of Damascus 118
John the Evangelist 13, 27, 46, 87, 114,
    123, 147–58, 181, 184 see also Me-
    tastasis 151–52, 160
John of Shmun 41–44
John the Theologian 113–14, 144–45
John the Younger 165
Julian Peter 107

Laodicea 57, 151
Last Supper 52, 84, 90, 109, 110, 111,
    117, 187, 191 See also Passover
Lazarus 52, 90
Libya 19, 61, 74
Life of Auxibius 62–66, 195
Limnetes 62, 64, 65

Logos Theology
– and Mark 92, 94, 96
– and John 95
Lucius of Cyrene 25–27, 30, 57
Luke 25–27, 30–31

Marcion 100, 190
Marcionites 17, 18, 23–24,
Mark, also named John 7, 27, 30, 55,
    69–72
– abandonment of mission 9, 42, 46–
    47, 56–57, 61, 76, 81, 181–82
– death 183–84
– house of 9, 60, 80, 89, 92, 117
Man carrying jar of water 60, 70, 76,
    82–83, 109, 188
Mark,
– exalted with respect to the command-
    ment 38
– priest 36–39, 94, 188
– and the sacerdotal plate 39, 124–25
– the stump-fingered 18, 100
– virgin 112, 188
Mark, of Apollonia 33–34, 78
Mark, of Byblos 33, 78
Mark, of Alexandria 7, 19–21
– date of death 21
– martyrdom of 20, 48–49, 74
Mark the Evangelist 7, 13–19, 26, 35, 7
Martyrdom of Andrew 153
Martyrdom of Mark 19–21, 43, 48
Mary Magdalene 130–31
Mary, mother of John 46, 91, 111, 129
– dormition of 118, 158–63, 168, 180–
    81
Mary, mother of John Mark 9, 28, 34,
    41, 45, 48, 60, 70, 80, 92, 181
Matthew the Evangelist 15, 35 57
Mawhub 50, 81
Maximos 115
Memorial of Saint John 96
Miletus 151, 171–72
Mingana Syriac 540 164–66
Monarchian Prologue to John 112
Monarchian Prologue to Mark 94–96,
    101, 189
Moses Bar Kepha 164, 166
Mount of Olives 60, 117–18, 162–63
Mount Zion 60, 89, 114–20

Nero 11, 59, 148, 155, 183
Nicene Creed 93

Odes of Solomon 133, 135–36
Odist 133, 137, 138–39, 144
Oecumenius 13
Origen 18

Pamphylia 56, 61, 71, 75, 176–77
Paphos 58, 178
Papias of Hierapolis 14–15, 18, 32, 94, 113, 164
Passover 52, 60, 70, 76, 82–84, 90, 110, 119, 134, 188 *see also* Last Supper
Passion of Mark 39
Patmos 96, 148, 152, 157, 166, 169–73
Paul, the Apostle 9–10, 30, 55, 66, 155, 178–79, 182–83
Pauline Corpus 10, 67
Pella 116
Pentapolis 19, 74
Perga 56, 76–77
Pergamum 154, 169
Peshitta 137, 140, 177
Peter, the Apostle   15–16, 18, 28–29, 30, 38
Peter, bishop of Alexandria 90
Philo 32,50, 113, 125
Phoenicia 33, 72, 175
Pityusa 57, 74, 75
Polycarp 151, 164
Polycrates 107, 123, 124, 137, 142, 145
Praenomen 8
Prochorus 156
Procopius the Deacon 33, 96, 108, 113
Prophecies Collected from All the Books 26
Protevangelium of James 91

Revelation, book of 12, 93, 114, 139, 149, 151, 159, 165
Rhoda 28, 30
Rhodon 58, 59, 62, 64,
Richard of St. Victor 169
Rufinus 125

Sacerdotal plate 39, 123–26, 133–35, 139–40

St. Mark's Monastery 120
Salamis 55, 58, 61, 64, 72, 195
Sedulius Scottus 94–95
Seleucia 56, 71, 77, 156, 169, 172, 175–76, 185
Septuagint 125, 137
Seventy or seventy-two disciples 24, 28, 30–33, 39–40, 50–51, 156, 190
Severus of Antioch 28
Severus of Nastrawa 44–50, 112, 159
Silas 10, 47, 55–56, 77
Simon the Canaanite 82
Simon the Cyrenian 51, 53, 82
Simon the Leper 83
Simon Magus 18, 28–30, 73, 79, 102
Smyrna 144, 151, 164, 169
Sophronius of Jerusalem, 33, 107
Stephen 175–76
– persecution following death 72
Story of John, Son of Zebedee 154
Suffering of John 153–54

Tertullian 17, 141, 148, 173, 183
Theodorus Lector 63
Theophylact of Ochrid 13, 34, 93, 180
Thomas, the apostle 60, 91–92, 110, 119
Tiberius 21, 164, 169
Timon 57, 64, 74
Timothy 11, 43, 65, 167
Titus 26
Trajan 157, 166, 183
Tübingen Theosophy 158
Tychicus 63

Victor of Antioch 27, 34, 110
Victor, bishop of Rome 107
Virtues of John 153–54

Witness of Holy John the Precursor and Baptist 87, 88

Young man who fled naked 109–10, 125–26, 129–31, 188, 189

Zebedee 107, 120, 190
Zion Church 114–120

Wissenschaftliche Untersuchungen zum Neuen Testament

Edited by Jörg Frey (Zürich)

Associate Editors:

Markus Bockmuehl (Oxford) · James A. Kelhoffer (Uppsala)
Tobias Nicklas (Regensburg) · Janet Spittler (Charlottesville, VA)
J. Ross Wagner (Durham, NC)

WUNT I is an international series dealing with the entire field of early Christianity and its Jewish and Graeco-Roman environment. Its historical-philological profile and interdisciplinary outlook, which its long-term editor Martin Hengel was instrumental in establishing, is maintained by an international team of editors representing a wide range of the traditions and themes of New Testament scholarship. The sole criteria for acceptance to the series are the scholarly quality and lasting merit of the work being submitted. Apart from the specialist monographs of experienced researchers, some of which may be habilitations, *WUNT I* features collections of essays by renowned scholars, source material collections and editions as well as conference proceedings in the form of a handbook on themes central to the discipline.

WUNT II complements the first series by offering a publishing platform in paperback for outstanding writing by up-and-coming young researchers. Dissertations and monographs are presented alongside innovative conference volumes on fundamental themes of New Testament research. Like Series I, it is marked by a historical-philological character and an international orientation that transcends exegetical schools and subject boundaries. The academic quality of Series II is overseen by the same team of editors.

WUNT I:
ISSN: 0512-1604
Suggested citation: WUNT I
All available volumes can be found at
www.mohrsiebeck.com/wunt1

WUNT II:
ISSN: 0340-9570
Suggested citation: WUNT II
All available volumes can be found
at *www.mohrsiebeck.com/wunt2*

Mohr Siebeck
www.mohrsiebeck.com